Praise for *Flex*

"*Flex* is based on real-life experiences of its authors. This book gives you a useful framework and real-world strategies for how thoughtful leaders should operate in today's global workplace. You will learn how to remove the interpersonal gaps that erode trust in business relationships. Every corporate and nonprofit leader must read this book before taking on a new post."

—Manny Espinoza, CEO, ALPFA

"*Flex* provides a thoughtful guidebook for the crucial leadership skill of developing 'fluency across differences.' There are applicable tools here for reacting with agility to a changing workplace that is filled with rich and divergent perspectives. Hyun and Lee offer a helpful resource for honing adaptive leadership behavior."

—Douglas Conant, Chairman, Avon Products, Kellogg Executive Leadership Institute; Founder & CEO, ConantLeadership; Former President & CEO, Campbell Soup Company

"Jane Hyun and Audrey Lee have mined their experiences as consultants, coaches, and first-generation Americans to write a compelling and timely book. The authors challenge twenty-first-century leaders to broaden their mind-set and acquire new skills if their organizations are to be successful in a world where the people they lead reflect cultural, racial, gender, and generational differences. Changing demographics have placed the United States on an inexorable path toward a genuine multicultural society. This book provides critical information and practical action steps for how leaders can make the journey productive for themselves and their organizations."

—J. M. Cobbs, MD, coauthor of *Cracking the Corporate Code*

"In the twenty-first century, a new type of leader will need to emerge to develop an authentic partnership with the new global worker who will drive innovation and growth. *Flex: The New Playbook for Managing Across Differences* provides the new era attributes of leadership that highlight the leadership agility required to master success in a global environment."

—Ronald C. Parker, President/CEO, The Executive Leadership Council

"Jane and Audrey courageously get at the heart of why we seem to be 'stuck' when it comes to effectively managing across differences. *Flex* provides compelling reasons why we need to more openly and honestly address our differences if we expect better organizational and societal outcomes. Insightfully using their own experiences as well as success stories from others, the authors offer a practical roadmap to bridge the power gap to build stronger, more productive, and inclusive relationships with employees, clients, and the community."

—Mary-Frances Winters, President and Founder of The Winters Group; author of *Inclusion Starts with I*

"If you are in leadership or want to remain competitive and you don't have a racially and culturally diverse board or staff, you are part of the past. We need to focus now on understanding the necessity for developing this untapped pipeline—we are losing momentum every day. This remarkable resource will set you on the right path."

—Frances Hesselbein, President and CEO, The Frances Hesselbein Leadership Institute

"I have known Jane and Audrey for about ten years, and they are thinkers. And when they think, others benefit. Flex is about thinking—managing one's thinking to meet the demands of business relationships inside and outside of your organization. It is about the twenty-first-century essence of the workplace: how do you work with, manage, and coach people who are different from you. From the conceptual rationale to the practical how-to, take this journey with them!"

—J. T. "Ted" Childs Jr., Principal, Ted Childs LLC

FLEX

FLEX

THE NEW PLAYBOOK FOR MANAGING
ACROSS DIFFERENCES

JANE HYUN AND AUDREY S. LEE

WITH LESLIE MILLER

HARPER
BUSINESS

An Imprint of HarperCollins*Publishers*
www.harpercollins.com

HarperCollins books may be purchased for educational, business, or sales promotional use. For information, please e-mail the Special Markets Department at SPsales@harpercollins.com.

FIRST EDITION

Designed by Renato Stanisic

Illustrations by Jerome Walford, The Blue Griffin

Library of Congress Cataloging-in-Publication Data has been applied for.

ISBN: 978-0-06-224852-7

14 15 16 17 18   OV/RRD   10 9 8 7 6 5 4 3 2 1

DEDICATED TO GARY A. PARRETT, WHO SHOWED US HOW
TO CLOSE THE POWER GAP.

AND TO MAUREEN BUDWAY, FOR YOUR INSPIRATION OF FAITH,
LAUGHTER, ARTISTRY, COURAGE, AND FRIENDSHIP.

ACKNOWLEDGMENTS

This book could not be completed without the work, support, and love from our community. It was truly a collective effort. We thank those who stood by our side and shared their talents with us.

For being an integral part of this journey, our friend, coworker, the go-to person, and the glue that holds everything together: Lisa Craig

To our clients around the world: Thank you for sharing your lives with us and teaching us lessons in return.

For giving voice to our work: Leslie Miller

For bringing this book to life: our agent, Stephanie Kip Rostan; and Colleen Lawrie and Hollis Heimbouch at HarperCollins

For providing our concept with art for our cover: Daniel Koh at agendanyc.com

For the graphics that highlight our words: Jerome Walford

For bringing wisdom to our work: Eva Chou, Jim Jones, Jimmy Lee, Juan Lopez, Connie & Kent Matsumoto, Gabi Page-Fort, Sri Rajagopalan, Guy Rockey, Thomas Tseng, Sheila Robinson, Mary-Frances Winters, Fiona Wong, Richard Wong, Asia Society, Daria Lamb & the Conference Board, Jonathan Beane and Lisa Quiroz at Time Warner

For being our mentors and friends on this journey: Ted Childs, Doug Conant, Dr. Price Cobbs, Deb Dagit, Manny Espinoza, Tom

Greco, Mitch Hammer, Frances Hesselbein, Ron Parker, Toni Riccardi, Melinda Wolfe, Sylvia Ann Hewlett, Lauren Leader-Chivee and Peggy Shiller, and the Center for Talent Innovation

For those who shared their stories with us: Ahad Afridi, Ray Bain, Linda Banion, Sheri Bronstein, Mary Jane Butler, June Carter, Heidi Casey, Eugenia Castillo, Jenny Cha, Ivan Chan, Fanny Chen, Joy Chen, Kuntesh Chokshi, Anne Chow, Wilson Chu, Lieutenant General Ronald Coleman (Retired), Flor Colon, Doug Conant, Peggy Craig, Orlando Crespo, David Cross, A. B. Cruz, Linson Daniel, Rafe Esquith, Raudline Etienne, Erby Foster, Michelle Gadsden-Williams, George Gaston, David Goderich, Linda Griego, Claire Gruppo, Tim Haahs, Mark Hershey, Rich Hille, Mae Hong, David Howse, Jae Im, Bill Ingham, Juan Roberto Job, Toby Johnson, Dr. Adina Kalet, So-Young Kang, Rich Kelly, Roger Kim, Rosaline Koo, Jackie Krese, Rose Kwan, Inwha Lee, Don Liu, Stephanie Lofgren, Emile Mack, Jeff Marcus, Drew McGregor, Pat McManus, Jackie McNab, Tim Minges, Steve Miola, Grace Chiang Nicolette, Jacob Pak, Lindsey Pollack, Bill Pollard, Marnie Raymond, Steve Raymond, Veta Richardson, Maria Rios, Quentin Roach, Christy Rutherford, Janet Salazar, Jim Schaefer, Steve Schloss, Ofir Shalev, Dr. Joseph Shin, Ray Short, Angel Stewart, Carol Tan, Nico Van der Merwe, Drew Wahl, Gloria Wahl, Mark Washington, Phil Webber, Bill Welder, Scott Wharton, Carol Wittmeyer, Richard Wong, Anne Marie Yarwood, James Yen, Robert Yi, Rachel Yoka, and many others we have met along the way.

FROM AUDREY:

——*I shall run the way of Your commandments,*
for You will enlarge my heart.
—PSALM 119:32

To my husband, Alan Wong—for being the one I've been waiting for. Thank you for the love that gives me joy and healing every day.

To Mom—Thank you for providing the foundation that continues to hold me up, even in the darkest times.

To Mom and Dad Wong, Connie, Zack, and Audrita—I'm so glad to be part of the family. Thank you for being so welcoming!

To Kathy Keenan and the team at Oak Ridge, Don Morrison and Tom Hamilton—Thank you for being my earliest mentors and setting strong examples for me.

To Jane Hyun—Thank you for the opportunities.

To dear friends who have supported me through this journey. Thank you for your listening hearts and helpful advice:

All Angels Inwood House Church (Jeff, Yavonne, Renee, NamHee, Erik, Bikki, Dan, and Rachel); the worship community at St. Ignatius of Antioch Episcopal Church; Suzanne Allen; Nancy Chan; Archelle and Monique Funnié; Georgetown Leadership Coaching Cohort 23; Alison Hwang; Jan Kang; Ina Kraus; Stephanie Lau; Agnes Lee; Ginny Lee; Walter Lee; Max Martina; Denine Monet; Soohee Kang-Nam; Kathie Ping-Heap; Toni Riccardi; Ray Short; Suzanne Timmer; Helen and Sam Tsang; and Deanna Witkowski

FROM JANE:

Yang Jae Kim, my Gomo, I will never forget the imprint you left on me as a young girl. I am forever grateful and miss you terribly.

Thank you, David, for extending your patience and wise counsel during all the late nights.

Abigail and Timothy, your smiles bring life-giving energy to me each day.

Mom, Dad, and Susan, thank you for showing me nothing but unconditional love.

Jewel and Gene Hyun, thank you for the many ways you support us to pursue our calling.

Alyce, Rob, Josephine, and Lowell, you are a blessing to me.

Audrey, thank you for the collaboration. After four years of stops and starts, we did it!

Wendy and Ali Ager, Charlie and Jeannie Drew, Liana Loh, So-Chung Shinn-Lee, Linda Kelly, Sue Yim, and Moon Sung were early cheerleaders and supporters along the way.

Our MIP group—Jane and Kristin, thank you for your faithfulness.

Special thanks to Carolyn, Alice, Sandra, and Sujin—I treasure our times together.

Our small group at EPC—Your good humor and grace helps me get through another day.

Thank you, God, for the opportunity to serve others.

Thou my best thought, by day or by night,
Waking or sleeping, thy presence my light.
—"Be Thou My Vision"

CONTENTS

Introduction xiii

Glossary of Key Terms xxv

PART I: GETTING INSIDE THE GAP: WHAT KEEPS US FROM CONNECTING

Chapter 1 What You Don't Know Can Hurt You: How We (Don't) Talk about Difference 3

Chapter 2 Managing the Power Gap 33

Chapter 3 Culture and Communication: Flexing across Styles 47

Chapter 4 Portrait of a Fluent Leader 67

Fluent Leader Profile: Rosaline Koo—Building Fluency Beyond Stereotypes 89

PART II: THE KILLER APP: FLEXING ACROSS THE GAP

Chapter 5 Power Gap Principle: Flex Your Management Style 99

Fluent Leader Profile: Don Liu—Bridging the Gap through Generosity of Spirit 126

Chapter 6 Navigate the Power Gap with Your Peers 131

Chapter 7 Go the Distance with Your Superiors 151

Fluent Leader Profile: Erby L. Foster Jr.—The Fluent "Agent" and Champion 170

Chapter 8 Connecting with Customers and Partners 177

Profile: Memorial Hermann Southwest Hospital—Health-care
    System Identifies Innovative Solutions for Patient Needs 197

PART III: MULTIPLYING YOUR SUCCESS

Chapter 9 Onboarding Your Employees—Getting It Right from Day
    One 207

Fluent Leader Profile: Steve Miola and Ray Bain, Merck Research
    Laboratories—Creating a Fluent Company Culture 227

Chapter 10 Mentors, Sponsors, Coaches, and the Gift of Feedback
    235

Fluent Leader Profile: Rich Hille—From the Baseball Fields to the
    Corporate Boardroom: Leading a Winning Team 257

Chapter 11 Leveraging Diverse Thinking from Your Teams to Drive
    Innovation 263

Conclusion 283
Bibliography 287

INTRODUCTION

You never really understand a person until you consider things from his point of view . . . until you climb into his skin and walk around in it.
—Atticus Finch, in *To Kill a Mockingbird*, by Harper Lee

We feel it's only right to warn you: this book might make you a little uncomfortable. This is a book about differences, a topic that ranges from awkward to scary to strictly off-limits for some people. And as we work more frequently with people who are different from us, we notice that people are still very hesitant to have an open dialogue about what makes us different, sometimes avoiding the topic altogether. But ignoring our differences at work doesn't make problems go away. In some cases, it exacerbates them—causing employees to feel misunderstood and unsuccessful, and managers to hit their heads against walls, stymied by how to get the best from everyone around them.

This book is about becoming curious again. It's about investigating what makes different people tick and respond the way they do. It's about finding common ground on which to build stronger relationships, and having positive dialogue with each person at the table who brings divergent, unique perspectives. It's about first recognizing superficial traits and behaviors, then valuing a deeper look beneath the surface. It's about suspending judgment until you get to really know the person. And it's about knowing how and when to put useful information and tools to work as you strategically shift how you respond to you and your employees' differences, whether they are cultural or generational, or whether they stem from the gender gap or even disparities in communication styles. This book offers what courageous, thoughtful leaders need in order to operate successfully in today's diverse, global workplace.

In life and in business, all great relationships are built on the essential principles of trust and respect. When trust is present, it's exciting to watch relationships flourish, people and teams become productive, and companies prosper. The problems start when there is a breakdown in trust, and when you fail to realize that people build trust in different ways. Miscommunication often occurs when respect is interpreted in a variety of ways by people with different backgrounds, and when those differences remain unstated and unobserved in relationships. For some, respect may mean taking the initiative to resolve project roadblocks without involving the manager—their way of showing their superior respect and protecting the boss's precious time. Another worker might show his respect by deferring to the boss's direction first, afraid that his superior might lose face by being shown up by an underling. Barriers arise when workers from different cultural contexts expect others to behave the same way they do, without understanding that while the intent might be the same (e.g., to show respect), the behaviors might look very different. We want to help remove these barriers that keep you from truly engaging colleagues who are different from you, and to do so in a way that strengthens, not hurts, the work relationship.

And the barriers are many. Male executives may refrain from giving constructive performance feedback to their female direct reports for fear that the women might get emotional. A boomer manager might assume that a Gen Y recruit lacks social graces. A project leader of a team of employees from diverse cultures could hesitate to bring up a misunderstanding due to a cross-cultural communication issue in order to be polite. Our consulting and coaching work has taken us into organizations around the globe, and what we have discovered in our mission to develop effective leaders is that most people—regardless of their title in the organization—experience extreme discomfort about having an open conversation about differences in the workplace.

To be sure, organizations have become more diverse—a global/multicultural workforce, more women, and a new generation of workers have entered our ranks in large numbers; but many businesses have not yet figured out how to best engage the talent that they have successfully recruited. Due to the speed of change in our current business environment, leaders must be adept at leveraging their employees who work throughout their local markets around the world for input, wisdom, and skills to survive. CEOs and senior leaders need to be more inquisitive and more reliant on their employees for wise counsel. As coaches, we have worked with a variety of organizations and helped managers wrestle with how to reach across differences to establish clear, two-way communication with their diverse teams. We find that it has helped them build and renew the trust with their teams and create the kind of fertile environments where their employees can build their careers.

IT IS NOT EASY to change the behaviors of people at work, even if business as usual isn't working out. But our experience has taught us that interpersonal dynamics can change when people with a drive for making a difference take the initiative and then influence others to multiply the effect. We've seen firsthand how, as companies seek to become more profitable and productive in an increasingly global landscape, different leadership styles are becoming more acceptable, impacting all aspects of employee development. This includes how you recruit and orient new hires, mentoring, modeling, and feedback; leading teams; and applying the same relationship skills to adapt to your clients and customers.

Though the idea of adaptive, fluent leadership is still a young concept, we are beginning to see the efficacy of this approach in generating out-of-the-box thinking that has created new business innovations. As we grappled with this concept, we found that our clients were trying to figure out how best to lead people who were different from them. Our directive became clear: we all need to learn a new skill set that will enable successful business interactions in our new diverse surroundings. Your country manager in Vietnam, as well as your finance director sitting in headquarters in Chicago, may lack the fluency required to work effectively with each other. We are simply not taught how to relate to people from other backgrounds, and these skills of *flex*ing are not adequately taught in our educational systems, undergraduate programs, or business schools. The world has certainly become "flatter," as Thomas Friedman posits in his treatise on globalization, *The World Is Flat: A Brief History of the Twenty-first Century*. But although we are more connected globally as a workforce through technology, managers aren't actually better equipped to interact and communicate globally with *people*.

Even as we write this, we realize the stakes are significant, not only in the work we do for our clients, but also because each of us has experienced, firsthand, the disconnect and dissonance of not matching up to dominant norms in our work environments. But both of us have also felt the exhilaration and empowerment of leveraging our unique perspectives in truly transformative ways. Our personal journeys compel us individually to bring these issues to the forefront.

JANE'S STORY

"You have to work really hard." That's the English translation of *yeol-simheehaeyadeh*, the Confucian work ethic that served as a refrain in my life nearly from my birth in South Korea, where I also spent my early childhood years.

When I was a first-grade student in Korea, the rules for how to do well and succeed were abundantly clear. I understood perfectly the expectations for how you treat your teachers, how you learn, and how you communicate in the Korean classroom. Always raise your hand before answering a question, and never interrupt the class or the teacher. Never disagree with teacher in public. Listen carefully to what is said and jot down your lesson plan in your notebook. There was no debate. These rules were instilled in all of us at an early age. The social distance, the gap between my teacher and me, dictated very specific rules for proper behavior.

When we moved to New York, I was the same person but I didn't know how much the rules had shifted. As a child, you can't pinpoint that uneasy feeling you have. When your environment (and the rules that accompany it) changes, you know that something dramatically different has happened, but you don't know exactly how to put it in context. Instead of recognizing external differences in the environment or in the behavior of others, a young child is only left to wonder, Is something wrong with *me*?

When the Old Rules Don't Work Anymore

So when my third-grade teacher, Mrs. Quinn, asked me after class one day, "Jane, how come you don't ask any questions in class?" I was dumbfounded. I thought I was doing the right thing by listening, not talking, in class. Participating verbally in class was not something I was ever encouraged to do before. I was following the rules of what I had been taught earlier as a schoolgirl in Korea. The distance between student and teacher in that Confucian Korean mind-set was a chasm I was taught not to cross. Perhaps Mrs. Quinn thought I had simply checked out, or was shy. Here was the disconnect. The cultural rules for how to behave in class had changed. Had my teacher pursued her line of questioning, or been invested in helping me learn the new rules, I might have been able to explain how what I was trying to do was show respect to her. But as it was, Mrs. Quinn couldn't figure out what was behind my unorthodox behavior, and I wasn't able to articulate my reasoning to her.

Even so, as many children starting over in a new country do, I adapted quickly. After some awkward attempts, I learned how to question and make inquiries in class even though I didn't fully understand why it was important to do so. Fast-forward to my first job, where, once again, these subtle cultural and gender messages that were ingrained in me surfaced in often unconscious ways. Over the last twenty-three years as an employee, manager, then as a consultant to mostly Western multinational corporations, I have found that a similar dynamic plays out every day in nearly every workplace whenever you enter a dominant cultural environment that is foreign from the one you grew up in, including aha moments that impact you in a major way, not unlike my experience in elementary school when I moved to the United States from Asia. People report to work every day having been raised with a specific code of behavior, cultural values, and rules, all of which represent the "right way to behave." However, they could be assigned to work for managers and coworkers (and direct reports) who have management principles that are at odds with that behavior. So when we're working with global business leaders, I remind myself never to forget how to put myself in the shoes of that eight-year-old girl trying to do the right thing, knowing she has fallen short but not understanding why, so that I understand the perspective of someone from a different cultural experience.

Nearly eight years ago, when I wrote *Breaking the Bamboo Ceiling*, it was primarily from the employee's perspective. I wanted to offer Asian employees a strategic guide for managing cultural differences at work, allowing them to better understand what was expected of them on a Western corporate playing field so they could navigate their own path toward success. Through that work I became more attuned to the differences, including social distance, that exist between Asian workers and their managers. Since most of the leadership paradigms in today's business world are Western in orientation, other cultural groups are often unfamiliar with the unwritten rules of this culture. In the same vein, managers of diverse employees can and indeed *must* play an active role in helping their employees succeed in the global workplace. *Flex* offers an important counterpoint from the manager's point of view, explaining to and instructing leaders how to navigate the differences between them and their diverse teams in ways that allow everyone to succeed.

AUDREY'S STORY

I was born in the United States but grew up in a family with strong Confucian values. My parents were from China, and, even after they immigrated to the United States, my dad made a conscious choice to preserve and enforce Chinese cultural heritage over Western culture. When it came to the most critical cultural values, we were sometimes "more Chinese" than the Chinese families in my community, which was often confusing for me growing up in a Western world.

For example, at home the idea of humility was paramount: one never talks about one's own efforts or accomplishments. My dad taught me from an early age that it is for others to validate you and your accomplishments. Thus, I learned growing up that in order for my accomplishments to count, an authority figure needed to assign them value. In fact, if I talked about myself at all or received a compliment, I was to downplay my achievements and talents. I learned how to wait patiently for acknowledgment and when that didn't always come, I was the first to criticize myself and anything I did. Once I entered the workforce, it took a long time for me to talk about what my work was worth—to assign it value. For years, talking about compensation and accepting acknowledgment for my work was uncomfortable and often embarrassing. I was almost more comfortable being criticized by managers or clients than with being asked to discuss my value.

My aha moment came when I started my marketing consulting business. I remember the process of creating a proposal for a project complete with scope, resources, and budget. I was well familiar with the process, given my experience in previous consulting and agency settings. And so it surprised me that I almost accepted the client's much lower counteroffer without questioning my own assumption that my experience and proposal weren't good enough. At that moment, I caught myself and suddenly recognized the roots of that particular mind-set in my upbringing. I was used to having superiors and clients define my worth; that was their role. But now that I was put in a different context, I realized the client wasn't necessarily trying to tell me I didn't have the qualifications or that I wasn't good enough. If that was his message, he probably wouldn't have wasted his time discussing the work with me and giving me an offer. He was simply negotiating a contract and trying to get the best price he could for his company. And he probably expected me to hold my ground and defend my value. So I held to my original bid, he paid it, and from that moment on I understood that though it often appears that we're playing the same game in business—negotiating a deal, developing a product—we're not always playing by the same set of rules or values. My realization gave me a deeper understanding of how my background impacted my responses, and that helped me change how I played the game.

But as much as these different cultural perspectives are often seen as detriments and barriers, I also have had the joy of experiencing what it feels like when managers reach across the power gap to help someone succeed, and I look back often at those examples for successful strategies for reaching out to those with different skills and backgrounds. When I started my career in business, the tech industry was exploding with new ideas and solutions. It set the tone for the innovative work and management lessons I learned as I began working for a small PR firm in Silicon Valley. It was my first job out of college, and with a background in music and Spanish, I was definitely out of the norm in terms of qualifications and, at least on paper, perhaps not the most automatic fit. But my manager, Kathy, and my colleagues were able to recognize that this green, quirky, Asian American college graduate with a different background had transferable skills of communication and quick-study abilities that would benefit the company.

When I think back on that experience, I remember that my manager not only had an open-door policy, as many do, but fostered an environment with an *open-floor* policy, by which I mean that everyone who worked there offered me advice and mentorship and found value in my perspective and opinion. Everyone in the firm was responsible for business development, and they told me to look around, find a circle or group, and get involved. Because of this, I got involved in an Asian entrepreneurial group that focused on manufacturing with an emphasis on the Pacific Rim. This was a manufacturing community, and not one that other members of the firm would have necessarily been drawn toward (since the rest of the group was Caucasian). This group proved to be very fertile ground for networking and building business relationships. The firm encouraged me to operate using my own experience and background. They never pigeonholed me but instead stayed open, applauded my style and unique background, and said, Let's talk about this, let's see what you have to offer, and let's leverage that. It was an incredible foundation that has stayed with me throughout my career and cemented for me the importance of reaching across the gap.

As I have transitioned from business and marketing roles to leadership development, I've realized that these early experiences of good management/mentoring have helped me formulate my own philosophies about inclusivity and reach across differences in work contexts. I notice the "outsiders" and the "interlopers" and those who seem like they don't belong. My experience enables me to have empathy, drives me to include them and find out their value under the surface. It expands my worldview and ultimately enlarges my heart.

HOW TO READ THIS BOOK

Before you dive in, we'd like to offer you a few words about how to use this book. The ideas of adaptive leadership behavior and learning to be fluent across differences are difficult and require more than acquiring a simple list of cognitive how-tos. In some cases, you will find that they may operate in ways that are counterintuitive to how you might respond in the same situation; you might even consider them strange at the outset. We want this text to be your playbook, to guide you in better and fluent ways of approaching all types of different people that you will encounter, first in the workplace, and later in your broader communities. Like a playbook, *Flex* will help you better prepare for interactions with workers who are different from you. Even if the live interaction may turn out differently than you expect, your preparation and thought process will yield greater awareness about your style as well as teach you something about how to meet that person partway.

Part 1 provides the rationale for why we need to acknowledge difference and learn to *flex* our management styles to those different from us. We will define the **power gap**—a critical relationship dynamic that managers need to understand—and teach you how to spot it. Using an assessment tool we developed just for this book, you can gauge your own power gap understanding and fluency. The assessment tool will help pinpoint areas in which you may need to devote more practice, education, and investigation. We'll also introduce the concept of the **fluent leader**—someone who is able to effectively bridge distances between themselves and their colleagues and get the most out of each employee.

In part 2, we get practical. We discuss not only *flex*ing down to your employees, but about *flex*ing across to your peers and reaching up to your superiors as well. We introduce you to a diverse array of real-life leaders who are living this out with their teams every day. You will find questions useful for engaging with your teams and colleagues, including a framework for modeling conversations and problem-solving, and you'll learn three critical questions to ask yourself when you encounter any new work relationship where you seek better understanding and communication. We will also share how you can apply *flex* concepts to relationships outside of your organization—including clients, suppliers, and customers—so that your impact will reach into the marketplace and community.

Part 3 is where we'll show you how to multiply your success and pass on what you've learned to others. These chapters will allow you to incorporate your *flex* skills in the way that you strategically think about mentoring and modeling the appropriate behaviors. We will end with how you can leverage the diverse thinking and communication styles of your teams so that you can create cutting-edge business practices.

And throughout this book, we'll introduce you to fluent leaders who closed the power gap effectively and have changed their organizations for the better. These are leaders that come from all different backgrounds, with varying personality types and leadership styles. Some are naturally more reserved, quiet, and thoughtful, while others have more forceful, highly expressive personalities, but each exhibits common fluent leader traits behind their effectiveness. Those traits can be developed, and we will show you how.

In the end, it is our hope that *Flex* will guide you and show you how to become a fluent leader. We want to help your businesses flourish by helping you build successful relationships across differences. We're excited to share with you this new playbook for skillfully and effectively meeting your employees partway and building stronger, more enduring work relationships. Whether you are a seasoned executive or a first-time manager, this book will help you play an active role in bridging the power gap, and in developing the latent talent of this emerging workforce. Our collective future depends on it.

NOTE: Except where affiliated with obviously identified organizations, all names and identities used in illustrations or case-in-point examples throughout this book have been changed.

GLOSSARY OF KEY TERMS

POWER GAP TERMS

POWER GAP: The social distance that separates individuals from those in positions of authority, whether in a formal or more informal structure, defined by gender, age, or cultural differences.

CLOSING OR MANAGING THE GAP: The ability to effectively read the power gap between yourself and other individuals, and respond in the most appropriate manner to reduce the social distance.

FLEXING: Adapting how one communicates, relates, and responds to others in a manner that takes into account an understanding of status differences.

FLUENT LEADER: An individual who investigates, without bias, the differences between her position and those of her team members in the organization. A leader who does not require others to adapt to her style, but instead adapts her own leadership style in order to meet her team members partway and helps bridge the distance between them.

CULTURE: The unique combination of attitudes, knowledge, behaviors, and strategies of a social group that are reinforced by the community.

DIVERSITY: A visible (gender, ethnicity, etc.) or invisible (religion, thinking style, disability, etc.) dimension that differentiates one group of people from another.

STEREOTYPE: A widely held but overly simplistic idea of how a person from a particular background behaves or thinks.

MULTICULTURAL PROFESSIONALS, MINORITY PROFESSIONALS, and PROFESSIONALS OF COLOR: Terms used interchangeably in this book to describe African Americans, Latinos/Hispanic Americans, Asian Pacific Americans, and Native Americans in the US workforce.

FOUR GENERATIONS IN THE WORKPLACE

TRADITIONALISTS: The generation born before 1946; also known as the "Veteran Generation" and the "Greatest Generation." This generation survived the Great Depression and is characterized by a sense of civic duty, respect for authority, sacrifice, and hard work.

BABY BOOMERS: The generation born roughly between 1946 and 1964; these workers are characterized by individualism, idealism, optimism, and a strong work ethic.

GENERATION X: The children of the older baby boomers, born between 1965 and 1976. Generally characterized as independent with a priority on work-life balance, Gen Xers are said to have a "free agent" mentality, are adaptive to change, and possess a healthy dose of skepticism.

GENERATION Y/MILLENNIALS: Also called "echo boomers," Generation Y workers were born between 1977 and 1994. Tech-savvy and social media–minded, they crave a strong team culture; eschew hierarchy (respects competence, not title); possess a sense of civic duty; and prioritize personal time.

PART I

GETTING INSIDE THE GAP: WHAT KEEPS US FROM CONNECTING

CHAPTER 1

WHAT YOU DON'T KNOW CAN HURT YOU: HOW WE (DON'T) TALK ABOUT DIFFERENCE

As individuals we can accomplish only so much. We're limited in our abilities. Collectively, we face no such constraint. We possess incredible capacity to think differently. These differences can provide the seeds of innovation, progress, and understanding.
—SCOTT PAGE, *THE DIFFERENCE*

Two senior-level managers read through the performance evaluations for their team members, preparing for upcoming annual reviews and a rankings meeting. As they comb through the evaluations, they keep in mind a mid-level managerial spot that has recently opened up, scanning for top performers they might tap to fill the position. "What about Ursula?" asks one. "Her numbers are fantastic."

"Yeah . . ." The other man pauses. "Maybe. She's a rock star—don't get me wrong. She's got tons of expertise. But I don't really get her. She doesn't really respond to my questions and feedback, so I'm never sure if I'm reaching her. Does that sound like leadership material?"

It's the reality of the new global workforce: many managers are struggling, faced with a playing field that looks dramatically different from the one into which they were hired. Even those who work for organizations offering access to cutting-edge management training programs find little guidance about the critical skills for doing business and leading on the global stage. Most programs focus on teaching employees to improve communication, manage conflict, manage their teams, promote their accomplishments, and hone their presentations. Yet workplaces feeling the effects of their employees not being understood, have missed opportunities to expand their markets: dissatisfied and disengaged workers perform poorly or leave. High-performing employees and fast-track candidates are getting derailed or pigeonholed because the organizations have not used their abilities to the fullest. Managers don't get what they want or what they think they asked for. Others simply don't understand their new employees.

The truth is that the landscape of the American workforce is changing. It's growing more multicultural, younger, and more female, and we are feeling the effects of the growing distance between frontline managers and workers from different backgrounds. As of June 2012, people of multicultural backgrounds (of Asian, African American, and Latino/Hispanic descent) made up 36 percent of the labor force, according to the US Department of Labor. Census data predicts that by the year 2050 there will be no racial or ethnic majority in the United States, and that between 2000 and 2050, immigrants and their first-generation children will be responsible for 83 percent of the increase in our country's working-age population. According to a McKinsey study, women held 37 percent of all jobs in the United States in 1970, and nearly half of all jobs in 2009. Right now there are about 40 million millennials in the workforce, with millions added every year. By 2025, three out of every four workers around the globe will belong to Gen Y. As of last count, medical school enrollment stands at just under 50 percent women. Even managers who in the past were consistently effective at leading their teams in the United States now face more communication problems, as well as more complex and multilayered challenges in developing their teams, than they did even as long as fifteen years ago. This phenomenon is echoed around the world, including in the UK, France, Japan, Brazil, and Germany. The same management techniques are not working, and the rules for engagement cannot be applied universally in this new playing field. Without a more nuanced understanding of the interpersonal gaps between people, managers will be at a loss as to how to bridge the distance between themselves and employees who possess different cultural values and drivers of success.

Large multinational corporations learned their lessons rather abruptly a few years ago, when hundreds of companies outsourced their back-office IT operations to Asia in an effort to cut costs. These same companies later had to invest enormous amounts of time and money figuring out how to work better across borders. They had failed to consider the human implications of this transaction—what their new partners expected, how they communicated, what were their decision-making processes, how they defined values such as trust and respect, and what were their measures of success.

THE HIGH STAKES OF LOSING OUR BEST TALENT

Perhaps you might be wondering at this juncture, Does this apply to me? Don't some management skills apply universally? Isn't this a problem only for large Fortune 500 companies with a global presence? But multiculturals, women, and the millennial generation are now, or will soon constitute, *an increasingly large percentage* of your workforce. Even if you are a small company and may not have as diverse an employee base, your suppliers, external partners, and customers will represent, in the near future, a broader cross section of your business. What are the costs of bringing employees onboard and leaving their development to chance? According to HR executives we consulted, costs to replace an employee who has left to go elsewhere can range from 150 percent to more than double an employee's salary. That can amount to approximately $250,000 (including salary, recruiting, training, and onboarding costs) to replace a management consultant within the first year of hire after graduate school. Multiply that by the number of new hires, and we're talking about a serious, make-or-break investment.

When highly competitive industries examine the turnover rates of their most recent recruits and find inordinately high attrition, they begin to question the effectiveness of their existing processes.

A manager of college recruiting at a health-care company reports, "We hired the same number of people this year as we have in years past, but we've already lost thirty percent of that class of trainees in the first nine months. It's hard to retain our new talent due to our top-down organizational culture, where power only flows in one direction, and where there's a lack of early engagement that the managers are providing the young hires. Our newest hires are eager to contribute, to communicate their opinions, and to look for a way to add value, but there are no mechanisms for them to have a voice. Why doesn't senior leadership pay more attention to them? After all, they have, just a few months ago, been on the outside, still have strong linkages to the outside and can therefore provide real-life perspective into how we can be more relevant to our consumers." Although companies might agree that they have done a decent job of recruiting a fair representation of women and multicultural employees, they are far from being certain about how to get the best ones to stay and realize their full potential. Moreover, they are not always adept at identifying the diamonds in the rough through traditional recruiting mechanisms. It is clear that we need to do things differently!

There is a solution to all this misunderstanding, miscommunication, and missed opportunity. The answer lies in valuing differences in the leadership development of your employees and developing the qualities of a fluent leader. She investigates, without bias, the differences between herself and those of her team members. He does not require all his team members to adapt to his style, but instead is able to adapt his leadership approach and management style in order to meet his team members partway and help bridge the distance between them. This ability to flex affects how we deal with power and status differences, and how we communicate and relate to each other. And while the concept of flexing appears simple enough at the outset, it takes an intentional commitment to refine that skill over time in order to maximize its impact and have the impact felt by colleagues from a variety of backgrounds.

THE CHALLENGE OF BUILDING TRUST

It takes courage to be a leader who inspires others to contribute their very best. Creating an environment of trust with employees (particularly with those with whom you are not as familiar) is not an easy task, even for the leader who manages a homogeneous team! It may mean setting aside personal judgments and assumptions about others while truth-testing the validity of those assumptions. And it involves a heartfelt belief and consistent follow-through on your commitments.

To give us all a reality check, a recent MBA we met posed an earnest question after a coaching meeting: "There are senior leaders in my firm who get away with a lot of garbage because they make a lot of money for the company. But no one touches them. Why should I aspire to be better than that when even bad leaders who mistreat their people get rewarded? Is it worth the effort?" We can understand his perspective; it's easy to get cynical about leadership practices when you don't see positive examples to emulate. Organizations need to be vigilant about instilling strong corporate values since employees look to leaders to demonstrate what those values look like in practice. It may mean holding people accountable for their most prized principles in the workplace. And it will be up to the individual leader to decide how he or she will demonstrate effective day-to-day management practices. No doubt, in that process, you may encounter some naysayers in your quest to develop principled leaders. If you want the managers in your organization to value fluent leadership, you may consider a firmwide strategy to instill inclusive leadership and cultural fluency as core values into your corporate DNA. If you are looking to build a profitable *and* sustainable business in this new global landscape, you will not be able to exclude the talent, resources, and perspectives that differ from the dominant environment. It is our sincere hope that you will see how flexing will make you a powerful, more respected leader in today's global business environment.

FLEXING IS GOOD FOR BUSINESS

Becoming a fluent leader requires personal integrity and a commitment to do the right thing as a manager. It just makes good business sense. It's worth repeating that the American—and perhaps global—business environment and workplace will never be the same again. In developed countries around the world, the workforce is aging and will be retiring in the next decade or so. Chances are good that your company will be comprised of workers from around the world as well as multicultural employees in North America; more women will be in the workforce than ever before and more young people will replace retiring baby boomers. No matter where your company headquarters are, you are also likely to be doing business with at least one overseas partner, vendor, or supplier.

The way you handle the social distance between yourself and employees (or clients) of different cultures, genders, and ages can make or break your company. This distance, or the power gap, is the "amount of emotional distance that separates subordinates from their bosses," as defined by Dutch social psychologist Mauk Mulder. Renowned intercultural expert Geert Hofstede added his research to the definition by showing that the power distance that is socially acceptable by the boss and employee depends largely on their national culture. For the purpose of this book, we will apply the power gap to discuss the chasm that separates managers and employees, men and women, as well as employees of different generations and different cultures. In each of these relationships, we will refer to this distance as the power gap. In some countries, for example, contradicting another senior executive in public can be enough to derail sensitive negotiations or to dismantle an existing working relationship. Similarly, in some workplaces around the world, a manager who is a woman will be viewed with less respect than her male peer.

A variety of academic studies and reports link diversity and diverse thinking processes to a higher return on investment, better communication, and more effective teams. More recent studies reveal that embracing different ways of thinking contributes substantially to creativity and teamwork. Fluent leaders who think innovatively are able to capture the unique perspectives that your people bring to the table (mining the gold, as it were). In *The Innovator's DNA*, authors Jeff Dyer, Hal Gregersen, and Clayton M. Christensen highlight that "discovery-driven" executives network with people who are *not* like them, seeing the importance of finding wisdom in unexpected places. As a manager, you can apply this in your own organization by actively and consistently reaching out to bridge the distance and difference that exists between you and your team members, not discounting those who may have fallen under your radar.

No matter how many scholarly data points and case studies we can present to you, perhaps the following example will best illustrate what we commonly hear in our leadership development sessions.

LEADING A GLOBAL TEAM

Jim is a senior vice president at Global Company, Inc., a large consumer products company with offices in nine countries throughout Asia, Europe, and South America. The Global Company Web site and recruiting materials emphasize global "interconnectedness." The head of his division, Jim manages a team of twenty-one direct reports. Many in Jim's team manage their own discrete global teams as well. Global Company has a stated mission of global inclusion and diversity, and managers are encouraged to hire from the widest possible pool of applicants. For his own part, Jim is proud to say his team includes a wide range of people, from Marc, an occasional golf buddy of his whom he closely mentors; to Mitra, a bright twenty-three-year-old originally from India; to Paulo, who heads up the Brazil office. Every team at Global Company undergoes mandatory diversity training in the first year of employment, and the company is proud of its blemish-free record with regard to discrimination. Jim takes advantage of regular, ongoing management training and executive education retreats. Personally, he's found that his generous open-door policy ensures he stays connected to his team and is brought in at the first sign of trouble with another team member, a product, or a client.

As part of a global diversity effort, Global Company's human resources department schedules Jim and his team to attend a panel discussion on "cultural fluency," an initiative in his organization where leaders make sustained efforts to understand and appreciate other cultures. The panel of senior global executives discuss the critical importance of cross-cultural adaptability for all managers, but especially for those charged with working in a global marketplace. Jim listens attentively during the talk, then approaches the presenters afterward to shake hands and thank them for a stimulating discussion. He grabs Marc to go have lunch, nodding to Mitra, who is hanging back and tweeting a line she really liked from the presentation.

"Interesting stuff," Jim tells Marc on their way back to the campus. "But I'm glad we're beyond all that here. We don't single out people's differences, and we never have. We abide by a simple principle: *We respect one another and work with integrity. It's all about respecting each other, and that's the heart of our value system. Everyone who works for me is a part of the Global Company family, period.*"

While there is much to admire in Jim's pride in his diverse team and his attempts at open communication, Jim might be making an all-too-common and shortsighted mistake in glossing over the differences in his team. Jim believes he is treating all his reports equally. But in the chapters that follow we will examine some of them, in turn, to see how Jim might be failing to connect with them as a manager, and at what cost to each employee and to the company.

An inherent problem with Jim's managerial style, which diminishes difference, lies in his belief that everything will go okay so long as everyone at the company simply respects one another. Respect is the right foundational value, but it is also highly contextual. Understandably, Jim had managed other teams throughout his career who were combative with each other and lacked cohesion. He had had to use the language of "respect" with his direct reports as a team "mantra" for building a collaborative work environment. With this new team, there is no appearance of "outward" conflict. However, what looks like respect to Jim might not look respectful at all to Mitra. Neither one of them might understand what respect looks like to Paulo, nor to the thousands of female consumers in Brazil whom Paulo is in charge of reaching. So many iterations of respect—which one to choose? By whose rules do we operate? Do we use Jim's because he's the guy in charge? That of the targeted consumers because they generate revenue? Or Mitra's because she represents the voice of the new generation? You can see how quickly the illusion of sameness breaks down. Though born of a well-intentioned desire to avoid making anyone feel bad or somehow inferior, the fix—to avoid any recognition, discussion, or even admission of difference—doesn't really fix much at all.

Though born of a well-intentioned desire to avoid making anyone feel bad or somehow inferior, the fix—to avoid any recognition, discussion, or even admission of difference—doesn't really fix much at all.

THE "EXTROVERT IDEAL" IN THE WORKPLACE AND IN OUR COMMUNITIES

Difference doesn't have to be as overt as your country of origin or your gender, but it encompasses communication values and styles that can also distance us from the corporate norm. In her insightful book *Quiet*, Susan Cain describes the journey she went on to research introverts. She struck up a conversation with a Harvard Business School student who simply assumed that there "are no introverts at HBS. You won't find any here," pointing to a particular success profile that appears to thrive in their school. Of course, that isn't true. We have encountered socially adept introverts who have attended HBS (and gone on to succeed as executives, even heads of organizations, in both the for-profit and nonprofit worlds). Yet certain professions or organizations reinforce a certain dominant "style dynamic" that is considered more attractive in that organization, which signals to new entrants (including prospective students) that only those who fit the "extroverted" profile need apply. Indeed, this "extrovert ideal" is ubiquitous and often rewarded in most North American business environments, schools, and society. Not surprisingly, individuals who do not demonstrate leadership in an overt, brash display of expressiveness are often overlooked in workplaces that value "strong, visible leadership qualities."

We hear this "let us respect one another" managerial philosophy all the time. To understand its prevalence, it helps to put this difference-diminishing instinct in context. Jim's line of thinking reflects, in part, a response to the history of discrimination and inequitable treatment based on differences. As recently as fifty years ago, women and minority professionals were just entering the workforce in the United States and all but missing in corporate boardrooms. The legal mandates that ensured equal pay and representation, as well as protection against discrimination, were a necessary foundation for building more diverse work environments. But they didn't go far enough to shield people from hidden biases in the organization. Companies have maintained an entrenched business-as-usual attitude shaped by dominant cultural norms that didn't make any space for workers who didn't fit the mold.

We've certainly come a long way since the early to mid-twentieth century. And it's easy to think that we have made it if gaining equal access and entry into certain professions for women and people of multicultural backgrounds was the ultimate goal. But there is more to this journey if we are serious about being successful in a global economy. We need a system that understands how to leverage what we have in common, while also learning how to recognize and utilize our differences.

The next step was the proliferation of workplace diversity training in the 1980s and 1990s, mainly about the concepts of race, gender, and privilege, guided by human resources and legal departments, aiming to eliminate the *isms* of difference and ferret out bias and discrimination. But the unintended consequence of framing diversity as a problem that only engenders bias, prejudice, and injustice, according to Harvard Business School professor Lakshmi Ramarajan, is that it negatively contextualizes any mention of diversity to the point that it makes people wary of having any conversation at all. One effect of this framing, says David Thomas, dean of Georgetown's McDonough Business School, has been for companies to implement defensive policies in which managers are coached to stop outwardly recognizing difference, period. Concurrently, the business case was steadily building in favor of a diverse workforce. In tough labor markets, a company's attention to diversity was cited by top candidates as a draw. The high cost of onboarding and training top talent meant that companies needed to understand diverse workers' needs in order to retain them. Increasingly, a diverse workforce was seen as able to accurately reflect the concerns and needs of a diverse consumer base. Thought leaders and researchers touted diversity as a must for top-performing companies at the same time that legal teams and HR departments erased or glossed over the language needed to frame and contextualize difference positively.

As a result, in our experience we see the impact of unspoken assumptions, crossed signals, and confusion inside companies large and small across three key groups: culture, gender, and generations. There are certainly other groups that present workplace differences, such as race, religion, disability, and sexual orientation, and research demonstrates the same lack of understanding and power gaps with the dominant culture across these groups. However, in this book we will focus on the first three areas as critical for leaders learning to recognize difference and flex their management styles appropriately.

WHAT WOMEN BRING TO THE LEADERSHIP TABLE

Though women continue to be actively courted and recruited into companies, and make up about half of the graduates entering the workforce up to the junior-executive level, a recent article in the *Financial Times* calls out the ongoing difficulty that UK firms have promoting and retaining women executives. Women make up only 6.6 percent of executive directors in the FTSE 100, and 4.6 percent of those in the FTSE 250, according to the 2012 Female FTSE Report of Cranfield University's School of Management. Research by the executive coaching firm Praesta shows that women have few leadership role models and suffer a crisis of mentorship when traditional models are used, leading some firms to engage in nontraditional mentorship arrangements such as pairing more senior women with junior male executives to help men understand the women's positioning, or having women mentor each other across companies.

Women are penalized, too, when they exhibit a leadership style that is seen as too soft compared to that used by men at the top. A more consensual style is still not perceived as strong leadership. There is an underlying assumption on the part of many that women simply can't handle the stress that comes with leadership positions. Yet this is a conversation companies are afraid to have, dancing around the beliefs surrounding women at the top. Without a candid conversation about the value of women's leadership styles, facilitated by an infrastructure supporting sponsor relationships, the high rate of attrition of female executives will continue unabated. IMPACT Leadership 21 CEO and founder Janet C. Salazar says the most common mistake women make in the workplace is assuming that men auto-matically understand them. "There is no way. As a woman, you can never assume that men understand you, your leadership approach, or where you are coming from. Men are wired differently, so you have to educate them, learn their language, and leverage these differences be-tween genders to work together." For men? "Same thing. Women use different language than men and you need to understand the unique-ness and impact on interaction, and how women give meaning to men's actions."

Gender expert Avivah Wittenberg-Cox discusses in her book *Why Women Mean Business* the importance of understanding the unique value that women bring to an organization. Women have tremendous purchasing power and offer different perspectives to leadership deci-sions. Recent Catalyst and McKinsey studies have also shown that having more women on your board or on your executive committees gains a significant performance advantage and increases your bottom line: 73 percent return on sales, 83 percent return on equity.

As one senior leader in a global consumer goods company ex-pressed, "The more our employees can look like and understand our customers, the more successful we'll be." He saw that leveraging dif-ferences inside the organization has a direct linkage to profitability.

A CULTURAL CRISIS

Gender is only one of the differences that companies need to take into account in measuring power gaps. In order for organizations to truly thrive, they need to exhibit not just cultural diversity but cul-tural proficiency, according to Cardea Services (formerly the Center for Health Training). A federal Glass Ceiling Commission study found differences that were both measurable and stark in the S&P 500: companies that rated poorly on diversity-related measures, in the bottom 100, earned an average 7.9 percent return on invest-ment, while those rated in the top 100 more than doubled that rate,

coming in at an average of 18.3 percent. Infusing cultural proficiency initiatives into company-wide values, policies, and programs
achieves a demonstrable effect.

In our own work, we see that a lack of cultural awareness can be
a barrier to effective business. Alex, a young investment banker of
mixed Latino heritage, recalls when he had to accompany his senior
bankers to meet a potential local client company in Brazil. During
that first meeting, the two senior leaders from the local company wel-
comed the team graciously and spent the first hour getting to know
the banking team, even asking questions about the personal interests and family backgrounds of the senior bankers. Alex could sense
his senior management team growing more impatient by the minute.
Given that the Brazilian business culture is highly relational and trust
driven, the leadership of the local organization did not feel ready to
talk business until they had established some deep personal trust with
their American counterparts. The Americans, conversely, were ready
to sign the documents in the first twenty minutes. Alex recalls, "We
almost lost that deal. Just as we were starting to warm up and get to
know each other, the senior managing director on our side pushed for
next steps in closing the deal. It was not necessary to move it along
so quickly. If we took that block of time to build that relationship, we
would have still had a successful outcome."

As an example of what can happen due to differences in cultural
expectations, we also found that Asians who work in Western companies become stalled in their career trajectories on their way to the
top. Today, while Asians are the most educated cultural group in the
United States (50 percent have college degrees) and make up 15 to
20 percent of the entry-level workforce in some industries, Asians
comprise only 0.3 percent of corporate officers and less than 1 percent of corporate board members. What's behind the disparity? The
2011 "Asians in America" study by the Center for Talent Innovation
(formerly the Center for Work-Life Policy) revealed that nearly half
of Asian men and women feel pressured to alter how they act, look,

and sound in order to conform to established leadership models in their workplace. Though Asians are still viewed through the stereotypical lens of the model minority and are consequently passed over for programs meant to support their professional development, these same qualities ascribed to Asians contrast with a US emphasis on an aggressive leadership style; on brash, overt displays of personal charisma; and an ability to tirelessly self-promote. Thus, according to a University of California, Riverside, study published in the *Journal of Applied Psychology*, while tapping into the knowledge and experience of racial minorities constitutes a clear competitive advantage in the global marketplace, stereotypes and bias persist regarding perceptions of who makes a good leader in business, resulting in significant implications for leadership advancement among ethnic minorities, and lost opportunity and market share.

THE GENERATION GAP

It's a conventional complaint that parents never "get" their kids or their kids' friends, who in turn can't fathom the opinions and perspectives of their parents—each generation has its own set of values, biases, and preferences that set it apart from the others. Consider, then, that the typical US workplace now employs workers from *four* distinct generations, each with a unique mind-set and approach toward work and workplace culture, posing diversity challenges that rival those of gender and ethnicity. While boomers are still apt to demonstrate their commitment with eighty-hour workweeks, Gen Y talent takes work-life balance and meaning of work too seriously to stomach that expectation without understanding the end goal of the work tasks. In fact, the generational differences that shape workplace values and retention loom large for today's companies, according to leadership development consultants and generational experts. "With Gen Yers, there's a change in the social contract between the company and worker," says Lindsey Pollak, Gen Y expert and author of

Getting from College to Career: Your Essential Guide to Succeeding in the Real World. "Loyalty for millennials doesn't mean staying at a company, building a career, and retiring. They want managers to think of them as individuals and to understand their contributions. They want their leaders cultivating each millennial as an equal participant, not just someone getting something done. They want to love their company because the company and brand reflects who they are." Boomers tend to do fine with Gen Y reports, she says; it's the Gen Xers who can't understand the generation that follows. Gen X bosses would do well to learn to "let go of what things were like when they got started—paying the dues and all that. Instead, think about how to make things easier for Yers. How do you leverage the knowledge that Yers have for the business objectives at hand? Put them on the committee you don't want to be on. These are the new leaders. Understand the new people! We need their knowledge!"

As increasing numbers of our leadership reach retirement age and we see an unprecedented brain drain, understanding what makes younger generations tick becomes increasingly important for companies intent on attracting and leveraging younger workers. Yet without understanding different styles and how they express each generation's values, clashes are waiting to happen. And, like it or not, your Gen Y talent will seek out and find a place that is better aligned with their values and work styles. Boomers might have rebelled against their more conservative and traditional parents, but they will still demand respect from their reports. These same teams, comprising Gen X and Gen Y, are by nature more entrepreneurial and may even chafe at traditional hierarchal structures within a company. Often labeled as entitled, self-absorbed, and tech-crazed by older generations, Generation Y workers tend to express their work values differently. They may leave work at five on the dot, only to be back online later in the evening to work until midnight. They are looking for meaningful work projects, with even the most entry-level hires wanting to feel connected to the greater mission of the organization. Their media multitasking may confound their older managers, but they truly hold the keys to accessing the 72 million consumers of their generation with money to spend. Organizations unable to keep workers motivated and productive lose an estimated $450 billion to $550 billion a year, according to a 2013 Gallup study. According to Birkman International's director of training, Matt Zamzow, companies that fail to address the generational gap in appropriate and effective ways will face unprecedented and significant retention problems.

HARDWIRED FOR SAMENESS

Judged against blatant bias and a backlash against diversity, Jim's we're-all-just-people framework might seem like the progressive response. After all, his team is diverse and we see plenty of goodwill expressed by Jim in his attitude toward his reports. However, when it comes to navigating across differences, research shows that goodwill and positive intent are not enough. While Jim comes with the best of intentions, we see in his management philosophy the subtle belief that his approach is the right approach, unconscious as it might be. After all, cultural, gender, and generational differences still remain between Jim and Marc and Mitra and Paulo. Jim expects those cultural outliers in his team to assimilate into the dominant workplace culture he shares, and to adopt the corresponding behaviors and expectations for how to succeed and get ahead. Leaders who are able to perceive and judge behavior through only one lens—their own—force employees outside the dominant culture to change how they behave in the workplace, whether or not they realize they are doing so. Women might be expected to assume a more aggressive or competitive style in order to be considered leadership material. Workers from other cultures have to adopt Western or American notions of acceptable behaviors and mannerisms, even those that clash fundamentally with their lived and learned cultural values. For millennials entering the workplace, assimilation could mean forgoing the use of common social networking platforms in order to conform to more accepted communication models in the company, or accepting a slower promotional path than they feel that they deserve. In the absence of an adaptive, fluent leader at the helm to encourage different viewpoints, there is tremendous pressure for employees to fit in to the existing leadership norms of the team. In an ideal state, both the organization and the employees of particular cultures or generations would flex mutually to each other.

While there is no magic formula, at the end of the day both sides need to do what is most effective for the business. Getting there means asking more questions and not automatically plugging people into the default system. It means challenging assumptions (on both sides) about the organization's default style, process, communications, and the unwritten rules governing promotion. Managers can ask themselves, and encourage their employees to ask, What are the strengths and weaknesses of each style? How does it affect the bottom line? How does it affect relationship building? Which approach will be most effective; or is it conditional, where different styles might apply in different contexts?

Most managers don't realize that they are forcing these changes in their team members' styles. After all, to see the change one would have to understand and appreciate the starting point these diverse team members are coming from. Others think it seems fair—they're at the top of the ladder, after all; why should *they* have to change? As we've seen, the simple answer is that there is clear risk in not doing so. The employees may not thrive under this management approach, or they may resent the changes they are forced to make. Over time, some will simply tire of constantly going out of their natural comfort zone to fit in to the new culture and find an organization (or manager) that can tap in to their strengths more readily. Consequently, they will underperform or leave. This is not to mention the untapped potential left lying on the table in the form of differences in style, values, and experience (something we call *underutilized cultural capital*) that could be leveraged to the company's benefit.

The old business case for diversity is no longer sufficient—that companies do not realize benefit from simply peppering their teams with diverse members from a few different backgrounds and hoping for the best. In fact, according to Robin Ely of the Harvard Business School, when put to the "empirical test," diversity without integration and two-way learning between groups can actually act as a destructive force. Research demonstrates that Jim's color-blind model that limits conversations about differences simply doesn't work; similarly, managers who direct diverse team members "appropriately" according to their perceived strengths and weaknesses and without investigation fall short as well, and in fact might experience more conflict than homogeneous teams without a corresponding bottom-line advantage. There is a need to move beyond the simplistic business-case argument for diversity, according to the Diversity Research Network consortium, because it lacks the complexity of what is found on the ground. If left unattended, the group says, research indicates diversity can negatively affect team cohesion and increase miscommunication and conflict. Instead, they found that "context is crucial in determining the nature of diversity's impact on performance," with some promising evidence that organizations that promote learning from diversity realize a direct benefit.

IN TODAY'S GLOBAL MARKETPLACE, if we don't get the small things right from a management perspective, we will have missed out on a critical element that can mean the difference between fully realized talent or disengagement and lost opportunity. Companies are tapping into their diverse employee population to gain cultural insights to unleash innovation. If we don't invest the time or effort to understand the cultural makeup of our team members, we will lag behind others in navigating global teams, and underuse the very people who can fuel innovative thinking and connect with a diverse customer base. Successful leaders must be willing to meet their team members partway. They acknowledge and reach across differences to give appropriate and constructive feedback to their team members while looking for every opportunity to leverage difference and enhance the bottom line.

TALKING ABOUT DIFFERENCES IS HARD

This willingness and intentionality on the part of great leaders is key. Because, in truth, it's not just legal departments in the defensive mode that have encouraged the rhetoric of sameness; it's an integral part of our human nature that steers us away from matters of difference. It has partly to do with language; as leaders in the American workplace, we lack a satisfactory vocabulary for talking about our differences. The words we do have all seem too loaded or don't express exactly what we mean. Many of the descriptions of cultural differences that we are exposed to in the popular media are exaggerated stereotypes or generalizations that stymie rather than help the discussion. Conversations about difference are uncomfortable. They seem almost destined to elicit conflict and enmity. We fear the negative response. In fact, we're so afraid we'll make an erroneous assumption or say something offensive that any natural curiosity we feel toward one another is stifled.

We're so afraid we'll make an erroneous assumption or say something offensive that any natural curiosity we feel toward one another is stifled.

And so, it's imperative that we develop a shared vocabulary for talking through difference in a productive way so that we can initiate these basic and necessary conversations. It's the first step toward fully understanding one another's perspectives and positions.

THE MYTH THAT "WE DON'T SEE COLOR"

It's no wonder we have difficulty discussing difference in the workplace. Some of us may also refrain from talking to our children about cultural and racial differences. Birgitte Vittrup, who as a doctoral student conducted a study on multicultural story lines and children's racial attitudes at the Children's Research Lab at the University of Texas, found that hardly any of the white American parents she surveyed had ever talked to their children directly about race. Their families used some general guiding principles such as "everybody's equal" or "under our skin, everyone's the same," but almost never called attention to racial/cultural differences, whereas nonwhite parents were about three times more likely to discuss race.

FEAR OF THE UNKNOWN

On a more basic level, while our disparate societies and cultures around the globe seem to be integrating with lightning speed, the processes of our humble brains have yet to catch up. Some neurobiological researchers believe we may have an evolutionary bias against difference, which supports the need for intentional learning and integration among diverse groups. The unfamiliar still functions to elicit in our brains a fight-or-flight reaction, meant to keep us out of harm's way in the face of a potential threat, according to David Rock and Dan Radecki of the NeuroLeadership Institute. Some studies have shown that that "threat" may appear to be a person of a different racial group. A joint research collaborative out of the United States and China showed an unconscious empathic bias of test subjects toward members of their own racial group. The research demonstrated that we subconsciously process information related to friends or those belonging to an "in-group" with us differently than we process the same information related to strangers. We are more accurate and empathetic in our processing when we perceive some sort of inherent sameness and make more errors when we process information for those we perceive as different.

If we consistently have an air of distrust and suspicion about someone, we're not going to be processing information that we receive from that person very well. If we accept that we are naturally wired to respond best and most accurately to those who are most like us, then it becomes even more important that we build the necessary skills and develop our management of diverse environments. We must be taught to view difference as latent potential, not as a liability. We must exhibit more than intentionality in understanding different perspectives. We need an insatiable curiosity about the perspectives and motivations of others, and the skills to navigate across leadership styles to elicit the best results from our teams. These are the characteristics of great leaders. These are the characteristics of fluent leaders.

We must be taught to view difference as latent potential, not as a liability.

THE KEY COMPETENCY: FLUENCY

We know now that it's not enough for leaders to ignore difference. We know that it also doesn't work for leaders to expect team members who fall outside cultural norms to blindly assimilate into the dominant culture. So what should be expected from a manager of a diverse team? When we work with managers like Jim, our goal is to enable them to achieve what we consider to be the key competency for today's leaders, what we call *fluency*. We know that with regard to language, fluency indicates the ability to express oneself readily and effortlessly. Like someone who is fluent in many languages, a truly fluent business leader is able to work and communicate effortlessly with many types of people who are different from him- or herself.

A truly fluent business leader is able to work and communicate effortlessly with many types of people who are different from him- or herself.

When we think about fluency, we are reminded of another linguistics term—*code switching*—that we think works well metaphorically in describing what can be achieved by fluency in a business context. Code switching refers to the concurrent use of more than one language during the course of a single conversation. You might have heard terms such as *Spanglish* and *Singlish*, to connote the concept of code switching. In the past, code switching was seen as a form of coping behavior performed by individuals, stuck between two linguistic worlds, who didn't possess mastery over any one language. To compensate, so it was said, they would switch between the two languages they knew, alternating terms and phrases in order to get across their meaning. Later research published in the *Journal of Early Childhood Literacy*, the *International Journal of Bilingualism*, and the *Colorado Research in Linguistics*, suggests that code switching is less a tactic of desperation than a conscious picking and choosing of words and phrases across languages in order to capture exactly the nuance the speaker wishes to convey. Thus, rather than bilingual speakers being seen as inferior in the context of mastering each individual language, their ability to speak more than one language becomes additive, sometimes providing them with the ability to create a *hybrid third language* that captures nuanced expression and meaning that would otherwise be lacking. They leverage their difference to their benefit. Like those who code switch effortlessly between different languages, culturally fluent leaders are able to speak and switch between the "codes" of different cultures, genders, and generations, communicating in the most effective manner that context demands.

Can you decipher these "codes"? Spanglish, Singlish, and texting have all become unique languages, offering a playful and specific way of communicating that goes outside the bounds of "normal" but is really quite purposeful and effective.

Spanglish
Vámanos a hanguear aquí—"Let's hang out here!"
Es muy heavy—"That's very deep (or terrible)."
Trajiste tu lonche?—"Did you bring your lunch?"

Singlish
Ah ya! Cen you help me wit fix car, lah?—"Oh no! Can you help me fix the car?"
Yah lah, can, can.—"Yes, I can!"

Texting
IMHO, ITS PROLLY 2 L8 2 CALL. SO GLAD 2 B HERE! LOL :)—"In my humble opinion, it's probably too late to call. I'm so glad to be here! Laughing out loud and smiling."
LUV UR SELFIES. SO ADORBS! VERY JELLY.—"I love the photos you took of yourself. They are adorable! I'm very jealous."

Code switchers seem to operate unconsciously in this way, using the most effective means available to express themselves fully. However as leaders we must undergo a journey and travel through several stages before we arrive at fluency. This journey mirrors the path we undertake as adults toward maturity.

STAGES OF LEARNING AND CULTURAL COMPETENCE

The strategies we use in working with our clients to get them to power gap fluency draws from both the Four Stages of Learning by William Howell (1982) and the Intercultural Development Inventory (IDI) developed by Mitch Hammer (2009, 2011).

William Howell's four "stages of competence" when learning a new leadership skill are described as follows: individuals begin in a stage of "unconscious incompetence"; they are unaware of how little they know. They move on to recognize where they fall short, reaching a stage of "conscious incompetence." They still lack ability, but they are now aware of this. The individual consciously moves to acquire a new skill or ability, practicing that skill until eventually, the individual achieves "unconscious competence," or the ability to perform a skill or possess ability without even thinking about it. When you arrive at this stage, you are barely aware that you are adapting to a different style, it becomes easier to practice the new leadership skill.

1. **Unconscious incompetence**: The individual does not know how to do something and does not recognize the lack of ability. This may be a "blind spot" for his development as a leader. The individual may deny the need to learn the new skill.
2. **Conscious incompetence**: Though the individual has not yet learned how to perform the new skill, there is increased awareness of the lack of ability.
3. **Conscious competence**: The individual has learned how to do something. However, demonstrating the skill or knowledge requires concentration. There is significant conscious effort in executing the new skill.
4. **Unconscious competence**: The individual has practiced the new skill so much and with greater frequency that it has become a lot easier to practice, and does not require as much deliberate effort.

Additionally, we find the Intercultural Development Inventory (Hammer 2011) helpful as we assess intercultural readiness of a team for leadership training. It provides us with a snapshot of the cultural competence of individuals, teams, and organizations. The Intercultural Development Continuum (IDC) identifies five worldviews of cultural competence: Denial, Polarization, Minimization, Acceptance, and Adaptation. The IDI instrument is grounded and adapted from the Developmental Model for Intercultural Sensitivity (DMIS; Bennett 1986, 1993, 2004), and has been developed by Mitch Hammer (2011). Here are the five mind-sets:

Denial: This stage reflects a more limited capability for understanding and appropriately responding to cultural differences in values, beliefs, perceptions, emotional responses, and behaviors. It is characterized by a lack of interest in, or in some cases avoidance of, other cultures.

Polarization: Polarization is an evaluative mind-set that views cultural differences from an "us versus them" perspective. Characterized by Defense (your own culture is better than others) or Reversal (your culture is inferior to others).

Minimization: Minimization is a transitional mind-set between the more Monocultural orientations of Denial and Polarization and the more Intercultural/Global worldviews of Acceptance and Adaptation. Dominant cultures tend to highlight commonalities in both human *Similarity* (basic needs) and *Universalism* (universal values and principles) that can mask a deeper understanding of cultural differences.

For nondominant culture members, minimization is a strategy for navigating dominant culture practices (i.e., going along to get along).

Acceptance: Individuals recognize and appreciate patterns of cultural difference and commonality in their own and other *cultures*.

Adaptation: Adaptation is an intercultural mind-set and is characterized by individuals who not only can shift their cultural perspective, but who have also learned to adapt behaviors in culturally appropriate ways to be more effective with other cultural communities.

In practice, let's take a look at your own leadership. Here is a description of the four management styles you might encounter. As you read, try to assess in honest terms where you fall on your own journey toward becoming a fluent leader.

STYLE 1: THE BLINDSIDED MANAGER

Working with people who are different from you makes you feel uncomfortable and/or you might have had limited experience interacting with them. You may not be aware of the gap existing between you and your direct reports due to the power distance, and are blindsided when things don't always go the way that you expect. Therefore, most of the time, you don't even notice your lack of ability in closing the gaps with them. You stick closely to what you know and don't bring up any unnecessary issues. To you, "no news is good news"; if people haven't complained about you or your management style, you must be doing all right. When direct conflict arises from differences, you may try to avoid it completely.

STYLE 2: THE JUDGING MANAGER

You find that individuals who relate differently to you annoying, or feel that there is a better way to do things. You may feel a woman engineer can't be as hard-nosed and logical as her male counterpart, or resent a Generation Y for texting all the time, thinking these young people could use a lesson in relating to people the old-fashioned way: face to face. You tolerate some differences, but when push comes to shove, you know that you have the right way of doing things. You expect your team to conform to your style.

STYLE 3: THE GOLDEN-RULE MANAGER

Diversity training and previous experience have taught you that it's probably safest to treat everyone the same. While people might be different from each other on the outside, we're all human, after all. You believe that differences should be deemphasized and that they don't really matter in workplace interactions. You emphasize "fair treatment" and also believe that most people will respond positively if you treat them the way that you would want to be treated. You may subconsciously use your own experience and position in establishing the "universal template" for managing people.

STYLE 4: THE FLUENT LEADER

You accept and are curious about potential differences across cultural, gender, and generational lines. Instead of resorting to stereotypes to judge these differences, you begin your exploration and appreciate difference on an individual level. You use this knowledge to help correct negative behaviors, engage employees' motivated skills and talents on a deeper level, and motivate them more fully. You are able to flex across the power gap to be more effective with your direct reports. You take a chance to put someone different from you on a high-visibility project, even though that person might be untested. You value their input and find ways to enhance your ability to work across these differences.

Respectful inquisitiveness is one of the hallmarks of the fluent leader, as exhibited by Kristin, a VP in the publishing industry. "Even though our team meets once a week, our accountant, Rosa, never says a word," reports Kristin. "Others on the team actively contribute their ideas and questions during these meetings. Yet Rosa seems hesitant to speak up, even though her written presentations are always excellent. As a result, people see her as ineffective and even disengaged." After several peer reviews rated Rosa as low-performing despite her excellent work output, Kristin decided to investigate. Kristin took Rosa to lunch, and asked why she was so quiet in meetings.

At first, Rosa seemed unsure of why Kristin was asking. Finally, she told her that she was brought up and educated in Mexico. In that culture, you show respect by letting one's superior have the floor.

Since Kristin often ran the weekly meeting, Rosa did not feel it was her place to interject. However, Kristin explained that American managers expect their team members to chime in, no matter what the circumstances. With Kristin's encouragement, Rosa gradually began to contribute her views and was later able to save a new venture from running over budget. Kristin also realized that Rosa's respect for superiors allowed her to listen well and "soak up" the wisdom and knowledge offered by those with more experience. Rosa was a quick study, and with some coaching, she was able to leverage her value of respect into building strong relationships with all her colleagues.

Rather than allowing Rosa to fail or assigning erroneous motives to Rosa's lack of participation, Kristin's investigation into Rosa's different style allowed her to guide her employee toward more successful behavior and help her develop necessary skills.

CHAPTER 2

MANAGING THE POWER GAP

Jim is frustrated by his weekly status meetings. First, even though he likes to start Monday morning off with status, he moved the meetings to noon in order for Paulo to "attend" via video chat at a reasonable hour. But it's Mitra that Jim really can't understand. She keeps taking on new projects and accounts yet isn't delivering results in a timely manner. During status meetings, Jim deliberately loads people up until they say no. Marc is quick to laugh and say, "I've got enough on my plate!" But Mitra never pushes back. He's received e-mails from her at two in the morning and she's missed some of her deadlines, but no matter what he asks her to do, she readily agrees. Mitra seemed like such a whiz kid when they recruited her straight out of school. Now Jim's starting to wonder if he made an expensive mistake. It seems like she's trying to show off in front of the rest of her colleagues at the expense of the company.

When Jim asks for a meeting with Mitra, he carries into the room with him far more than his BlackBerry and a cup of coffee. He carries with him twenty-three years of experience at Global Company and the weight of his opinions. When people describe Jim, no one mentions where he's from (is it Ohio?). Instead, they talk about his ideas. Jim is a friendly guy, but they still speak in hushed whispers about the cutthroat manner in which he rose to his current position. Jim is a bit of a legend. He has a ruthless desire to win, and demands a lot from his team. In fact, when Jim was Mitra's age he took on every project and account he could, pulling eighty-hour weeks so that he could wow his boss.

Jim describes Mitra to a colleague as "that whip-smart kid" they hired out from under the nose of the competition. He knows her parents still live in India, though Mitra has lived in the United States since she arrived to attend college. She speaks English fluently, and writes better than a few of his American team members. He doesn't know much more about her, though. In meetings she never joins in when they're talking about politics or sports, Jim's favorite warm-up conversation, though he's heard her laugh about some video on You-Tube while chatting with another coworker. He's never been quite sure if she doesn't meet his gaze on purpose or because she's always texting or tapping or doing something on her phone, even during meetings! Jim loves that she never turns down a project. In fact, she always smiles and agrees to take it on. But if she's overburdened, why doesn't she just say so?

What exists between Jim and Mitra is what we call a **power gap**.

IDENTIFYING THE POWER GAP

In the previous chapter, we talked about differences between the styles, perceptions, and cultural values of managers and their employees. The power gap is the social distance that separates individuals from those in positions of authority, whether in a formal or more informal structure.

While we might recognize the social distance between a vice president and a junior associate in a formal organizational hierarchy, for our discussion we want to make an additional distinction between minority and dominant culture, since often people more closely aligned with the minority culture may not be given as big a voice in these organizations.

Conventional wisdom would say that the outliers from the dominant culture—the multicultural workers; the more junior people; or perhaps the young, entry-level team members—should work to get their styles, values, and communication in sync with their managers and feel empowered enough to close the power gap, i.e., they should assimilate into the existing culture of the organization, to "fit in" to the group.

However, in our work we have noticed that conventional wisdom might not be right and may not always work. We chose multicultural, gender, and generational groups to talk about in this book because these are the most common perceived outliers already being delineated by organizations across the globe and set apart from managers by an increasing power gap, although there are certainly others as well. In our work we've seen that the same dynamics repeat themselves time and time again as the unique perspectives of different groups are not understood by their managers, to the frustration of both sides.

Hierarchical Style

As we examine the power gap dynamics as it relates to these three groups, it is helpful to note the management and communication styles that exist at either extreme in the spectrum. Hierarchical management styles depend on standardized systems, value a great degree of control, and expect integration of others into the established system or order. Great deference is given to people in authority, and decision making is generally top-down. Hierarchical management styles roughly mirror traditional corporate company structures. Though the United States is not viewed as very hierarchical when compared with cultures, such as India or China, the truth is that the American business landscape still supports fairly traditional hierarchical management styles. Many companies still operate in a very directive, top-down fashion. People in the highest positions are afforded the most power in decision making, and set the tone for how the company should look, feel, and operate.

Historically speaking, the way that gender and age interacted with these structures is that women and younger workers have been lower on the pole in top-down organizations, and both sides knew it. That has changed somewhat over the past few decades, and continues to shift and evolve. Younger workers, for example, now largely eschew hierarchical models, favoring more egalitarian environments even when they work for a company with hierarchical structures in place. Women now outpace men as college graduates, and can even go to battle for their country. While there is still progress to be made in empowering women, American culture purports to offer them full equality in the workplace.

Egalitarian Style

Egalitarian management styles are based in the doctrine of egalitarianism, a term that derives from the French *égal*, "equal." In general, in a flat organizational environment, workers may share fairly equal authority in decision making. Managers who lean toward a more egalitarian style seek to minimize the power gap between themselves and their team members. In organizations, some leaders are more comfortable in hierarchical environments; the structures inside that hierarchy feel comfortable to them. Other managers exhibit a much more egalitarian ethic. Even if technically, on paper, they have more power, authority, or decision-making authority than other colleagues in their organization, they may treat employees of varying rank in the same manner. In the same way, egalitarian employees may feel comfortable questioning the manager and interacting less formally with him or her, whereas employees who are more hierarchical might wait for the manager to assign work, and maintain a safe distance from the manager. Gen Y's are said to trend toward egalitarian models, while multiculturals from hierarchical cultures might find the same models confusing or even disrespectful. The key lies in knowing your own individual preference and being able to judge the preferences of those around you correctly.

HOW THE POWER GAP MANIFESTS ON YOUR TEAM

With a power gap, the more hierarchical your culture or background, the greater the power gap is apt to be. This is because hierarchical cultures reinforce the differences between managers and employees. If you tend to be more hierarchical in your orientation, you tend to put those in positions of authority at a higher level, and there is more respect for that status or position, divorced even from the person who occupies it. Distance is seen as *good* if you have a hierarchical preference. It wouldn't be proper for a manager to be too familiar with his reports. The effect is that any power gap that exists is magnified through the lens of this dimension. A greater power gap can result

in decreased communication as well as increased misunderstandings
and conflict, potentially leading to missed opportunities for building
significant business and career relationships.

What does the power gap look like in the workplace? Here are
some more examples of workers caught on the wrong side of the
power gap in their organizations. Misunderstood and undervalued,
these are workers who could offer tremendous assets to their companies. Fluent leaders who can spot them and are able to close the power
gap with them can leverage their diverse talents to the benefit of the
company's bottom line and the workers' career. Managers who refuse
to budge stand to lose key talent and market share.

1. Gina is a marketing executive at a major auto manufacturer. She
   often sits in on design meetings with the all-male engineering staff.
   In the meetings, she's made a few suggestions about car accessories
   that would appeal to women. She's also asked that they add a new
   step in the design process: taking into account information drawn
   from female focus groups. The VP thinks the system is fine as is.
   After all, that model has run without a hitch for years. He thanks
   Gina for her suggestions, but never follows through on them.

   What's lost: Gina's perspective on how women, a critical demographic, make purchasing decisions; a sense of inclusivity that
   makes the customer feel part of the product design. Gina feels
   devalued in her team.

   What her manager could gain by closing the power gap: A
   new approach to innovation. New insight into buyers' wants and
   needs. A leg up on the competition by listening to customers' specific feedback.

   It can't be denied that almost every culture around the world
   is rooted in a patriarchal history. And if you start with a patriarchal framework in which women are inherently less valued
   and are even seen as inferior, it takes a sea change to shift that

perception in the workplace. Though a lot has changed in this country since the 1960s, we are by no means entirely free of this legacy. In addition to being subject to lingering perceptions of inferiority, women are still socialized at a young age to follow instructions and be attentive. They are rewarded for these "good student" behaviors. Yet some of these behaviors may be at odds with some of the traits expected in a high-risk, high-reward corporate environment. Increasingly, research seems to suggest that men and women communicate inherently differently. Because there has been so much tangible progress with regard to women in the workplace, talking about the power gap between men and women can be very uncomfortable. People don't want to highlight the differences between men and women—they want to point out the similarities. Yet this obfuscates the differences and minimizes the fact that dominant communication models in most boardrooms are still essentially "male." It's no wonder misunderstandings continue to arise along gender lines.

2. John is a twenty-three-year-old recent college graduate who hit the ground running. He's already put himself on the fast track and continues to press for an international assignment. Yet most days, at exactly five o'clock, he's out the door. He sits on the board of a start-up nonprofit that provides after-school tutoring for inner-city middle school kids. John has been coming in late recently, but instead of picking up the phone and calling his manager, he sends a text. In fact, John seems to spend a huge amount of time tapping away at his iPhone instead of getting out there and building relationships with clients face-to-face. No one confronts him about this behavior, thinking, Kids are just like that. Yet no one is fast-tracking him to the international assignment that he has been vocal about pursuing since he was recruited, either. If he can't build in-person relationships with people in the United States, how will he be successful in another culture?

What's lost: An opportunity to channel John's energy and team spirit and extend it outward into client relations and outreach into the broader community. John feels dismissed and grows increasingly disengaged.

What his manager could gain by closing the power gap: John's ability to work 24/7 to meet a deadline. He can go full steam ahead when he's excited by a project and can work on it, with no rules or restrictions, in the company of his peers. An added plus is his ability to get the word out about a new product using technology and social networking.

As companies welcome growing numbers of Generation Y into the workplace, we come up against yet another "ouch" point. In a hierarchical culture seniority is afforded respect and, traditionally speaking, age equals experience. The older you are, the more revered you are in your organization. Yet millennials are often frustrated by what they see as business as usual. They crave flatter organizations where collaboration can occur organically across different departments to solve business problems. They exhibit more fluid decision making, and have the ability to use new technology and new systems of communication to change the way business is conducted. You can see what often happens when the expectations of a new recruit clash with the traditional mind-set of a boomer boss. Managers who "did their time" may chafe at Gen Y employees who expect to contribute significantly and meaningfully even early in their careers. The new generation that expects to hold multiple career positions in their lifetimes, likely in different companies, expects responsibilities perhaps more senior to their level of experience. They want to be promoted quickly, and become frustrated when they are held back, told to wait their turn because "it's the way things are done."

3. Justin is second-generation Chinese American with an MBA; he works as a senior financial analyst. He finds his company highly political, with everyone jockeying to win the favor of the senior VP.

"Although I grew up in the States, I grew up in a very traditional Chinese family where we were rewarded for keeping our mouths shut and never questioning authority," he says. In Justin's culture (and countless others), junior people defer to senior people—even if those senior people are sometimes wrong. For these employees, *not* speaking up means showing deference to the boss.

What's lost: Justin is a top-notch analyst. If he doesn't feel recognized, he will leave.

What his manager could gain by closing the power gap: Justin's bicultural assets; language abilities and a larger, unrecognized external network, including his family connections in Asia.

Multicultural workers who are expected to promote their own accomplishments in order to get ahead, drop by the boss's office to shoot the breeze or pitch an idea, may find themselves completely at odds with their own deeply ingrained value system regarding respect and authority. The result is dissatisfied managers, bewildered workers, and a systematic breakdown of communication.

With all this in mind, let's return to examine Jim's situation with Mitra and the power gap that exists between them. There are disparities and difference in seniority, culture, gender, and generational values between the two of them, and there is a clear formal hierarchy as well. Jim enjoys an advantage because his positioning is much closer to the dominant cultural norm at Global Company and in traditional US corporate culture. Because Jim doesn't acknowledge difference in his team, he is unable to recognize the different values and assumptions Mitra carries with her as part of her lived experience as a female millennial South Asian immigrant, nor can he understand how the difference between their values and experience affects how she operates in the workplace.

You'll note that in assessing the motives behind Mitra's "problematic" behavior, Jim defaulted to his own past behavior to guide his assumptions. Instead of considering her point of view, he assumes she must be taking on too much in order to wow him and get ahead, just as he did as a junior-level executive. While Jim admires the grit, he is frankly annoyed that her competitive spirit is affecting his team's performance. Jim's inability to bridge the power gap between them and investigate the reasons behind Mitra saying yes too often is holding both of them back. And Jim is certainly not alone in failing to address the power gap in managing multiculturals or team members of a different gender or generation. It is not just Jim who is risking losing skilled employees and existing customers. If you are not bridging the power gaps within your team, you might be losing new market opportunities with customers as well (more on that in part 2).

Perhaps you're already feeling defensive of Jim. Mitra is the one taking on work she can't handle, so why are we saying Jim needs to change? Mitra certainly has her part to play in the solution. But often managers don't want to make the effort to close the gap. After all, in many settings, the gap serves to elevate the manager's rank. The social distance is sometimes viewed as an acknowledgment of authority or respect. But when managers choose to close the gap and meet their employee partway, they are *not giving away authority or respect*. Closing the power gap need not make a leader more vulnerable; in fact, it can do the opposite, creating trust and communication where before there was only conflict and poor performance. We have found that leaders who can flex to a variety of thinking and communication styles are more respected and more effective, overall, because they are able to tap each person's potential in unique ways.

When managers choose to close the gap and meet their employee partway, they are *not giving away authority or respect*. Closing the power gap need not make a leader more vulnerable; in fact, it can do the opposite, creating trust and communication where before there was only conflict and poor performance.

For example, a fluent leader in Jim's position would investigate Mitra's behavior free of any preconceived notions or judgments and without aligning it with his own history. There exists a problem—Mitra piling on work and then missing deadlines—but the solution is not yet clear. If Jim could acknowledge and investigate the difference and distance between them, he might discover something new or unexpected that he could then try to leverage to the benefit of the team, a process we call *managing the power gap*. As a fluent leader, it is critical that you innovate how you think about managing people, and rethink the actions you must personally take to manage people who are different from you. For managers of today's diverse teams, this means taking direct action to assess and investigate the power gaps between you and your team members. As we saw with Justin, Gina, and John, not only may managing the power gap correct unwanted behavior, it may uncover untapped skills and unrealized potential.

In this case, a fluent leader might have asked about Mitra's superhuman willingness to take on more work, even when she was clearly overburdened, and discovered that if asked to take on work by her superior, Mitra would never feel comfortable uttering Marc's "I've got enough on my plate!" If her manager needed someone to take on a project, she felt it was her job to help get it done. Jim and Mitra were playing the same game by two different sets of rules. Jim's tactic was to pile it on with the expectation that his team members would say "enough" when they hit their limit. Instead of choosing to take on more work to show up her colleagues, Mitra was accepting work no one else was volunteering to do, even when she was maxed out, because she didn't want to let Jim down.

Let's stop and think of the effect of discovering the true motives behind Mitra's behavior. Jim's feelings about Mitra could change dramatically. She's not putting the team at risk deliberately; she was willing to do more than anyone else in order to fulfill Jim's wishes! Coming to an understanding about why she was acting that way would allow Jim to work with Mitra in a more informed way to manage how much work she takes on, and even redistribute the load. He would be able to communicate to her that she need take on only enough work to be successful and show off her considerable skills. In the end, the behavior still needs to change, and Mitra would need to let Jim know when she's reached her capacity. Managing the power gap allows a manager and an employee to work toward productive solutions together with increased trust and improved communication. Jim is still Mitra's boss, he still has her respect (perhaps even more), and now he might also get the results he always wanted from her.

We've seen these situations play out similarly time and time again. Robert, a senior vice president at a large insurance company, recalls how he reached out to engage a newly hired Latina manager in order to unearth her knowledge in more detail in a meeting:

> I found that we had a relatively new person at our organization, a manager who had come from another company. At one of our status meetings, I noticed that she was very quiet. But I had enough info about her and had some insight into her considerable background and skills. So, after a while when she was still quiet, I invited her to come to the floor and told her, "My understanding was that you had this kind of experience in your previous job and, based on that, you would seem to have some insights into our current business problem." After I had acknowledged her expertise and told her we needed her help, she became a great asset to us! That helped to onboard her as an expert in our company.

Recently, we held our signature Cultural Fluency roundtable sessions focusing on leading virtual, multicultural teams at a large communications company in New England. We knew through the group IDI results before the training that the team was in the Minimization stage of cultural competence. During the lunch break, a senior vice president of a major communications company came up to us and pulled us aside. During the training, he had been sitting there and taking in all the information, and not saying a whole lot. Now, he described his aha moment, his face lit up with understanding:

> Our company is considered a model for diversity, a leading-edge company that leverages diversity to enhance our business. And over the past ten years of diversity training, I've been taught what to say, what not to say, and most important, how critical it is to treat everyone the same way, regardless of background. In the past, that's a management style that has always worked for me. But when you explained how the power gap works, and how it's okay to adjust my style to communicate more effectively with my new Asian manager, I realized how it fundamentally conflicts with my old modus operandi. I also finally got why the results from that manager were well below expectations.

How important is it that leaders understand how to manage the power gap? The simple answer is that if you intend to stay in business, it has to be one of your top priorities. Understanding the power gap dimension is *the* must-have survival skill in the high-stakes game of leading in the new age.

Too often managers don't believe they should have to make any sort of effort to take an active role in examining how to bridge differences. You'll remember that Jim felt a little put out that he had to shift a meeting time to accommodate the different time zone of his direct report. In puzzling over his problem with Mitra, Jim wondered why she didn't come to him to say she was in over her head, but he didn't take the critical next step to approach her to talk through the issue. As you move along your journey toward fluency, we encourage you to shift your mind-set from the fear-based and conflict-avoidant model of the past and adopt a fluent leader's curious, proactive investigation of the new American workplace. In her paper on reframing diversity policies (quoted in Nobel 2011). Harvard Business School professor Lakshmi Ramarajan urges leaders to reframe the direct engagement of diverse employees as a means of "increasing relationships" or to "create ways in which people have open communication," recasting managers' efforts to bridge the power gap as critical steps toward the advancement and growth of their teams.

Hiring diverse teams and then hoping for the best is not working. As a result, women, multicultural employees, and younger generations of workers are not getting the right management they need to rise through the ranks inside the organization or to do their best. Managers need to play a much more active role in examining their way of interacting across these differences, and provide stronger leadership and mentoring of these individuals in order to do their best to leverage diversity for the good of the company. This can be done if we can fully understand the power gap dynamic and work toward developing the skills of fluent leadership.

CHAPTER 3

CULTURE AND COMMUNICATION: FLEXING ACROSS STYLES

Say what you mean and mean what you say.
—AMERICAN PROVERB

He who knows, does not speak. He who speaks, does not know.
—CHINESE PROVERB

Don't beat around the bush.
—ESTONIAN PROVERB

As these proverbs so aptly show, there are a myriad of styles and manners in which people build trust, relate to one another, and communicate their needs and expectations. We find it helpful to apply insights from social psychology and anthropology—the notion that we have communication styles that might differ from our coworkers—to the business world. We borrow the styles and dimensions researched by various cultural anthropologists, such as Edward Hall and Geert Hofstede, who identified recognizable patterns and traits that emerge among different cultural groups. Understanding differences in communication should give you a new understanding and a new vocabulary to describe the personal differences you encounter in the workplace, allowing you to address different perceptions in a way that is not threatening for either participant and gets results. Your first step toward flexing, as a manager, is to learn to identify and examine the different styles and preferences of your employees through this lens. If we are successful in this, we can move beyond bias and stereotypes to see difference for what it is: just another way of being in the world.

In addition to sorting out your reports and colleagues according to their own styles, you should analyze your own interaction preferences. Are you a group thinker or an individual decision maker? When you take credit for your work, is it about what results you attained, or more about what the team accomplished together? When you have to give tough feedback to your colleagues, do you tell it to them straight or do you try to soften the blow? Are you expressive or more emotionally restrained? This self-examination is critical as you seek to flex your preferred style to ensure that your message is heard and increase the likelihood of getting the desired result.

IN BEGINNING TO UNDERSTAND these dimensions more fully, we would like to introduce you to a new vocabulary for differences. As we go forward and define these terms we will present them as dichotomies, e.g., someone is said to have either a *direct* or an *indirect* communication style, or to be more *individualistic* or *collectivist* when it comes to making a decision. You may recognize people in your organization who fall on one extreme of the spectrum, or you may realize that some people use different styles depending on context (e.g., people may communicate more indirectly with their superiors, but very directly with others). Others will fall somewhere in the middle. Understanding the nuances of each person's style will aid you in your ability to practice flexing in your leadership, and with practice and time, you will become more adept at recognizing the differences. While there is no one right or wrong way to communicate, chances are you have experienced already that individual leaders in your organization demonstrate a strong preference for a particular interaction style.

Below are some of the style preferences we will explore in this chapter. We'll explain what may be unfamiliar modes of communication and the assumptions around them, then offer examples and techniques that show you how to bridge the gap along the spectrum of the following styles, preferences, and behaviors:

- Direct vs. Indirect Communication
- Expressive vs. Restrained Styles
- Task-oriented vs. Relationship Trust Building
- Individualism vs. Collectivistic Behavior
- Low-context vs. High-context Cultures

A PREMIUM ON DIRECT COMMUNICATION

The acceptable norm in most American organizations is to employ a direct communication style. Overall, in American culture, we are more willing than in indirect cultures to confront a difficult situation, have it out, and get the issues on the table. Direct communicators expect that whatever words they say comprise the entirety of their message. So it's really no surprise when they are stymied by a co-worker whose style is more roundabout, by someone like Kamran.

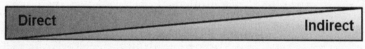

Direct   **Indirect**

The Direct vs. Indirect Spectrum

Kamran, a second-generation Pakistani American, is working to bring a new piece of software to market. Kamran happens to be a more indirect communicator. In his culture, it is more important to keep your head down and solve a problem on your own, without questioning the boss. Kamran might hint to a colleague that he's overwhelmed, saying, "This is more work than I expected." But he'll never walk into the boss's office and admit he's in over his head. How does this play out?

At the last minute, Kamran hits a glitch in the programming. Instead of informing his manager, he practically lives at the office, working 24/7, to debug the product. He works all through the weekend and finishes late on Monday, only to find out that he won't be able to make the delivery date and has set the project back significantly. Kamran is now sitting in your office, resignation in hand, waiting to find out if he still has a job. As his superior, where do you begin?

In general, while it's true that American managers and leaders are more direct in their style than those of other cultures, individuals actually fall along a spectrum, and can even shift at various points in their career. If you tend to prefer directness in your communication, you prefer to tell it like it is and expect that others communicate their needs to you in a similar way. If a directly communicating manager believes her employee is having difficulty with a project, she would probably approach him like this: "Kamran, stop by my office. I need to talk to you about the deal you're working on."

Indirect communicators may rely on other signals, signs, codes, and even third parties to communicate their meaning, and depend upon the receiver of the communication to decode their meaning and understand what they are trying to say. If you have a preference for indirectness, you may drop hints to others about your feelings about an issue, and refrain from explicitly verbalizing your intentions. It's important to note that indirect communicators are distinct from those who are passive-aggressive or conflict avoidant. Passive-aggressive and avoidant communicators are those who do not actively deal with the issue at all. People may mistakenly assume a coworker is passive-aggressive or avoidant when messages are actually being sent indirectly through various other means. In cultures where direct messages are preferred, people tend to distrust indirect communicators, as they are viewed as too vague or as intentionally deceptive or even manipulative. However, we should keep in mind that most indirect communicators are trying to get their message across just as clearly as their direct-communicating counterparts; they are simply using a different style.

BENEFITS OF THE INDIRECT COMMUNICATION STYLE

Instead of asking an employee to come by the office and asking him about a problem with a project, as our direct communicator did, an indirect communicator might instead ask Kamran to swing by the office so she could get his advice on something. "I'd like to pick your brain about a situation with somewhat similar issues to those we're experiencing with the component you're working on. . . . What do you think I should do in that situation?" The indirect communicator is stating very clearly, if you decode the phrasing, that the employee she is talking to is really the issue, and she is asking him to do his own problem solving related to the issue at hand. This is the business equivalent of the old saw, "So, I have this friend with a problem. . . ." You can see how, depending on context and the style most comfortable for the employee, one of the two approaches might work better in getting the desired result: the employee fixes the issue related to the component.

Because America is a very say-what-you-mean culture, we can feel a disconnect when we are on the receiving end of indirect communication. But in practice, indirect approaches can also be very effective, another means to get the message across in a different way. In the world of business, sometimes we are actually less direct than we think we are. In fact, leadership coaches may use indirect approaches to invite people to consider a situation, rather than directly confronting them on certain behaviors. It encourages both parties to actively participate in thinking over a problem rather than telling someone that what they'd done is wrong; often, people can get stuck on this first step—thinking what they've done is wrong—without moving on to changing and striving to model more appropriate behaviors.

One example that contrasts direct and indirect communication styles beautifully was relayed to us by Betty, a brilliant Chinese operations senior manager who works both in China and in the United States. Betty's boss, a Caucasian North American executive, asked her to translate for him in a very important meeting with a top Chinese client. In asking her to do him this favor, Betty's boss overlooked the fact that in Chinese culture, acting as the interpreter would lower Betty's status in the eyes of the client. Interpreting for her boss would create the perception that she was merely an interpreter and not the experienced authority figure that she needed to be. And since she was the primary relationship manager with this client, that misperception would damage her credibility.

But that is not what Betty told her boss. Her own deeply embedded cultural values would never allow her to point out to her superior that he had made such an obvious error. She simply told him that she was perhaps not the right person for such an important job of interpreting, and he found another interpreter for the meeting. In being indirect, Betty was expecting him to know what she was really saying. And because he was a fluent communicator, he understood clearly the intent behind her words. With this response, Betty found a way to still attend the meeting but not as an interpreter for her boss. She preserved her own credibility with the future client relationship without challenging her boss's request. Fluency means understanding how to communicate both directly and indirectly, depending on the receiver of the message and also on context.

Direct communicators may see their style as the most open and honest approach. But being indirect is about mitigating your message to soften it—and that has its value, too, because the focus is building and maintaining a relationship. Betty addressed the issue indirectly because she didn't want to challenge her boss's judgment. But her message was delivered *and* received by him, and the desired results were achieved.

There are plenty of Kamrans and Bettys out there. A variety of cultures communicate indirectly, and studies show that American women generally prefer more indirect communication styles as well. In the States, regional differences also exist, such as between those who grew up in the Northeast and those in the South. Chances are you have more employees than you think who fall into the indirect category. If you start out as a direct American manager and can master the art of indirect communication, you will develop one of the critical planks to becoming a fluent leader, and better able to bridge the power gap and work effectively with a wider range of people.

SOFTEN THE BLOW

Mitigation is a tool useful in multiple contexts when a more indirect communication style is warranted. Mitigation techniques soften the impact of a message, request, or problem statement, sometimes to the point that the initial "ask" or the person about whom you're speaking is not present in the speaker's language at all.

Consider the apology, a hallmark of mitigated speech. Georgetown professor and linguist Deborah Tannen has written extensively on what she sees as clear differences in the way men and women communicate publicly, especially in the workplace. She argues that the different styles are important not only because they prevent miscommunication, but also because they influence the perceptions of the skills and abilities of the speaker. One common example is that women tend to say "I'm sorry" frequently, though they often aren't actually apologizing when they do so. And apologies don't always convey that someone has made an error.

Tannen found that sometimes women say "I'm sorry" when the *other* person has done something wrong, asked for something, or caused an inconvenience. In those cases, the words are about connecting and offering automatic reassurance that they weren't put out by the other person's actions. Colleagues from other cultures might also use "I'm sorry" to convey an intent to preserve the harmony in the working relationship.

Understanding when and how to use mitigated speech is important, however. Tannen notes that women's overall more indirect and even apologetic style can make them appear less confident and competent. Too much mitigation can also become annoying or seem condescending, especially to direct communicators who just want you to come out and say it. Indirect communication is not always the right style for the situation.

What is the right style? There are times when being more indirect is warranted, such as when the other person is an indirect communicator. Culture and gender can both be factors. You can use mitigation to help someone save face in either a public or private situation. You can use it to avoid appearing confrontational or rude, especially with someone apt to challenge you directly and make the conversation more difficult. You can be indirect when speaking with a person of higher rank in order to show respect, or to offer politeness and propriety.

For the times you need it, here are several examples of how to soften the message and get heard:

Phrase a demand as a question.
Direct: "Do this by Friday."
Mitigated: "Can you do this by Friday?"

Make it conditional—*would, could, maybe, sometimes, possibly.*
Direct: "Give me the report by COB."
Mitigated: "If possible, I'd love to get the figures in time to look them over tonight."

Hide the message in a subordinate clause.
Direct: "I have more experience and education in this area. I would like to lead this project."
Mitigated: "When I was at Stanford getting my MBA, we worked on a test case similar to this one."

Yes, this is the equivalent of hiding vegetables so your kids will eat them. But if they get them into their bodies, isn't that what matters?

When Direct Is Best

In his book *Outliers*, Malcolm Gladwell makes the argument that avoidable plane crashes occur as a result of mitigated or softened speech—either on the part of the pilot when talking to air traffic control or a copilot speaking to a higher-ranking pilot who relied on deference and indirect speech in "hinting" at solutions for what became clear emergencies.

Okay, a plane crash is a fairly dire result of using mitigated speech when a more direct approach is warranted. But there are times when beating around the bush will only hinder the process and won't get you to your goal. If you're an indirect communicator, you may need to amplify the urgency of your message to be heard by the more direct person. Emergent or urgent situations often call for clarity, as the example above illustrates. Pay attention to how the other people are communicating with you. Are they direct communicators? They may be annoyed or put out if you don't respond in the same manner. If you've delivered a softened message once or twice and it doesn't seem to be getting through, a more direct approach is warranted. Sometimes, direct communication is necessary in situations where appearing anything less than direct could make you appear less confident, less competent, or incapable of handling the situation. Direct communication is also necessary when there is a great deal of urgency or there are time constraints (e.g., project deadlines, meeting time frames). Here's what direct expressions could look like:

Don't offer an implicit alternative.
Mitigated: "You know Suresh pretty well. Would you be able to speak to him about this project? What does he think about the deadline?"
Direct: "Please speak to Suresh about the project or we won't meet our deadline."

Drop the qualifiers.
Mitigated: "If you have time this week, let's go over your process on that last assignment."
Direct: "We didn't meet our objectives last week. Please get on my schedule tomorrow morning and we'll do a postmortem on your last assignment."

> **Don't apologize.**
> Mitigated: "Sorry, just bear with me, but what if we went in a totally
>   crazy direction here?"
> Direct: "Our old approach isn't working. We need to get creative
>   about a new direction for this campaign if we're going to connect
>   with our market."

EXPRESS YOURSELF

The good thing about highly expressive communicators is that you know them when you see them. These are the people who can't ask you for the time without gesticulating, laughing, or showing lively facial expressions. And you know exactly how they feel. Even in business contexts, expressive communicators can be highly animated. They have great variation in tone of voice. On the extreme end, expressive communicators might shout or pound tables (a stereotypically "male" response), or cry, shrink back, or leave the room (a stereotypically "female" response) to communicate displeasure or embarrassment.

In an American context, expressive communicators can find some validation and some barriers. As for facial expressiveness, it is acceptable in American culture to smile, even with strangers you encounter in public. However, people from Eastern Europe might find that gesture unusual, even suspect behavior. Expressiveness is often used to gauge enthusiasm for a project, a product, or a client. Similarly, expressive bosses may be easy to read in terms of whether they are pleased (or not) with performance, or whether they seem to like a particular employee. And these responses may be valued in different work environments. If you're a manager at an ad agency, or a sales director, where your competence is measured by your creativity and group presentation skills, you have to be upbeat and expressive and show that you are excited about your product.

The Expressive vs. Restrained Spectrum

Emotionally restrained communicators are different. Their mode of communication is focused on delivering the words and emphasizing facts. Restrained communication styles result in the coveted "poker face" that may be useful in negotiating deals or in dealing with clients. Restrained communicators may be unfairly judged as cold or unfeeling, but they also may be perceived as more rational or logical than their expressive counterparts. Certain cultures are deemed more expressive, such as Latin American cultures or the French and Italians, while others are regarded as restrained, including some Asian cultures, the British, and Germans. Men, as a group, fall to the restrained, while women are usually socialized to be expressive.

Brian, a Korean American educated in Asia, was an entrepreneur before he took a position as a manager at a telecommunications company. Working in his first position in an American company, Brian realized he was not comfortable looking people in the eye, and preferred a brief nod in the hall to talking to executives. He soon realized how important it was in his workplace to reassure people with body language and demonstrable excitement, a point brought home to him by his supervisor, who told him he needed to show more enthusiasm. Once he was told how important it was to his success, he began to express his passion in the words he chose to use and in the way that he presented his thoughts in in-person meetings. The result was that his ideas were received better, and his superiors trusted him with bigger projects.

Though Brian's ability to flex toward a more expressive style helped him to connect better with his leadership, there are times when too much demonstrative behavior will hurt, not help, your cause. A fluent communicator will deftly assess different situations and players to make the right call.

COMMUNICATING WITH GLOBAL PARTNERS

Eliseo, a VP in the Buenos Aires office of a US consumer goods corporation, was about to be promoted, but first the CEO wanted him to become a better global leader. We were hired to coach Eliseo, who was very effective in his home country, and prepare him to deal with his partners and direct reports in the United States, Europe, and Asia.

To begin we did a 360-degree analysis, interviewing staff, his peers, and his senior managers. As we spoke with a Mexican employee who worked with Eliseo online, and with others who worked with him in-house, we heard nothing but positive assessments. Of course his direct reports wouldn't dream of saying anything negative, but we got a very different picture from his boss, as well as from his Canadian counterparts. Eliseo could sometimes be gruff and bark out orders, and at times he was quite intimidating. Stories were circulating that he'd lost his temper at a worker and had engaged in a shouting match with him. It became obvious that he would have to learn other tools of management to be more effective outside of his current sphere of influence.

Because of his family connections in Buenos Aires and his position in the company, no one was ever going to challenge him. He was also helping the company to grow, and led the office to double its revenues in the past two years. But he was a real closed-door guy. He put out the word that he wanted "to hear from you and have a good, collaborative working relationship," but in practice, he wasn't as welcoming as he said he would be.

He was very expressive and passionate during his phone calls with his colleagues in North America, western Europe, Mexico, and Brazil, yet some members of management found him hard to handle. For example, in the United States, his peers expected that he would work better "through the system," and Eliseo found that difficult when his local offices were able to implement his ideas much more quickly. As we talked with Eliseo, we pointed out that he was underestimating people who weren't as vocal and as passionate as him. He had been assuming that they were not committed to the project and that they weren't as good at marketing themselves or the products.

His aha moment came when we explained that he was a highly expressive manager, and we noted that many of his new clients and colleagues outside of Argentina would likely have a more rational, matter-of-fact style. He also realized that his highly intense style wouldn't bring out the best in his counterparts in the other regions to which he was now accountable.

Eliseo was a very charismatic, charming guy. But if things weren't going his way, he'd lay down the rules with peers and direct reports. He would lose patience with colleagues who had difficulty with his ideas, and his way of doing things. With an American colleague, we told him, he'd have to elicit what they thought, get input. He might have to start with a question rather than with a statement. In short, he would have work on his communication style.

The company's home office in the United States had its own power structure and its own set of values. Eliseo had risen as high as he could in Argentina, and he would have to flex his approach if he hoped to get this big promotion.

HOW DO YOU BUILD TRUST?

The dimension regarding relationship or task-oriented styles speaks specifically to how you built trust with your coworkers, with your employees, and with your bosses as well. This can be described in more succinct terms as tension between "being vs. doing." Do you delve into the business agenda right away after an introduction, or do you require a more developed relationship before you feel comfortable advancing the business relationship? In general, Americans are very task- and results-oriented when it comes to building trust. An existing relationship isn't required in order to sign a contract or make a big business deal: if the terms are agreeable and if you can get me what I want, then let's make it official. The trust is implicit and quickly formed. Other cultures are much more relationship focused. Someone might need to know everything about you—from the background of your family, to the college you went to, to your entire career trajectory—before they would dream of putting pen to paper.

The Task vs. Relationship Spectrum

There is a phrase in Chinese, *guan xi*, which translates as "relationship." This speaks to the primacy and importance of whom you know—your network, your family, your connections, and your relationships, all of which are foundational in helping define your place in the world and how you are received. In China, you cannot do business unless you understand the importance of *guan xi* and how to navigate the web of relationships. What seems like wasted time to a results-oriented boss might be critical networking and relationship-building time to an employee who believes he or she simply can't move forward without it. Conversely, a relationships-oriented manager might find an employee who is a "doer" insubordinate or rude when he or she tries to accomplish job tasks without paying proper respect to the business culture. We see it play out with gender differences as well. Men are often deemed as task-oriented and look for results in evaluating worth, while women place great importance on building trust first through establishing relationships—and often get good results by doing so.

It's important note that "doers" still care about building relationships, just as relationship-oriented people may still want to get down to business. It is a matter of how trust is built and what it is built on. In some cultures trust is more quickly built and often implicit, while in others who you are forms the basis of trust, not the role you play.

Sometimes a long period is required for that trust and relationship to build.

Different generations as well as cultures fall to different sides of this dynamic. Gen Y workers are often posited as much more task-oriented than their older counterparts who take the time to build respect within a company and establish a network of important relationships. Younger workers may need to understand more fully the relationship-building aspect of your company culture. You could encourage formal check-ins, or ask them to move more slowly with clients who need to get to know them better before feeling comfortable. Conversely, you might try to take advantage of Gen Y's willingness and desire for an immediate rise to the top, and harness that energy.

Making the distinction between "doing" and "being" preferences is critical not only inside your workplace; it is extremely important when you are dealing on an international level. Teams in India and Hong Kong want to see their American partners more; not to go over facts and figures, or set up a new project, but simply to be in their presence. This is how they get to know you, and how they develop confidence that they have chosen the right partners. American managers, who prefer efficient conference calls and e-mails, too often fail to build rapport. Asian managers even cut off a business deal if they feel their need for face time isn't being honored.

A. B. Cruz is the former general counsel of a global media company, and as a rear admiral in the US Navy Reserve was the deputy commander of the US 4th Fleet, which serves the Caribbean and Central and South American regions. Through his military experiences, AB noted, "there's this introductory period that other cultures have that Americans don't always get. We go in there and think that there's really only one purpose for us to be in this country—to get our work tasks accomplished! And we don't really bring a lot of our personal side to the table. We get to the boardrooms in the country after we arrive and it's, 'Why are we here? Let's get this agenda going!' Other cultures are uncomfortable with our sense of urgency and some want to get to know you, especially if you're visiting them; *not* talk about *business*. These differences are more important than we American managers perceive them to be." A big part of his navy job during peacetime has been about developing trust. "A lot of efforts in Latin America are less about hardline military stuff and more about building relationships so that if something happens, then you know how to proceed." Understanding the being/doing dynamic is critical for AB's work. "In the US we think of work as really being as efficient as possible. That is not so with the people I've with in Latin American countries. They often begin 'business' with a dinner or social event because they really want to develop a personal relationship with you."

THE RUGGED INDIVIDUALIST

There may be no more American a trait than individualism, a cultural dimension in which your value stems from your own unique and distinct contributions to society or to a group. Pull yourself up by your bootstraps, the classic Horatio Alger story—many American narratives stem from the belief that one individual can make his or her own destiny and rise as far as he or she is willing to go. In collectivist cultures, identity stems from and is defined by being part of a group. Whether you see yourself as individualistic or collectivist influences how you behave and make decisions, and makes up the prism through which you cast the behaviors and actions of yourself and others.

The Individualistic vs. Collectivistic Spectrum

In general terms, we've already stated that American culture is highly individualistic. Most Asian cultures, as well as many European, Latin American, Middle Eastern, and African cultures, tend to be more collectivist. Men are often encouraged to strike out on their own; women are generally socialized to act as part of a group. Women might be encouraged to seek consensus before moving forward with a project or idea, for example, rather than simply taking the initiative to begin the work on their own. Depending on the values of the company and on her manager, that might be seen as good relationship building and acting like the consummate company man. Or it might be viewed negatively, as lacking in initiative. Older generations tend to exhibit more collectivist tendencies, even in the United States. As the business world has shifted, this value has, too. Millennials also trend highly toward individualism. What younger workers may perceive as anti-bureaucracy commonsense, or behaviors that take into account work-life balance, their managers may perceive as rogue or even lazy. Understanding the differences of these styles as rooted in culture, gender, and generations will help you avoid rushing to negative judgment and allow you to flex toward others as appropriate.

CONSIDER THE CONTEXT

The theory behind high- and low-context cultures postulates that in low-context cultures, little is taken for granted or assumed by each party.

If you have a high-context cultural preference, you are guided by a multitude of unwritten rules that are readily understood by those who are also from your particular high-context culture but may seem opaque to others. Often this is a result of living in a group culture where relationships and age, status, and hierarchy build and define the interactions of the people within the group. Some examples of high-context culture in practice might include relying on nonverbal communication—such as body language, tone of voice, and the pacing of interactions—to get your message across.

The Low-context vs. High-context Spectrum

In Japan, for example, lower-level workers know that when the CEO walks into the room, they walk out. They would leave out of respect, minimizing their presence in deference to a leader so far above their level. They wouldn't dream of taking the same elevator as the CEO. No one would order a lower-rung worker off the elevator or gesture for him to leave a room; it would simply be understood. If these unwritten rules govern who can occupy the same space, you can imagine all the dimensions that may come into play in negotiating a business deal or in talking through a problem with an employee, or how bewildering the behavior might seem to someone unfamiliar with the rules.

As a consequence, to operate well in a high-context culture, it's necessary to first identify what it takes to become an insider in that culture, and it may include developing deeper relationships with others over time in order to grasp the unwritten rules. The stronger your high-context preference, the more unwritten rules there are!

In low-context cultures, behavior and beliefs are explicit and defined. Often, the relationships may be defined more by tasks and actions taken than by the nuanced relationships in a high-context culture. Because of this, lower-context cultures are easier to enter than higher-context cultures because the relationships are more easily formed in a shorter span of time.

If you think about it, very few business environments are strictly low context, and there are always unwritten rules. Not only do we depend upon a hierarchical system to guide our business communication, but we are expected to interpret many different signals—including body language, the title of the person we're talking to, the office surroundings, tones of voice—in order to deduce meaning. Yet some cultures are higher context than others, with Asian cultures being notably higher context than American culture. If you're both highly formal as a culture and highly hierarchical, you can be sure you are operating in a very high-context environment. Said differently, in these contexts, all of the classic journalism questions apply—where, what, why, how, when—as every one of them matters in setting the tone and ensuring you are sending the message you want to send.

Though American business culture still tends to be hierarchical, many American leaders and managers like to think of themselves as low context. This is also part of the reason American contracts are so explicit and lengthy—nothing is assumed and therefore everything needs to be spelled out in writing. But even in the United States we have some unwritten rules when it comes to casual conversation. It's tacitly encouraged in the United States to drop by the boss's office to chat about the World Series or about family and holiday plans. This is the type of everyday banter many American bosses depend upon to build trust and deepen relationships in the office. Yet this is not true in a large number of countries around the world. When working in Latin American cultures, cozying up to the top brass may not be considered in good form if you're lower in the reporting chain. In Mexican business culture, you show your respect for the boss by maintaining your distance—respecting the power gap. He comes to you when he needs you. In all business environments there are keys to behavior that are valued, but perhaps not directly requested.

As you examine and sift through the different preferences and styles, remember that this isn't about worse or better, it's about accepting difference without judgment. By saying you should learn to appreciate and understand others' ways of interacting, we aren't saying you must abandon your preferred style, abolish hierarchical levels or set customs, or advocate for one set of behaviors over the other. In fact, fluent leaders will simply add to their toolbox of means and methods in order to get the best result possible depending on the context.

Remember, opening your curiosity and learning how to flex your style will make you a better and more effective manager and leader. Ultimately, it's about getting results while preserving the dignity of your employees, and increasing their chances to succeed. Learning these skills will also help you connect on a better and more intuitive level with your overseas partners, clients, and markets. If you take the time to learn about different cultural dimensions, you will broaden your thinking regarding assumptions about the behavior, motivations, and values of those you work with. In the next few chapters, we will discuss in greater depth how to apply your knowledge of these dimensions to everyday workplace situations and flex your management style.

CHAPTER 4

PORTRAIT OF A FLUENT LEADER

If we are to love our neighbors, before doing anything else we must see our neighbors. With our imagination as well as our eyes . . . we must see not just their faces but the life behind and within their faces.
—FREDERICK BUECHNER, *WHISTLING IN THE DARK: A DOUBTER'S DICTIONARY*

In light of uncertain conditions and a slower-growth economic environment, today's senior executive faces many challenges. One of the greatest hurdles that leaders (CEOs and first-time supervisors alike) will face lies in knowing how to engage with people from other backgrounds. The question you will have to ask at every step is, How do I define and/or identify what gap exists in my department, my division, at every level inside my firm? Then, what do I do to bridge that gap?

Becoming a fluent leader takes much more than just knowing the best way to hear from everyone on your team or reaching out to your direct report instead of waiting for her to come to you. The small things that we say and do make a difference in the way people perceive us as we conduct business on a global stage. Adaptive, fluent leaders can integrate these and other practices to remove the barriers that exist when working across cultural, generational, and gender differences to build stronger work relationships. We have found that truly fluent leaders consistently demonstrate a core set of beliefs and mind-sets that guide their actions in the workplace and in their communities. These collected traits, along with an intentional focus on improving their management skills form the basis of the tremendous influence, admiration, and respect given them by their teams and, for some, by their clients and suppliers.

In narrowing the scope of the core fluent leader traits, we examined a half-dozen existing leadership models and paradigms but saw no one single model that fit the bill. For example, in many models, it is important that a leader demonstrate emotional intelligence. But a fluent leader is more than just someone who is emotionally mature, demonstrates empathy, and is able to make an accurate assessment of people and their emotions. The fluent leader may also demonstrate elements of innovative thinking, but there are other aspects of his style that go beyond creativity and thinking outside the box. Hence, we developed a new combination that captures the full range of characteristics and leadership beliefs and behaviors we feel a truly fluent leader possesses. At the end of this chapter you'll find a discussion of those attitudes and beliefs, as well as a tool meant to gauge your own fluency in assessing and adapting to the power gap.

THE ART OF FLEX

In addition to studying the belief systems intrinsic to fluent leaders, it's important to look at how they adapt to accommodate the power gap, a set of behaviors we call flexing. When we talk about fluent leaders flexing, we mean that you have the ability to switch behaviors and styles in order to communicate more effectively with those who are different from you. It may help to think about flexing as "stretching" your interpersonal style or "reaching out" to meet someone else partway.

In order to do this, you have to find a part of yourself that can connect with your colleague; you need to be able to find common ground. There are a couple of different ways you might do that:

- Connect with a trait, communication pattern, or cultural dimension that you share.
- Search for a common interest, be it your shared love of music, sports, the arts, your alma mater, or the mission of the company.
- Discover a shared experience.

Self-aware leaders know it is easier to spot points of commonality in others if you refrain from positing your way as the only way to get things done. They also understand that this rapport is needed to appreciate and reconcile differences. This is a critical component of flexing across the power gap.

It can be helpful to compare the flex model to some of the other popular leadership models out there in order to highlight the critical part the power gap plays in becoming a fluent leader. You might already be familiar with the idea of *situational leadership*, a term and idea popularized by leadership expert and author Ken Blanchard. In situational leadership, you adapt your leadership to the maturity of the people you are leading by interacting with them via one of four ways: telling, selling, participating, or delegating. In the situational leadership model, you might use a "telling" approach with a new hire because they are unfamiliar with your organization and need direct, very hands-on management, while a more "participating" approach would be useful with someone who has been in the company longer and has more experience working on projects within the corporate culture.

The flex concept differs in that it encourages you to shape your style by viewing difference through the lenses of culture, age, gender, and other differences, not just seniority, and by identifying the subsequent power gap between you. We have found that in addition to seniority and experience, leadership has a cultural context rooted in an individual's deeply ingrained messages embedded since childhood. Someone from another cultural experience might have different expectations from his manager. After all, not all new recruits will exhibit nor respond positively to the same management and communication style, nor will they act from the same set of values and beliefs. By ignoring the nuance of difference in your new recruits, you could underutilize existing talent or miss an opportunity to get the best out of each employee.

The concept of flexing across the gap differs, too, from leadership styles that vary based on personality type. The Myers-Briggs Type Indicator, for example, assigns people one of sixteen personality types based on their answers to a psychometric questionnaire. We use the Myers-Briggs Type Indicator in our work, and we think there's a lot of good in recognizing how those extroverted, from-the-gut ENFPs can communicate more effectively with their more analytical, data-driven ISTJ counterparts, to cite one example. The best part of the Myers-Briggs typologies and other personality inventories is that they expose people to the idea that it's okay to use and apply different mind-sets with different people. The limitation of these inventories is that they seek to identify the personalities we are born with, and doesn't take into account the socialization, family, and cultural influences that play a part in leadership. We know too well that people who hail from different cultures, women and men, or people who are raised in different generations, and are shaped by different events and trends, are influenced and socialized in different and profound ways, forming distinct sets of belief and thought processes that drive their behaviors based on these differences. For these reasons, the flex model can gauge your ability to recognize the differences as well as your ability to first assess and then bridge the power gap through your actions.

HOW MUCH DO I HAVE TO CHANGE?

There is no silver bullet for developing fluent leadership capabilities and building a culture of fluency in an organization. We will give you the tools you need, then leave it to you to synthesize the information and insights to put them to work for your organization. With that said, the first question many people ask us when we explain the concept behind becoming a fluent leader is, Are you asking me to change who I am? Well, yes and no. Think about it this way: the key word here is *flex*. We don't advocate tossing your morals, ethics, or values system out the window. Nor are we advocating that you contextually morph into a completely different being depending on whom you are talking to. Similar to a strong rubber band that can stretch and flex to different lengths depending on what it needs to contain, you can adapt your style to meet others partway, stretching more as the situation demands.

FLEXING WITHOUT COMPROMISING YOUR CORE VALUES

You can retain your value system and still stretch your style to meet someone different from you partway. In fact, one common theme that we have discovered about fluent leaders is their astute sense of self and strong personal moral core. Their behaviors are rooted in a value system that they stand by, regardless of whether it is aligned to their company culture. What might change according to the situation is *how much* and *in what way* you flex your style. To fully engage some people and close larger power gaps, you may have to do nearly all the heavy lifting, especially in the beginning as you build trust and create new communication pathways. For others, you may have to alter your way of doing things only slightly or only once in a while. When and how often you flex might also depend on who is in the room with you.

It has been our experience, however, that some people consciously opt to change their management style for good as they become more fluent. To help illustrate, let's return to the language metaphor from the first chapter. Remember that for code switchers, their way of speaking becomes a distinct way to communicate, essentially a different tool at their disposal to use when appropriate, or when an impending situation is high stakes. A person fluent in both Spanish and English might use Spanish at home and English at school, or might speak Spanglish in either context, incorporating both languages and her unique ways of conveying meaning to get her point across most effectively. It works similarly with management styles.

In order to flex your management style, you may choose to

- Go back and forth between different management styles while maintaining your core preferences or style, *or*
- Create a new hybrid management approach that blends different perspectives into a new style. The new style can be a powerful tool for managing across difference in various contexts.

WHEN TO FLEX

In the first scenario, you don't really fundamentally change your own preferences or styles. Flexing is situational and may be a fairly infrequent endeavor. For example, perhaps you don't deal with Germans on a daily basis in the workplace, but you need to collaborate on a global product launch with your counterparts based in the Berlin headquarters. You may notice and take into account cultural differences in communication and decision making you experienced the last time there was a face-to-face meeting, and reach to work better with those differences while your teams are engaged. Then you might store that information away for later, better prepared to flex in any future interactions you may have with a German team or when you encounter similar situations. Or perhaps you notice that two of your Gen Y employees crave a more flexible and informal model for intraoffice communication. Of course, U DNT NEED 2 TXT your employees instead of writing memos (LOL!), but you might decide to disseminate information in a multitude of ways to employees, or even clients, in order to ensure your message gets across.

In the second scenario, as you gather more information about difference, you start weaving other styles into yours and create a completely new, personalized management style that works on a different level. Sabrina, a vice president in the banking industry, would hardly be recognized now by those with whom she grew up. In her earlier years, she was shy to the point that she actually cowered in the face of authority. Withdrawn and reserved, she reacted badly to any sort of criticism or correction. The woman Sabrina has become is very outspoken and opinionated—and very comfortable in any social situation. She still calls herself an introvert. She needs more time than more naturally outgoing colleagues to go inward to gain new energy for the times that she needs to be "on" at work. As she entered the workplace, she was good at assessing what was needed, and realized how much her chosen industry could be unforgiving of a shy or retiring demeanor, and definitely of someone unable to take correction. And so through her leadership experiences, from school clubs and organizations to her early work experience, Sabrina began to take on more leadership roles. Through flexing (observing and adapting) to the requirements of leadership such as project management, team leadership, and leading with different styles, she developed her own voice. And though occasionally she goes back inside to that quieter self in new situations, she quickly finds her equilibrium again due to years of practicing her new style.

This example is illustrative of how frequency might play in to whether you alter your style for the long term. If you work with people from different cultural backgrounds or collaborate across generations or work in a global context, you might need to create a hybrid style. Frequency definitely becomes a factor in how often you adapt your style. Or you may find that you completely leave the old you behind, taking on a new persona that offers the best path toward leadership success.

FLUENCY DEVELOPMENT

We find that developing a truly fluent style is important . . . and difficult. For example, how do you internalize the efficacy and efficiency of social media as your Gen Y reports do? Do you have to eschew your more traditional methods of communication? Not necessarily. However, we have found that if you just change your behavior but don't link your behavior back to what's beneath the surface, the change is not sustainable. You might put out a detailed report behind an upcoming reorg through a variety of channels (including Twitter and LinkedIn) but still believe that *real* workers with a strong work ethic would take the time to read a full news article rather than depend on a tweet to hear the news announcement. If that bias still lingers—that social media is for the lazy—it is unlikely you will put the full force of your convictions behind using social media effectively to shape your team's feelings about the reorganization, and might still judge those who rely upon it. Conversely, sustainable change begins with shifting our thought process, which in turn drives our behavior, which influences the perceptions and actions of others.

THE PROCESS OF CHANGE

As a leader in your organization, you can influence your team in many ways. You may be able to motivate, mentor, inspire, educate, or guide the people in your organization, but the one thing you cannot do is control what they do. The only person's behavior you can control is your own, and your behavior starts with your internal thought process. As the image on page 75 demonstrates, our thoughts and feelings guide our behavior. Those actions are, in turn, judged by others, who translate them into their own perceptions about who we are. Fluent leaders are aware and checked in at all stages of the process.

The "Thinking Path," a framework developed by Alexander Caillet, provides a helpful model from cognitive/behavioral psychology and neuroscience that breaks the human thinking-and-doing process into discrete steps to help people create sustainable change. We've modified it in our work.

Thinking, a cognitive and mechanical response our body has in response to stimuli, is the starting point. That cognitive response, in turn, elicits feelings—emotional and physical manifestations throughout the body. Our brain signals our body to increase our heartbeat or produce stress hormones (making us feel anxious or nervous) or release dopamine (making us feel a natural high) among myriad other physiological responses. The reaction begins through routes in our brain called neural pathways, which we form through the repeated mechanism of thoughts and attitudes. Our feelings, the product of chemical chain reactions caused by these neural pathways, become our body's go-to response as our brain utilizes the most-used neural pathways to gauge a response. This is what is happening on the inside, beneath the surface. Only you know your exact thoughts, and as those translate into feelings, others begin to see something on the surface.

We then behave in accordance with our thinking and feelings and perform an **action**. Our action, in turn, delivers the impact onto a situation or a person, the measurable outcome of our behavior. In the workplace, this affects how others perceive us, impacts the results we're seeking from our teams, and contributes to the general reputation we hold among our coworkers.

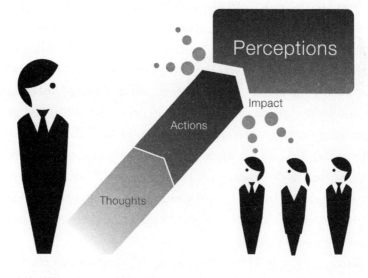

Identifying Areas of Change

This is why real internal change is difficult. It requires you to rewire your brain through your thoughts in order to coax your body into using alternate neural pathways and create new behaviors. People come to interact with this path at different points and can experience changing thoughts and behavior as a bidirectional relationship. For example, you can work for change on the inside, and question/alter your own thoughts at the moment you have them. Noticing and questioning your thoughts arrests the process in time for you to produce a different emotional response, which guides a different behavior, which produces different results.

Many people tend to begin at the end of the chain. To illustrate: you desire better relationships with your coworkers or you want your team to raise its sales numbers. Those are results. From there you would begin to work backward and identify the actions that would elicit those results. Perhaps people need to work more cooperatively together, and share more client leads with each other. What feelings are causing the team members to work independently? Maybe one team member always dominates the meetings, so the others dread attending the meetings and start to avoid meetings with that team member. Or the most capable team member doesn't feel comfortable sharing her ideas, so she goes underutilized. Underneath those feelings are the assumptions, beliefs, and values that make up our thoughts: The boss only wants to hear from the more senior person, not from me. Since our sales numbers are low I need to watch my back and hoard information. The way to get ahead in this company is to outmaneuver the others. It's every man for himself, because if you don't put out, you get cut in the next quarter. These are all defensive responses, but if the underlying belief is that the company is struggling and the team doesn't get rewarded for collaborative behaviors, it is understandable that the people in the organization will act as if this is only a zero-sum game.

However, even by exhibiting different behaviors you elicit different reactions from the people around you, and these external changes can work backward along the path to shift your feelings and thoughts based on the new interactions. For example, Anna is a domineering team member who monopolizes all the time during a meeting, frequently interrupting and only focusing on her own ideas and thoughts. She believes that others are important, but that doesn't translate into her treatment of her teammates; her confidence in her own ideas and identity is stronger than her belief in others. Through feedback processes, however, she discovers that she has a bad reputation for being narcissistic; her behavior makes other team members feel disrespected and trampled. Her manager asks her to share the floor in future meetings, ask others directly for their input, and listen closely to their ideas. In the beginning, Anna might begin to practice these behaviors with good intentions, perhaps only to create the perception that she is *not* domineering and that she *does* value others. But as she makes this a habit and hears really solid input from her coworkers, those behaviors can begin to challenge her original thoughts and change her attitude about herself and others.

CHANGING FROM THE INSIDE OUT AND OUTSIDE IN

Like Anna, some people are initially concerned with managing others' perceptions or producing immediate results. Yet, if they are able to take in the lessons learned from changing their own behavior, they might ultimately be able to make an internal shift as well. It works the same way as smiling in order to improve your mood and overcome negative emotions. Some psychologists have found that smiling even when you're feeling sad makes a difference in your psyche. As well, making a change to the outside can have an impact on your inside.

Others place more value on their attitudes and work to change the inside first, a worthwhile task that is harder to do and may not produce immediate changes in behaviors immediately recognizable to others. It's also possible to feel completely at ease with your values and belief systems and not realize that your behaviors are still having a negative impact, however unintended they may be.

As you continue to practice these leadership behaviors with others, you will see results—improved outcomes, positive responses from your team members, and increased trust—and you will become more open and even eager to embrace alternative mind-sets and points of view.

The goal for change and authenticity is to be as congruent as humans can be—up and down, inside and out, all along the pathway. There is no precise formula. You will need to decide for yourself how best to model fluent leadership behaviors and flex across the power gap, even if at heart you have not yet fully embraced the core fluent leader beliefs and attitudes we will now discuss in detail.

 DEVISING THE RIGHT GAME PLAN

Pre-engagement—The Three Critical Questions

As a starting point, if you find yourself in a new relationship with someone different from you whom you don't quite yet get, here are three pre-engagement questions to ask yourself before you open your mouth to say anything to the person in question. At this stage, keep an open mind about the person until you get to know him or her, and refrain from making hasty judgments. This process alone can yield meaningful results in your future workplace interactions.

Used whenever you confront a situation or behaviors you don't understand, these questions help you unearth your attitudes and examine your thought process *before* you act.

1. What are they thinking?
- What's behind the action?
- What perspectives and assumptions might he have that are different from mine? What is the context? Are there cultural, gender, or age differences at work here? Are there specific experiences in his background that affect his interactions?
- What's lying beneath the surface behavior that I just witnessed?

2. How should I connect?
- How will I break the ice with this person?
- What can I say to express my desire to reach out to her?

3. How can I put myself in the other person's shoes?
- What can I do and say to demonstrate positive intent?
- How will I show my willingness to meet him partway?
- Are there underlying fears or barriers that I need to take into account?

THE FLUENT LEADER MIND-SET

During our research for this book, we discovered six critical traits for a fluent leader that encompass the attitudes and behaviors needed to flex up, down, and across. Connecting back to the idea of sustainable change in terms of aligning your beliefs with your behaviors, we hope that understanding these common traits and how they contribute to fluency will aid you on your own leadership journey. Also, as you encounter the range of leaders (diverse in experience, sector, age, gender, ethnicity, and global experience) profiled throughout this book, we hope you see that these individuals are not only beloved and revered by others, but that their common belief systems and behaviors contribute greatly to the health of their organizational culture and to the bottom line of the company. These common fluent leader traits are within reach of every manager who is willing to do the work.

Fluent Leader Master Trait: Possessing Self- and Other-awareness

Fluent leaders have a good grasp of their own strengths, weaknesses, and preferences. Additionally, they are able to quickly discern the preferences of others in order to know how to flex their style. This is a critical component to fluent leader awareness, since some managers may have a high degree of self-awareness but may not be able to take the next step to discern how someone from another culture or generation responds to authority, or may not be able to investigate the underlying beliefs behind their team members' behaviors, or may not elicit the result they want by approaching an employee in the right way. This trait in action shows a leader's cultural competence and emotional intelligence.

Orlando is a mid-level manager at a nonprofit organization that works with college students, primarily focused on Latinos. When connecting with students, he draws from his own experience in college twenty-five years before when he was the only Latino/Puerto Rican student at his small liberal arts college, when other students didn't know how to engage with him. He knows how isolated he felt then and realizes how that impacted his identity and interactions throughout college and even into the workplace. Fast-forward a couple of decades. He seeks to build relationships with Latino students so that they begin to connect with him and allow him to help them help themselves. At work, he also has begun to realize that there are a lot of hierarchical behaviors based on cultural values and that his style leans toward an egalitarian style, especially when working with his team. "Sometimes my team holds back on telling me what I really need to hear. It's a hierarchical respect-your-elders thing that can be great unless you need to be told you need to do better. I am older and have a few more years of experience, but I'm certainly not always right. If I give a talk and it's not good, I need someone to give me feedback that it wasn't my best work." Orlando works to debunk the misconception that all Latinos communicate in the same way, being both Puerto Rican and a direct communicator. "I've asked people who are junior to me for their advice directly, and sometimes they will be honest with me. However, there's always a level of respect when they give me feedback, even in the way they talk to me. They are more hesitant, which is based in our culture of honoring your elders and trusting your parents. But in our organization, our culture values direct communication styles, so I'm totally used to getting in-your-face feedback!" Through Orlando's self-awareness of his background and experiences, he is able to assess and discuss the preferences of others in order to flex effectively.

Fluent Leader Master Trait: Adaptability

Adaptability is a key component of fluent leadership, indicating an ability to adapt to stretch your styles and preferences and sometimes exercise other styles in order to better interact with others. Though often in powerful positions, fluent leaders also have the humility to admit faults and use information from others in order to adjust to the needs of the situation. Fluent leaders are not only able to admit their mistakes, they recast them as teachable moments and are able to adapt to shifting styles and circumstances, often thinking of themselves as working in service of their employees, the organization, or the client. Adaptable leaders are teachable and open to change.

Bill Pollard's early days as a senior executive at ServiceMaster were not spent in meetings engaged in formulating high-level corporate strategy. Instead, he was out in the field, on the front line, doing the work of serving customers and experiencing the feelings and challenges of the service workers of one of the world's largest residential and commercial service networks. At ServiceMaster, all operating managers were expected to do the hands-on work of the front-line service workers so they, too, could better understand the emotions and mind-set of those they were managing. This connectedness allowed them to better know how to motivate and develop those working for them.

Similarly, every employee at ServiceMaster, regardless of title, years of service, or position, was expected to spend at least one day per year working in the field serving customers. The company referred to it as We Serve Day. Bill called this service opportunity "keeping your hands in the bucket." It ensured that people in leadership positions or at "corporate" were never out of touch with what service employees were doing and being asked to do in serving the customer.

For Bill, working alongside the service worker gave him new insights and helped him to shape his thoughts on what should be added or changed to help the service worker excel in not only meeting customers' expectations but exceeding them.

Fluent Leader Master Trait: Comfort with Ambiguity and Complexity

As we discussed in chapter 1, talking about differences honestly and earnestly requires a special courage and a particular skill set. In general, difference is a subject people are trained to avoid. Fluent leaders are unique in that they are able to break down complex situations and uncertainty. They know how to get to the root of the relevant issues and priorities in any given situation. They manage even tough situations and search for reconciliation.

In the wake of the 1992 LA riots, Deputy Mayor Linda Griego was tasked with beginning to rebuild a fraught community, actually a collection of communities at the time. There were lots of minorities and each stuck together in its own groups, siloed. There was no crossover. "Part of it was that people thought they needed to look out for their own constituencies. Instead, I sought to get learning between groups. They come from different backgrounds, some very religious and some with strong politics. There were still lots of tensions there in the neighborhood." The Korean community felt that it got neglected by the fire department and that it was the buffer that protected other communities during the riots. There was unified anger toward the police. "Black and Korean leaders were in the room, pastors, nonprofit and business leaders. Everybody sitting around the table with body language that said, I don't want to be here."

Linda tried to find a way to meet the needs of the disparate communities with all these functions in the room. One strategy was to rebuild and expand the community. People wanted to have a store to go to where they could buy fresh fruits and vegetables. "We started to think outside the box: can some of these liquor stores be turned into corner grocery stores with fruit and fresh produce? It took many points of view to approach this. How do we meet the needs of Koreans who come from Korea? How can they make money? If African Americans don't want the liquor stores, what kind of store do we want, and how do we create it?" With Linda's leadership they settled on corner grocery stores and reduced the number of liquor stores in communities. It took different thinking from both sides of the table and was a complex process fraught with tension, anger, misunderstanding, and need. She was able to navigate that environment and help negotiate a compromise that could begin to knit the communities back together.

Fluent Leader Master Trait: Unconditional Positive Regard

As a group, fluent leaders demonstrate *unconditional positive regard* (UPR), a term coined by psychologist Carl Rogers that signifies the unconditional acceptance of others, even in their vulnerable and weakest moments. Rogers believed that this attitude of grace is essential to healthy development. By providing UPR and full acceptance, managers can create the best possible conditions for their team members' personal development. Fluent leaders can turn failures into teachable moments and maintain an ability to see the promise of their teams, and help guide them toward a place where they can flourish. Fluent leaders with UPR are able to envision the future state of a situation or of a person's development, give feedback, and imagine future leadership potential for others.

Rafe Esquith has taught fifth grade for over thirty years at Hobart Boulevard Elementary School in downtown Los Angeles. Ninety percent of his students are below the poverty level and none of them are native English speakers. Yet Rafe believes he needs to do more than just fill the kids' heads with facts. "I am trying to teach my students to be honorable in a world that isn't teaching them that." As a teacher and a fluent leader, Rafe both empowers his students and gives them room to make mistakes, learn, and grow. As a teacher,

Rafe encourages questions rather than telling his students what to do. "At the same time, I try to create the right environment where they're not afraid to fail. I want to teach them values—such as humility, honesty, and working hard for something."

Rafe is not afraid to teach valuable lessons to his students when one of them breaks a rule in his classroom. They study economics, and each student earns "cash" (which can be redeemed for gift cards) as incentives. Depending on certain tasks they complete, they earn cash in the classroom, and they have to pay "rent" to sit in preferred seats or buy other desired opportunities. One day, a student stole the class cash. When it was discovered, Rafe quickly took action. Due to the gravity of the situation, he told her he would need to call her parents in. He took away her extracurricular privileges. However, he never forced the student to apologize. He waited for her to come to him and to initiate that part of the reconciliation, knowing that once she did so it would signify that she understood the ramifications of her actions and that she wanted to move forward in making amends. Eventually she approached him and asked if she could apologize to the class, which he allowed her to do. After that, he fully accepted her into the class and treated her as if nothing had happened. It wouldn't be a bad thing for some leaders to replicate Rafe's teaching methods and take them from the classroom to the boardroom!

Fluent Leader Master Trait: Innovation

Fluent leaders are not rigid, constrained, or trapped in a single-mode way of thinking. This is a fairly conventional definition of an innovative mind-set. Additionally and as important, fluent leaders are marked by a tremendous and insatiable curiosity in other people, in their approach to differences, and in their innovative ways of building relationships and doing business. Fluent leaders are open to engaging in new processes and methods that they might not have used before. When they encounter something or someone they don't understand, their first reaction isn't avoidance—it's interest.

Former president and CEO of the Campbell Soup Company Doug Conant was renowned for his positive leadership style and personal touch. But his ability to close the gap and his tenacious pursuit of alternative opinions and divergent points of view also paid off by helping spur and direct innovative thinking that captured the consumer's attention and turned the company around. When he took the helm of Campbell's, he said, "We weren't delighting our consumers. We had aggressively priced our products and compromised quality. Sales were declining." In order to make earnings, they were cutting consumer-brand-building initiatives, as well as research and development spending—most important elements for maintaining brand vitality. "We were trapped in this circle of doom," Doug said, "with a clear need to reinvigorate the conversation with the consumer." For three years, Doug focused on the consumer, focusing on seeing the grocery store aisle from her perspective. And it was *her*. "Eighty percent of our soup is bought by women and all of our soup products were designed by men. We had a focus group of women with men sitting behind the glass." Doug listened when Denise Morrison, president (now CEO) of North America Soup, Sauces, and Beverages, recognized an opportunity for women to have a greater voice. The result was Select Harvest soups. Featuring natural ingredients, it was named product of the year in the food industry in 2009 by Information Resources, Inc. "We recognized that we needed to hear that voice more clearly. If you want a different performance, you have to do things differently. With the market, we had to evolve to more completely include women, and we got innovation from this change."

Doug and his key executives asked the tough questions and had top-level-to-top-level conversations with senior leaders about what wasn't working and what was needed, characterized by candor and a fresh start. He met varying levels of resistance along the way, and it was frustratingly difficult when he was confronted with all the problems and excuses for why things needed to be done a certain way. He had to keep saying, "I hear you, but we need to move forward and things need to change." Gaining insights from suppliers, he and his team had similar interactions and reinvented those relationships, as well. The end result: a better product and advertising, and Campbell sales started growing again. Campbell's introduced a new retail shelving system that organizes soup cans differently on store shelves and helps shoppers more quickly locate the soups on their list. They developed easy-open lids and convenience microwavable products for consumers on the go. The company innovated sodium reduction and expanded the Healthy Request brand. This cavalcade of innovation stimulated growth and won over the customer.

Fluent Leader Master Trait: Flexing across the Power Gap

Fluent leaders are comfortable owning a leadership identity and effective at managing up, down, and across the organization, as well as with customers and vendors. They understand their power gap preferences and those of others on the hierarchical vs. egalitarian spectrum. Equally at ease with their senior leadership as well as with administrative assistants, they close the power gap and forge trusting relationships with all levels, through empathy, trust, and integrity.

Nico Van der Merwe owns the H.A.S.S. Group, which specializes in preventative and curative hearing health care, and serves as the founder and director of the Eduplex School in Pretoria, South Africa, a fully inclusive school that accommodates both hearing and deaf children. Nelson Mandela officially opened the school in March 2002. As a businessman based in South Africa with global partners, he has had to make profound adjustments in his management style in the relatively few years since apartheid was abolished. His experience with Eduplex has taught him how the educational system can flex to meet the needs of all children in a country where disability can have a profound effect on the power gap that already exists between teachers and students.

His experiences flexing down to accommodate racial, cultural, and socioeconomic differences with his employees and global partners demonstrate managing the power gap fluently in the most challenging of circumstances. "I personally struggled with reaching out across cultural differences after apartheid," he admitted. "I had to really learn how to genuinely engage with my staff on a different level and learn to love and accept them and embrace each person's unique challenges, and let go of some preconceived ideas of others." As a manager, you have to have difficult conversations in order to understand fully where they are coming from and what lies behind their behavior at work. "You might have to ask your employee, What are your monthly transportation costs? How many people are depending on your salary at home? And look at each person's situation on an individual level to determine an equitable level of pay."

 ## KNOW YOUR POSITION: TAKE STOCK OF YOUR POWER GAP FLUENCY WITH THE FLUENT LEADER INVENTORY

To aid you on your own path toward fluency, we have developed a tool that allows you to map the power gap between your managers and employees while also helping you gauge your current ability to flex across the power gap. That instrument is available on our Web site www.flextheplaybook.com free of charge. Simply register on the Web site.

Some of us like to *think* we lead in a certain way, yet how others perceive us can be quite different from our own perceptions of ourselves. To get you thinking before you take the self-assessment, here are some questions to ask yourself as you consider your own propensity toward becoming a fluent leader.

- How would I describe the power gap between me and others in my organization?
- Do I notice the different leadership styles and preferences of

those around me? How do I react when they are different from
my own?

- How comfortable am I with people who are different from me
  (culture, gender, generation, lifestyle, habits, etc.)? What differences am I comfortable with? Which differences make me most
  uncomfortable? Why? Do I find difference difficult to talk about?
- Do I actively seek out situations that are new, even when they are
  sometimes uncomfortable? How do I behave in those situations?
  What do I learn from them?
- What keeps me from openly engaging with these people and
  discussing differences? How have previous diversity training efforts, the legal aspects of discrimination in the workplace, or the
  stigma of talking about differences impacted me as a manager?

Fluent Leader Profile: Rosaline Koo—Building Fluency Beyond Stereotypes

Leaders must earn respect while giving respect.
—ROSALINE KOO

When we first met Rosaline Koo, now founder and CEO of Conne-XionsAsia, based in Singapore, we were struck by her dry, droll sense of humor that immediately puts you at ease. With Rosaline, there is no facade; perhaps because early in life, Rosaline learned there is no hiding your difference. Like many other leaders who are masters of navigating the power gap, Rosaline had the formative experience of standing out from the majority culture around her, growing up during the Watts riots as a Chinese American in the primarily African American area of South Central Los Angeles. She jokes, "There were many times where I had to quickly assess whether I should either stay and fight or flee for my life!" Yet while her childhood taught her how to navigate differences in the broader context of her community, Rosaline's truly extraordinary trajectory is rooted in the lesson of a difficult position early in her career, an experience where she was not successful. Instead of accepting defeat, she was able to leverage these early experiences and launch a highly successful career overseas, where she now exhibits a rare cultural fluency and ability to build bridges with colleagues and clients alike.

After working at Bankers Trust in New York, both Rosaline and her husband were given expat opportunities in London. Excited, they prepared themselves for the move to England. However, the day the packers came to move all their belongings, they were told to move instead to Singapore. Rather than letting the change devastate them, they remained open to the new assignment, demonstrating flexible and adaptive behavior. They refocused their direction quickly and got ready for their new lives.

Rosaline's situation turned out to be very different indeed. At

Mercer Marsh Benefits, Rosaline's job was very complex and in-volved managing four hundred employees based in fourteen different countries. Before she took her position there, Mercer had grown to only $11 million in sales over the previous thirty years. By the time she left eight years later, Rosaline had taken the business to $88 million in annual sales. Her team exceeded budget targets every single year, becoming the dominant player in the industry with 50 percent greater market share than the next competitor. How was she able to turn around the business and accomplish such quantum growth? In part, it was because Rosaline had arrived overseas with more than just her bags; she unpacked some early lessons from her childhood and her twenties.

KNOWING WHAT YOU DON'T KNOW

Though Rosaline is truly a global leader—with twenty-five years in Asia and the United States working as a leader across many different industries—her first job was in the Midwest, where she was tapped to manage several production lines at Procter & Gamble. Put in charge of packing Crest toothpaste, the job was a stretch for the then twenty-one-year-old, who had moved from her native Los Angeles to Iowa and, once again, found herself in a workplace with few people like herself. In fact, she was the first Asian to ever work in that plant. Yet Rosaline threw herself into her job with gusto, managing a team of thirty-three people, all of whom were much older. However, she soon realized that she was in way over her head, feeling like a substitute teacher struggling with an out-of-control classroom.

Rosaline looks back on this early foundational experience as the motivation that led her to seek out future stretch assignments that would help to shape her into a great leader. One of her takeaways was that the best learning comes from leading in the face of ob-stacles and failures. During these crucial learning experiences, her manager drilled the importance of gathering feedback and support from the ground. "You need to establish these relationships within your team one-on-one. You have to learn to recognize what you don't know—and you don't have to know it all. Build trust with your team and create a climate that brings out the best in them, so that they're willing to experiment in order to find new and better ways of doing things." In giving Rosaline this early advice, he set her up for future success. He urged her to model collaboration right from the start rather than differentiating herself as "the boss," as many may have been tempted to do. She learned to lean not only on her manager but also on her team, growing to understand that as a young, inexperienced, Asian woman in that particular environment, she had to "earn respect while giving respect."

On top of her lack of experience and her age difference, she was again confronted by stereotypes tied to her ethnicity. Many people in her workplace would ask her what China was like. Rosaline had no experience with China at that point, but she turned the stereotypical assumptions into a chance to grow closer to her team. More importantly, her boss let her explain her background when she was faced with these types of assumptions. He didn't jump in and explain that she was born and raised in California; instead he let her tell her own story and convey her personal values.

Looking back on that position is humbling for Rosaline. She feels she was too young and didn't have the capabilities needed to handle the leadership responsibilities, and acknowledges how the role was eye opening in helping her understand how much she still needed to grow. Although this could simply have been marked as a failure, Rosaline had both the humility and a clear-sightedness regarding her own shortcomings to turn this failure into a stepping-stone. While she may remember being too green to succeed, she also knows that in the end people respected her efforts to get back up after every fall. She wasn't able to bridge every gap, but because she tried so hard and cared so much, "the team was finally inspired midway through my tenure to start working together with me." The skills and resilience she developed through challenge and risk taking made her fearless and helped fuel her subsequent successes. We've found that the most fluent leaders are able to assess their mistakes and missteps honestly. Then they work hard to continuously improve themselves through challenging experiences instead of seeking out a scapegoat or trying to minimize mistakes in order to look good to colleagues and superiors.

BRIDGING THE POWER GAP THROUGH CULTURAL FLUENCY

At Mercer, Rosaline succeeded in part because she was able to connect everyone with the vision, implement a succession of quick wins to blast through decades of inertia, and eventually built up enough momentum that change became unstoppable. She also zeroed in on relationship building, a trait she had mastered over the years. All over Asia she found that trust and relationships are core to everything you do. While expertise is a given, understanding people with different perspectives and attaining personal closeness is crucial, and much more so in Asia than in the United States. To be a true leader in Asia, you need to know how to get things done in hierarchical, high-context cultures. There are plenty of dictatorial managers, Rosaline said, "but the ones who are respected are the ones who work closely with those on the ground to problem solve and help move things forward." Even in Asia, people respond to a leader who reaches out to close the power gap. Rosaline remembers a strong, highly rank-fixated sales manager in Hong Kong who knew how to control his sales force using the status of position/title that he had at his disposal. However, once he went outside his area of influence, he found he lacked the relationships and skills needed to get his work done. His biggest mistake: he didn't listen.

Thanks to the strength of her convictions, Rosaline was able to engage people in a very collaborative, egalitarian manner in an extremely status-oriented work environment. There's a difference between imposing your ideas and introducing a Western style, and for Rosaline, this wasn't a stunt but good business practice. Driven by a vision of dominating the region, she used all the skills at her disposal to get every country to work together on launching a first-to-market, pan-regional solution. She admitted that when she did business with her teams and clients in Japan and Korea, she had to flex a bit more to their more hierarchical culture, especially with her threefold disadvantage of being female, Asian, and American. She realized she had to slow down in some countries to localize the solution in order to better fit the culture. At the same time Rosaline was able to take her difference—her American background—to push through new innovations in order to fulfill more sophisticated client needs. She prompted leaders to examine their strategic value to their clients. In every situation they would ask, as she did, How can this new innovation be useful to me and my clients? How can it be adapted to resonate in my market?

In this way, bridging the gap as a business strategy didn't just reflect the more egalitarian style she was used to; she used it strategically to raise the bar in each market. Sometimes she received a lot of pushback to her style and her approach. When she did, she would retool her own strategy and behavior, reflecting a different and necessary type of flexibility.

Rosaline constantly assessed, gathered information, and gauged the best approach. For the first ninety days she was at Mercer, she was confident in her vision for the business, but also remained collaborative in the way she extended herself as she traveled to meet the management and teams in all of her countries. She spent her time listening and then integrated other people's ideas into the vision, giving them credit and acknowledging them publicly. Every quarter for eight years, she made it a practice during the quarterly webcast to update the region's employees on the progress toward realizing the vision and showcasing employees for their contributions. Listening worked well not only with her team, but also proved critical to understanding the needs of her clients. "I brought my own practices to the job but used my Asian values as a lens and used my Asian face to relate to the local teams. My Asianness was a point of entry into the new people I was working with. I then leveraged my relationship skills to connect with them personally." Again Rosaline confronted stereotypes, but this time the difference rested not in her being Asian, but in her foreign nationality. Instead of shying away from the misconceptions people had about foreigners, Rosaline found it helpful to understand these underlying stereotypes in order to deal with them effectively. For example, she found that the stereotype of the expat manager is one of a person who is not too heavily or emotionally invested in their job or in the locals. People initially believed that she, like most other expats, would work her stint and then move on when she achieved her personal career goals, and so questioned why they should spend any time helping her. Rosaline worked against that stereotype and was very conscientious in building her team, taking a genuine personal interest in investing in those with whom she worked. In fact, many of her team had followed her from previous dot-com start-ups and corporations.

In building these cross-cultural relationships, Rosaline's hybrid style worked very effectively. According to Carol, her regional HR business leader, offices are a *very* big deal. Singapore is an extremely status-oriented culture where titles and corner offices tell people a lot about who you are and how much you matter. When Rosaline arrived, she was given a prestigious space that symbolized the honor and power attached to her role. Rosaline, however, rejected working in an office, and in fact tore down all the offices for her business. Instead she was the only regional business leader who sat in the trenches with the team and walked over to everyone else's desk to have conversations. When Carol asked her about this choice, Rosaline replied that she didn't believe in "turf or power games." She said she wanted to be with the team to unleash positive energy, initiative, and idea generation. She saw walls as a barrier to innovation.

UNCONDITIONAL POSITIVE REGARD FOR OTHERS

Rosaline is able to flex so readily in these different situations in part because she has abundant unconditional positive regard, understanding the inherent potential of each team member. Rosaline personally recruited every week and worked hard at finding the right people for the right roles. If you are able to integrate the best talent into a high-performing team, she said, "then you can accept each other's pace and style" and deal effectively with direct and indirect communicators alike.

Ellen, one of her country leaders, said Rosaline "was pretty supportive of anything you wanted to do as long as it aligned with the vision and you were willing to drive it. If you had a good suggestion, she would give you freedom and authority to run with it," allowing her reports autonomy and the ability to take risks. Rosaline focused her leaders on adapting to the rapidly changing client and competitive environment in Asia. "Working with Rosaline made me more culturally adaptive," Ellen told us, because her business experience in the United States and Asia was so diverse. As a result, Linda became more conscious of her own style and learned to adjust it when necessary. Rosaline was very passionate and cared deeply about the team and the business, yet at the same time she had a tremendous drive toward excellence. Rosaline wanted to win, but she also connected the team member's personal growth and development to the business goals.

"She was really great at coaching me in how to be successful in Asia," Ellen said. "In North America we are more of an adviser to companies and employ more of a consultant style. In Asia clients want things to be more prescriptive and more productized." There were other differences as well. "Working in Asia you have to be extremely adaptable and resilient and learn to achieve much more with less. We were being asked to rapidly expand market share in new emerging markets without the luxury of the infrastructure in the

United States. As a result, you need to be really resourceful in building new services and do a lot of educating of the market regarding the services we provide." Rosaline helped Ellen see this difference and flex to the different needs.

Universally, her former employees told us that if you didn't know how to do something, whether it was a client presentation or firefighting, Rosaline would roll up her sleeves and do it with you, teaching you how to do it by yourself the next time. She enabled others to take on more risks and to stretch their limits by being there to remove obstacles and help them along the way. Consequently, initiatives moved rapidly to fruition.

Rosaline was able to bring a very personal touch to her work in Asia and found unique ways to form a style that mixed Western values with an Asian perspective. In a place where most people did their work because that's what you were supposed to do—making an impact and achieving at work itself was the motivation— Rosaline put her own humorous spin on it, asking of her colleagues the deliberately hyperbolic and slightly tongue-in-cheek question, "How will we become masters of the universe?" By consistently forging the connection between personal and business goals, Rosaline tweaked the highly hierarchical culture in which she worked, and reached in and grabbed people's hearts. She closed the gap and gave people the tools, the training, the leadership, the communication skills, and the inspiration to really envision how they might personally grow while making a difference to the business. "Rosaline had very high standards," Ellen said, "and it became an honor for us when we met those standards."

PART II

THE KILLER APP: FLEXING ACROSS THE GAP

CHAPTER 5

POWER GAP PRINCIPLE: FLEX YOUR MANAGEMENT STYLE

We judge others by their behavior. We judge ourselves by our intentions.
—Ian Percy

THE NEW OPEN-DOOR POLICY

Jim has always lived by the empowerment principle, which he describes like this: He tells his direct reports that he has an open-door policy, and encourages people to drop by and speak their minds. He often asks for their ideas on how to improve operations. However, there is a problem. Two years ago, he added a new finance associate to the team who seemed to have impeccable credentials, including education and a great work history with her previous employer. But she doesn't seem to be taking advantage of his wide-open door and desire to hear from his team members. He wonders if is there a disconnect somewhere. Or did he simply misjudge her?

Like Jim, many managers try to close the distance between themselves and their employees by employing one strategy, in this case the classic open door. Maybe you use a similar approach. By setting aside a certain time each day for casual drop-ins, many managers let employees know they are available to hear complaints, progress reports, and pitches for new ideas. Others make it even less formal and say their "door is always open," and assume their team members will approach them with their problems, questions, and concerns.

If we've learned anything after profiling leaders and multinational companies, and as you learned by assessing your own communication styles and preferences, it's that we all have a default mode of relating to people. The art of flex lies in noticing when your preferred mode of relating to people is not shared by those different from you, and then reaching across the power gap in search of a solution. It takes willingness, time, and practice to develop mastery in the art of flex. Though some managers come to it more easily than others, when we first ask managers to initiate the dialogue with an employee and to consider adjusting their management approach with some of their employees, we often encounter resistance:

"What you're suggesting to me seems fake and contrived. It's not my personality."

"It's not my job to change. My employees need to remember that I'm the boss! They don't need to be coddled."

"I'm not great with people, and that's not the focus of my job."

"Do I need to use a different management strategy for all my employees?"

Our response to all that resistance is simple: you may not need a total makeover, but you might need to change your approach. When working across differences, the same strategies may not work and may not have the same outcome you intended. It's imperative that all of us develop the ability to flex our styles if we want the best performance out of those who work for us.

PRINCIPLES OF FLEX

- Anyone can learn to flex his or her management style and learn how to adapt to a changing workforce.

- Flexing requires decreasing the power gap with your team members.
- Flexing is about exercising a variety of responses to make you more adaptable and fluent.
- Flexing is about context: customizing and individualizing your approach to the person and situation, as you might do when raising three very different children, each with distinct learning styles and personalities.
- Flexing always starts with authenticity. Show who you are and what you value and then extend your curiosity toward others.

LOOK FOR CREATIVE WAYS TO BRIDGE THE POWER GAP

Many managers depend on one go-to way for expressing their accessibility to their reports. In Jim's case, he felt he had messaged clearly to his team, "I'm always accessible! Just come in and tell me what's on your mind and how you're doing. I want to hear your thoughts!" He offered; it was now *their* job to take him up on it. If they played their part, Jim would be aware of their questions, issues, and concerns.

Jim had tried to demonstrate the value of inclusion through his approach, and he had good intentions. What he wasn't taking into account was the power gap between some of his team members and him. The power gap is the reason some employees still weren't approaching him and communicating freely. It explains why they weren't offering ideas and solutions that might better their careers, and why they weren't engaging in problem-solving or sharing issues early on that might help the whole team's performance. You can probably identify some of your own employees, right now, who don't seem to play by the same set of rules as you. Perhaps your one-size-fits-all approach to management is having the opposite effect that you intend and, without realizing it, your open-door policy might actually be shutting a fair number of your employees out. We know you have the best of intentions. So how do you go a step further to close the social distance between you and the employees who are different from you?

Without realizing it, your open-door policy might actually be shutting a fair number of your employees out.

Ask the question: Who's not in the room?

Getting back to Jim's predicament, let's identify something he did right: Jim noticed the absence of his finance associate in his communication loop. As we outlined in the previous chapters, the first step to bridging the power gap lies in identifying these possible misfires, miscommunications, and missteps as we go about our work instead of waiting until an employee quits or we have to give them a poor performance evaluation. Jim knows his finance associate is bright and talented. It's why he hired her! But the means by which Jim has arranged to get information from his team members is not being used by those whose opinions and status updates he wants. In this complex business world, it makes no sense to assume that no news is good news and wait for the problems to arise.

As a first step toward confronting the issue, we suggest starting with the three-step pre-engagement questions we described in the last chapter. That exercise will help you try to get at the values and beliefs behind the other people's actions and think of ways you might flex to them in order to get heard. This process can help you identify key elements to bring up in your next one-on-one with them.

Before you can investigate the motivations for their behavior, you must embrace the fact that we often work with individuals who view the world through an entirely different lens—not better or worse, just different. It's critical you not judge their behavior as wrong, and first simply allow yourself to see the difference. This can be the tricky part. Most managers and executives are now trained to eradicate or ignore difference in our workplaces as a defense against legal action. Our personal defensiveness also pushes us to try to assign blame. However, it is only by forgoing assumptions and judgments that we can explore the potential motivations behind that behavior, then identify solutions.

Steve Raymond, president of Raymond Handling Concepts, is a fluent leader committed to his internal values and also interested in ideas and people he doesn't know. He actively seeks out those not in the room. "I'm open to ideas. I make sure to talk with people; I *want* to hear the stupid question." Right now, Raymond Handling Concepts does not have much generational diversity. Yet Steve's automatic response to the absence of a Gen Y presence in his company showed his fluency. "I don't 'get' the younger ones," he told us, followed by the unusual reaction, "We don't have enough of them! We need to recruit more into this business." Under his watch, his company is always trying to reach out to the people whose opinions aren't being heard and seeking difference rather than avoiding it.

How Steve handles every issue—by investigating and exploring options rather than making assumptions or placing blame—flows down from the top level and permeates the company culture. A sales contact told us, "When I had a problem on the floor, I would go in to talk to him just to communicate what the issues were. Steve would ask questions and press the issue. He wanted me to come up with not only the answer, but several alternatives and options in defining the problem. Now that is part of my style, too. What are we thinking of to solve the problem? What else can we do? At first, my reaction to Steve was, What do you mean? I just want the answer! But he had a better approach. He didn't really answer my question, but engaged me in the process of solving it."

Sometimes, your personal experience working in different regions urges you to flex your management style. Scott Wharton, head of global procurement for Citigroup, has a large, geographically dispersed organization and ten global direct reports. Because his team is so widely dispersed and encompasses so many different cultures, Scott has made several adjustments to his management style. While before he might have checked in only as much as he perceived was necessary and used the most efficient means of communication, he now calls himself an overcommunicator. Some of Scott's reports think he communicates *too* much, yet this approach is a shift he has consciously made in order to work more effectively across an array of employees from diverse cultural backgrounds and connect meaningfully with different country norms. He has regular communication with his management teams but still found he needs to spend a lot of one-on-one time, face time, with key individuals around the world. It has taken both extra effort and time on his part, but he knows he can't be effective without doing it. "You really need to set aside your biases about being effective and being efficient. When you're working across many different cultures, you need to change your opinion about what constitutes effective and productive time commitments to your employees and what is essentially an inefficient use of time." Those in-person meetings and increased communication are yielding results, proving invaluable in building trust with his employees.

"You really need to set aside your biases about being effective and being efficient."

As Steve and Scott demonstrate, a fluent leader feels enough comfort with difference to effectively navigate through a variety of cultural contexts. Remember, fluency is an art—it's not a rigid prescription of behaviors. Perhaps the best way to prepare yourself for reaching across the power gap is with an honest examination of your own expectations for the other person. Why am I feeling offended by his actions? Is this behavior personal, or might it stem from a different set of values or preferences?

HANDWRITTEN NOTES: A PERSONAL WAY OF CLOSING THE GAP

Doug Conant models how even a C-level leader can maintain a highly personalized approach to staying close with his people. During his tenure at Campbell's, every time an employee did something above and beyond expectations, Conant wrote him or her a personalized note of gratitude. He would also write notes to encourage struggling workers to continue to persevere, to welcome a new hire, or to congratulate someone on a promotion. Each missive took the form of a handwritten note card from his office; they were not typed by his assistant—each held a personalized message intended for the employee. Despite his exhausting schedule of meetings and constant travel, he averaged ten to twenty personal notes a day and over his tenure as CEO, Conant wrote thirty thousand personal notes to employees, customers, suppliers, and others! His gesture of bridging the power gap paid off. His in-touch approach helped turn around the Campbell Soup Company, and placed it on a positive trajectory to increased market share, employee engagement, a more inclusive work environment and improved total shareowner returns.

Curiosity: The prerequisite for a productive dialogue.
If a millennial employee e-mails you a project update when you were expecting an in-person report, check yourself before labeling him as impudent. What you may consider disrespectful might just be his easy and preferred way of communication; it may seem informal to you simply because it's new. For another example, let's say your first-year high-performing Gen Y recruit approaches you about his interest in an assignment in a different region of your company that would provide more challenge and exposure. He has barely been at the company long enough to learn the internal systems, and his background and education were unrelated when you took a risk in hiring him. How

will you respond? Laugh at his bravado and artlessness, knowing it took six years of hard work for you to land a similar position?

In general, younger workers today seek and expect more challenge, meaningful work, and promotion at a quicker pace than those of previous generations. They may not see working your way up the ladder or paying dues as prerequisites. Instead of chafing at this and reacting negatively, is there another way to address his enthusiasm for the organization and immediate willingness to contribute? Could you come up with an approach that might include alternative career paths and a reasonable plan and timeline that allows him to make the best of his skills? Are you willing to flex your transfer policy to not lose this valuable resource?

Sometimes it's as simple as sharing what you know. When Lieutenant Commander Christy Rutherford, an African American woman in the US Coast Guard, spoke to a group of new Gen Y recruits, she closed the gap with them by telling them plainly how their generation was viewed by the older generations and asking them to respond to these stereotypes of Gen Yers. She then shared with them the unwritten rules of operating in a hierarchical environment. In doing so, LCDR Rutherford demonstrated to them the importance of understanding their environment, while giving them specific keys for success. She told us, "It's assumed by some in the Coast Guard that everything you are asked to do is mandatory, to the minute and to the detail. That may seem obvious, but that's the unwritten rule here for success. And it goes against many of the younger generation's habits. Someone needed to share that with them explicitly."

In some cases the "problem" behavior isn't imprudent action or dialogue, but a lack of communicating expectations or sharing ideas, such as with that finance associate of Jim's who isn't bringing problems or ideas to him in a consistent manner. If your best female marketing director isn't as aggressive or speaking up as boldly in the weekly meeting as everyone else, you need to also consider: Is she the only woman in the room? Do I just expect her to fall in line with everybody else? What are the ramifications of her not speaking up? As you consider how you might flex your style to work more effectively across differences, recognize that other factors may play a role in her behavior. In addition to differences in communication style, is it possible she is reacting from the perspective of feeling invisible and doubts that her opinions will be heard even if she spoke up?

Some managers fall into the trap of immediately writing off those who don't act, talk, and think the same way as simply high maintenance and a waste of time: if she needs so much help, perhaps this may not be the right job for her. Some employees truly aren't a good fit. However, it is just as possible that your marketing director has some special knowledge or new insight into your market that she might need your encouragement to share. You could let things go on as they are and see if she changes her behavior to match the other participants. You could also wait until her performance review to make your displeasure known. You could hope she'll quit once she's passed up for better opportunities, sparing you the trouble. In each of these cases, not only will your marketing director not be successful, you will have lost a rich opportunity to mine her different way of thinking and communicating. You will have lost your investment in her talent as well as potentially helpful and insightful ideas that could improve your performance and the company's bottom line.

Linson Daniel, a leader of a national nonprofit student organization, was born in the United States to parents who emigrated from southern India. Very self-aware, he's also skilled at calibrating his approach with individuals within his broadly diverse team. Linson is very reserved in his own communication style, and he found he needed to use a more direct style with one employee who took his more low-key requests as suggestions and not directives, leading to a lot of misunderstanding. However, when he initially used the more direct approach with an East Asian woman on his team, she constantly felt like she was in trouble. She didn't need the direct approach from him as a manager, because even a subtle suggestion from Linson was taken to heart. "I've had a different experience with all these different ethnicities in my team, so it's not a one-size-fits-all thing." Currently, with a white female report who needs development coaching, he takes a stance somewhere in between the two approaches. "As a woman she needs to be empowered. I really had to show her that I value her and her contributions. Once she had that assurance, she became very autonomous and is now willing to take bigger risks, knowing that I'm behind her."

Don't judge—investigate.
Once you've noticed who's not in the room or who's left out of the conversation, you need to start investigating why they aren't there. Ask that first question: *Why* is Jim's finance associate not availing herself of the clear and egalitarian communication channels he's put in place?

As a fluent leader, you can envision multiple reasons for this scenario. You recognize that for varying reasons, different employees may not feel that they have built sufficient rapport with their bosses to just "drop by." They may feel uncomfortable striding through that door, unable to confidently showcase their idea, propose a better way to launch the new product, volunteer to run a meeting, or ask for additional resources to complete a project under deadline. They may not feel like they have an "in" to approach their boss, such as a shared interest or a more comfortable, informal relationship. They may feel it's their duty to solve problems on their own and spare you the aggravation and potential embarrassment. Or they may feel that the more space they give you, the more respect you are shown. And all of this could have grave implications on the assessment of their potential.

The reason you need to flex is that many management styles reflect the preferences and comfort levels of the manager who puts them in place. Jim's open-door policy works for direct reports with extroverted personalities or those who happen to come from a culture that values speaking up, taking initiative, advocating a position, and voicing opinions. It's a good strategy for employees who expect, and have had, the experience of being listened to and taken seriously for taking the initiative. In short, *it works only if his direct reports are wired like Jim.* As we've seen in countless examples, those style preferences are not a given with today's changing workforce. Chances are, a difference in culture, gender, or generation has created a power gap that limits the usefulness of Jim's communication policy with his team.

Is it cultural?

Perhaps Jim's finance associate comes from a high-context, hierarchical culture where the informal act of dropping by the boss's office would be unheard of. These values are passed on from generation to generation as well. We spoke with Cristina, a second-generation Mexican American, who was raised in a home where she was encouraged to be very respectful of authority figures, which meant allowing them to approach her if they wanted to engage. Though she is a director-level manager in her retail company and manages a team of twelve, she still feels somewhat awkward whenever her "big boss" comes into town. Her marketing team has an all-hands-on-deck meeting once a month, and she still finds it difficult to initiate an informal conversation with Tom, her senior vice president, in this relaxed setting. She was taught and socialized to be deferential to superiors, to show respect by being humble. She observes, however, her peers taking the opportunity to connect with Tom, and she struggles with the notion. Asking questions, challenging the boss, and speaking up are considered disrespectful and even inappropriate to Cristina. If Tom were to judge Cristina's behavior by his own standards, he wouldn't have the chance to see her behavior as a sign of respect; she would simply look passive and disengaged.

Cultural subtleties like these make plain that for some, dropping in to air issues or problems with a superior is a last-resort option. These workers are more comfortable staying in the background and keeping their focus on the job. Because of their deference to authority, they may feel less comfortable with being singled out and asked to provide a different opinion.

Is it rooted in gender?

Sometimes the power gap isn't culture-based, but arises from gender-specific messages that girls receive since the time they are babies. Traditionally speaking, girls are raised to be rule followers. The International Center for Leadership in Education confirms this in their "Gender Differences and Student Engagement" report, stating plainly, "Girls and boys are different. They learn differently, they play differently, they fight differently, they see the world differently, they hear differently, and they express their emotions differently." According to psychologist and family physician Leonard Sax, who has studied gender differences in children, "ignoring gender differences does not break down gender stereotypes; ironically, neglecting hardwired gender differences more often results in a reinforcement of gender stereotypes." This plays out not just in sandboxes for girls and boys but in boardrooms across the country.

Drew Wahl, founder and president of IG Partners and an experienced executive in management consulting, has clear advice for organizational leaders: "You can affect the culture of the company and how others promote women. It's propagated by the top. If you reach out, it will permeate the culture and others will know it's an okay thing to do." Drew has observed some of the unwritten rules for women that don't allow them to be promoted, like the attitude that they're not tough enough to put up a good fight. Drew counters that what others think of as deficits, he plays as strengths. "I say, put them in there. Women make great negotiators. We were just at a conference for MBAs and I said to them, 'When you had a problem with siblings, did you go to Mom or Dad? You know it was your mom.' "

As a woman, perhaps Jim's finance associate has gotten negative feedback in the past for being overly outspoken or for taking the initiative to approach her superiors in the past. Maybe she prefers raising issues in larger meetings where she can gather everyone's input and have the team come to a consensus on new plans, ensuring support for the change of direction. Women subordinates may need to search for a conversational hook when they try to informally bond with the boss despite markedly different cultural values or experiences. "In my division, the VPs are always talking shorthand," a rising female engineer in a predominantly male company confided to us. "If you don't have an MBA and a real familiarity with finance, it's hard to start a conversation. I have to go in with an agenda to feel comfortable at all." While we don't know how much is nature and how much is nurture, there is enough research that points to behavioral and communication differences in men and women that it must be considered as a factor.

Is there a generational gap?

If Jim's finance associate is part of a younger generation, that open-door policy may appear less a generous opportunity than an outdated holdover from more formal, hierarchical organizations of the *Mad Men* era. Millennials are more apt to follow their own paths and problem-solve independently than spend time winning the boss over or trying to get management's ear when there's a crisis. American millennials generally demonstrate more egalitarian behaviors, and as a result may be perceived by some boomers as "entitled." Gen Y workers may communicate frequently, but they may do so in ways that are not immediately recognizable to a boomer boss. Instead of coming through an open office door, millennials may opt for an open portal instead, and rely on technology (e-mail, chat, or texts) rather than face-to-face communication to make their points and get their questions answered.

BEYOND THE OPEN DOOR

Though the open-door policy is a common managerial tool meant to solicit feedback and dialogue with subordinates, studies show that it's a pretty ineffective one, strengthening the case that flexing to meet your employees on an individual basis is a skill you need to develop. A 2010 *CBS News* report, "Is Your 'Open Door' Policy Silencing Your Staff?," highlighted the research of Cornell professor James Detert, who found the "chances are high that your direct reports are keeping potentially crucial feedback close to the vest." Detert determined that employees often stay silent out of fear, "even when their criticisms would serve to improve their organizations."

The *Harvard Business Review* has featured many managers increasingly discouraged by the limited results of the open door, and laid bare some assumptions about this common policy in 2010 in the article "Debunking Four Myths about Employee Silence," which built on the Cornell study.

We've seen the same limitations in our work. Here are some commonly held beliefs that we encounter with our clients:

Myth 1: If your employees are communicating with you, you're hearing the whole story.
Managers make decisions based on what they hear, but they aren't always getting the whole truth. The *HBR* article reports that 42 percent of survey respondents said they withheld information from their bosses when they thought there might be repercussions for speaking plainly, or even when there just wasn't anything in it for them to elaborate. And those are the employees who are *talking* to you. For the rest who aren't walking through your door, don't assume they lack issues or problems that need attention. Their absence might mean you haven't yet found a way to connect.

Myth 2: Having an open-door policy or an open form/suggestion box is enough to encourage employees' input.
This approach is far too passive; it puts the onus on the employee to identify the problem and speak out. There are those who, due to temperament or power gap distance, may choose to maintain the distance with you, and may share their ideas only with their peers, hoping they will eventually "filter up."

MAKING THE FIRST MOVE: FIVE STEPS TO PRODUCTIVE DIALOGUE

So you've noticed the problem and now want to investigate the issue and work together toward finding a solution. If an employee is failing to participate or hasn't given you a key piece of information, here's a step-by-step framework for engagement.

1. Initiate a one-on-one conversation about a situation you have observed that you are interested in exploring.
2. Describe the impact of these actions on you and connect it to business objectives; make sure you avoid blaming the person.
3. Investigate what is beneath the surface of the behavior; examine the intentions, values, and motivations that might be driving the behavior and the barriers that might be keeping the employee from developing new, effective behaviors. If your colleague is not ready to disclose at this first conversation, use the opportunity to share something about your own developmental experience. This can be the first step in connecting with your employee.
4. Explain why this behavior is so critical to your productivity and to your team dynamics.
5. Develop a plan of action for new behaviors that the employee can practice in order to bring his or her intentions, values, and core motivations into alignment with the impact of the behavior.

We realize that step 3 is the trickiest to broach yet in some ways is the most important piece of the conversation. Omitting the third step gives you a plan for superficial change, but getting to the root of the other person's values and motivations creates sustainable change. Nico van der Merwe, the South African businessman mentioned earlier, admits he personally struggled with reaching out across cultural differences after apartheid, since the power gap was so large. Because of the economic and political environment, Nico closed the gap by getting very personal.

BELOW IS A PRACTICAL demonstration of how a closing-the-gap conversation could unfold. Roger, a senior VP at a new energy company, has just finished up a biweekly conference to update the global innovation task force on new project deadlines for implementation. Anjali, a newly recruited engineer, is working on a new database for energy monitoring.

Roger (after everyone leaves the conference room): Can I talk to you for a moment?

Anjali: Of course.

Roger: I noticed that you didn't say anything in the last few meetings of the global task force. Even today, I know that you've just begun to work on the LAUNCH initiative in the Pacific Northwest, but you didn't mention it on the call.

Anjali: You're right. But you know the pace of these meetings, and how these meetings get really heated. I come into the meeting with a few things I want to say, but there are so many experts in the room, and a few of them are at the VP level with all of your top people. My comments would be redundant.

Roger: Understood. But, Anjali, I know you've got great ideas, and in our one-on-ones I can tell that you've really added value to the project and it's only been a week! Think about which of those concepts you'd like to highlight and, at the next update, I'd like you to speak up and contribute one of those! It's a high-profile project. Let's begin to get you out there.

Anjali may be holding back because she feels it's not her place to speak up in a room full of VPs. Or she might need a few moments to process some of the thinking before she expresses her opinions, particularly given the fast-paced nature of the meetings. Not doing so could cost her important sponsors at the VP level who understand her worth and could serve as her champions.

A boss like Roger can say, "Tell me about yourself, I want to get to know you personally. And I want to hear more of your ideas before we go into that meeting," then help Anjali understand the critical need to insert her thoughts in the meetings.

If an employee does not wish to be singled out, try using some of the mitigation techniques from chapter 3 to help take some of the pressure off. Share an example of how you handled a similar issue early on, or offer that in the beginning of your career those large meetings were daunting for you as well. Demonstrating humility and showing concern for your team members may invite the team member to open up. You can also set the tone by creating an air of openness and disclosure in your group meetings. Broadening the focus is yet another way to encourage communication. Put the focus on the team instead. That way, you put the spotlight not only on the individual's performance, but on the collective contribution of the group, a primary value in many other cultures and often for women as well.

As you'll notice from the examples above, one of the hallmarks of a fluent leader is the ability to develop people by asking probing questions in a neutral and nonjudgmental way. If this is new territory for you, you may want to revisit the techniques offered earlier in this book for softening your language and using a more indirect communication style: "I am eager to hear what problems you are having with the project, as I've not heard from you yet. When we go to lunch tomorrow, I'd like to know what you're seeing. I need to know if you think we're going to make the deadlines, and if you have everything you need."

Asking employees to weigh in gives them permission to start addressing important issues in their own way.

FLEXING IS ABOUT SEARCHING FOR SOLUTIONS TOGETHER

Say that you, like Jim, have identified a team member who, for some reason, does not feel comfortable approaching you directly or coming to you with problems or issues. This team member may also be reluctant to celebrate her accomplishments or relay her good work to you or to other managers. How do you deal with this different orientation in your own workplace?

Let's say you're holding a biweekly status meeting with your direct reports. You want to keep a pulse on how your people are doing, as well as create a lively forum for team members, encouraging them to challenge and learn from each other. Wendy, a young woman in your group, gives an update on her projects. But during the ensuing Q&A with her colleagues in the meeting, she refers all the difficult questions to you. The more she is challenged, the more she clams up. You know that she knows the answers to the questions, but you can't figure out what is going on. What happened to her backbone? Your immediate verdict is that she wilts under pressure and may have a hard time with conflict. You start to worry about how she might be faring with your most critical clients. How can you decrease the power gap and determine Wendy's true value?

Identify her behavior and specify its impact.

Wendy is not speaking up; therefore she gets no credit for her own ideas. This creates the perception that she is not leadership material, even though you know she has skills and talent.

"Let's debrief the last few meetings that we've had this week. I noticed that in the final meeting that we had yesterday, you lobbed all the questions back to me. I know you knew the answers, and I wondered why you did that."

It is important that in the course of this discussion you clearly link the behavior back to its impact on the business; point out that the problem doesn't exist in a vacuum. By doing so, you are giving her feedback in a way that links to her future success in the organization, and not just demanding that she change her habits or style because they're not like yours. This makes it more difficult for the employee to shrug off the feedback by blaming it on a personality issue between you.

Describe the impact of observed actions on you and the team, and connect it with your business objectives, avoiding blame.

Discuss this behavior with her with great sensitivity, and without *blaming* her. You may have underlying assumptions regarding her behavior. If done skillfully and with an earnest desire to understand her, you may find out something new about her perspective. Try probing beneath the surface in order to discover those motivations and values that are acting as barriers to her success in this context. Let Wendy know how much you need her participation, and then discuss how she might change her behavior in order to contribute while staying true to her values.

The rewards come once you start to really talk about what's at stake: Wendy's personal transformation as she understands how to create a better future in the company and improve her chances of advancement.

Provide clear input on how the employee will need to flex, and partner with her to develop next steps.

As a manager you must be specific when you lay out the consequences: "This is how things work at this company. We need your feedback, and we need you to take more initiative on this project and help the rest of the team to better understand your needs. If you don't do this, it may hurt your chances of getting ahead. Now what can I do to help?" You have flexed by identifying the issue, investigating the underlying causes, and by looking for a solution *together*. Your team member can meet you partway by implementing changes to correct the behavior while not compromising her values.

Today's leaders are being asked to manage a tremendous variety of people and management styles. To be effective, sometimes it will be up to you to make the first move. It is up to you to go *to them* to start a conversation. That initiative is what makes you a flex leader. But note that in the above case with Wendy, while you may take the first step, the goal is connection and working toward common ends. Flexing isn't about letting your employee off the hook; it's about sharing responsibility and clarifying expectations.

STRATEGIES FOR FLEX SUCCESS

You can successfully adapt your management style and learn to deal creatively—and authentically—with diversity. If you become fluent in these skills, the rewards are great: you can cut down on attrition rates, keep your top hires and learn how to grow them, and even end up with a secret weapon: the strengths and insights of people who are different from yourself. The following are tried-and-true strategies for flexing to meet the needs of your diverse team, from getting out from behind your desk to coaching candidates on interview techniques.

DON'T WAIT FOR EMPLOYEES TO COME TO YOU

Today's most successful leaders are known for meeting their employees partway. They engage in management by walking around, leaving their offices and walking the halls to ask their direct reports how things are going, if there is anything they can do to make their tasks go smoother, to help the teams run more efficiently.

One of the first CEOs to practice management by walking around and engaging people where they work is Syrian-born entrepreneur Omar Hamoui. In the 2010 *New York Times* column "The Corner Office," Hamoui, founder and chief executive of the mobile advertising network AdMob, explains that he gets better results by actually moving his desk around—setting himself up, out in the open, in various departments. How does this work?

"If you make yourself available to people, they'll tell you what

Close the Gap by Meeting Partway

they think. . . . I just pick up my computer and sit somewhere else," he says. "If people see you just sitting there and you're not doing anything, they walk up to you and talk to you. It's pretty effective in terms of hearing how things are going and how people are feeling about the company or how people are feeling about you."

This is a superb example of how companies can profit from closing the power gap and adopting wider cultural viewpoints. This technique is used by many of the fluent leaders we talked to, from Rosaline Koo in Singapore to Rafe Esquith, the fifth-grade teacher in Los Angeles whom we mentioned earlier.

Neil, an HR executive we worked with, took a similar approach. He decided to spend at least one day a week on the shop floor with his company's internal clients at the plant. When he was in his office,

Close the Gap by Meeting Partway

people tended to not call him about sensitive human resources issues. Going to HR connotes something *bad* happened or that there is a problem, and the culture of the firm had created a huge power gap between the HR people and the company's internal client population. Neil decided that he would create the pathway for others to come to him by going into their element. He reached out to his internal clients, with the goal of becoming their trusted adviser.

Once he started walking the halls of the "main business floor," it created approachability in his style, and more people felt comfortable confiding in him. With the trust that he built over time, various individuals were able to ask questions that would have a big impact on their careers. He was also able to keep close tabs on a few of the new external hires that he had brought into the business. During one of his visits on the floor, seven individuals stopped him to ask about such significant issues as the tuition reimbursement policy, the new performance management process, and the process for initiating a transfer. While these visits did not always yield the most innovative human capital problem for him to solve, he connected with his client group in a way that his counterparts hadn't. He had built credibility and trust. Not a bad return for a forty-five-minute investment!

FLEX TO HELP RECRUITS AND NEW HIRES

Consider this news from some of the country's foremost business schools. International students accounted for 45 percent of applicants to full-time business programs at US graduate schools in 2011, up 6 percent from 2010, according to the Graduate Management Admission Council. *U.S. News & World Report* found that international students comprised, on average, about 30 percent of the incoming students at US business schools in 2012. In some programs, first-year MBAs are given a comprehensive program on how to conduct informational interviews and networking meetings. Yet such meetings are not commonplace in Asian countries, like China, where the school you attended and your entrance exam scores are the criteria by which you are judged. Students may need additional guidance about how to go about initiating direct contact with potential employers. The international students might need coaching and practice to help them learn how to pitch themselves in an American context. Some are given access to alumni in banking and consulting, and are required to conduct at least five to six informational interviews to find out more about the industry. These are closed industries where you need to know people to get your foot in the door.

Another key issue to consider in recruiting and hiring: just because someone isn't proficient at self-promotion does not mean he is incompetent or ineffective. In North America, it is acceptable for the job candidate to openly promote his skills and experiences. In fact, you are expected to toot your own horn, since it is your responsibility to convince the hiring manager that you've got the qualifications for the job. In countries outside of Asia, it might be considered arrogant, even inappropriate, for a candidate to promote himself to the hiring manager. In those local cultures, it may be enough that you graduated from the top undergraduate or graduate institution, as gaining entry into those schools indicates a level of proficiency. You may want to reach out to help elicit this information and build a complete picture of what each candidate offers in order to ensure you're capturing the best talent available to you.

TAP INTO HIDDEN POTENTIAL AND PROMOTE THE RIGHT PEOPLE

Some of the same issues you may be having about communication and performance with workers different from you can also arise when choosing whom to fast-track or promote. The same people who might hesitate to drop into your office and talk through a problem might also go underrecognized for their achievements, and might even get passed up for advancement. In order to get the most from everyone who works for you, it's critical to reach across the power gap when it comes to reviews, handing out bonuses, and promotion time.

We have defined six proficiencies most managers look for when identifying high-potential candidates to move to the accelerated track or consider for promotion. We compiled this list from our own experience in examining corporate practices and how promotional decisions are made as well as on input from HR leaders, leadership consultants, and recruiters across seven industries. Many of you will recognize these basic rules for getting ahead on the job. When you measure the following skills and weigh their importance for each employee, pay particular attention to the power gap. We call this GARP (Generally Accepted Rules for Promotion). After each are some questions to ask yourself and steps you might take to close the power gap between you and these employees to better connect GARP and their performance.

1. Take initiative.

Does your employee always pitch new ideas in group meetings and not just to you? Are they performing exceptionally well on a project or wooing a client, but simply haven't told you about it? Communicate to your employee why demonstrating initiative matters, while considering the different forms initiative can take and whether you have all the information.

2. Demonstrate confidence in your communication style.

Confident communication is often equated with direct communication. If your employee isn't a direct communicator, investigate the reasons why. Is he actually demonstrating intuitive skill in connecting with different types of people? Does he alter his communication style depending on who's in the room? Is his indirect style simply in deference to you? Is he judged harshly by others when he employs a direct style? Perhaps his style belies his actual confidence level in his work.

3. Be aggressive about building your own network.

Look outside traditional circles for evidence of good networking on the part of your employees, and ask them to share with you networking they might not have thought connected to the workplace. Do they have strong ties to a culture-based group? Do they volunteer in a nonprofit? Or maybe they seek out only female mentors? Your reports might be taking advantage of resources and information and getting support in unconventional but helpful arenas. Look for opportunities to tap into that employee's network to gain access to diverse talent, new or innovative ideas, or build cross-company alliances.

4. Showcase your accomplishments.

We've already seen why self-promotion might be a problem for many people. Is there a way to allow your employee to communicate her wins without feeling threatened? Can you teach her the skills and techniques for reaching up to her superiors?

5. Take charge of your own career development.

Conventional wisdom may say no one's going to hand you your next job, but in some cultures that is *exactly* what would happen. A superior, not an individual, would dictate someone's career path. Does your employee not feel confident enough to look for opportunity, or does he not feel empowered to do so?

6. Say yes to stretch assignments.

In some companies, without some experience in the front-line sales function, you won't be able to run a P&L. In many high-tech companies, regardless of your academic background, it is expected you will take positions outside of your existing area of expertise and work in a variety of teams. Anecdotally, we've found that women are more apt to think through the logistical hurdles before signing on to a big assignment; while men offer a quick yes, then deal with the details later, even if it means taking on a special project or overseas assignment in a different region. Millennials may agree to positions beyond their skill set, based on their expectations for quick advancement.

THE PREMISE OF GARP is firmly embedded in traditional American corporate culture. Time and again, we need to remind our clients that employees who are from a different culture, gender, or age group can be at a disadvantage when it comes to meeting these demands, and may respond to such expectations differently. Take the time to communicate these values and unspoken rules to your employees, instead of making the assumption that they are understood. Also, look for ways these values are being demonstrated by diverse workers in just slightly different manners than those you are used to. That difference could be hiding a rich area of opportunity, or a path to success you hadn't thought of before.

VIEWING YOUR TALENT POOL THROUGH A WIDE-ANGLE LENS

If you see a problem in a certain arm of your company—lots of employees are leaving and you don't know why—culture might very well be the cause. In addition to engagement surveys and other cultural assessments, perhaps it's time to reach your talent differently. To find out, you'll need to spend time with various employees throughout the company to understand their perspective. For example, try connecting with each of your company's employee resource groups (ERGs) or affinity networks and ask for their insights. (See chapter 11 on innovation for best-practice examples.)

Some sample questions you might use to jump-start a dialogue with your ERG leaders: What don't we know about your needs and aspirations? What can we learn about this particular group of employees? What can we do to better engage them?

We did some digging into a large manufacturing company that had a high percentage of Latino workers in one of its departments, as well as an unusually high attrition rate. We found that these workers expected the boss to come to them and ask for their advice, especially when things went wrong. They didn't have the same ease as their counterparts when it came to reaching up, so they didn't know how to offer unsolicited advice.

The result was many unhappy employees who felt that their expertise was not respected. Meanwhile, managers were frustrated by what they felt was an unwillingness to "go the extra mile." The managers also complained that their staff failed to give them a heads-up about potential problems—and enough lead time to fix them, before incurring critical cost overruns.

Echoing what we'd seen in the field, in 2009, Google embarked on Project Oxygen, an intensive study that analyzed performance reviews and surveys, delving even into nominations for best-manager awards. When the findings came out, the simple directive "be a good coach" rose to the top of the list. The importance of being a good coach is certainly not a new discovery in the management space, but it was an aha moment for Google's management, who had assumed that technical ability alone drove management excellence. Their management strategy used to be, "Leave people alone. Let the engineers do their stuff. If they become stuck, they'll ask their bosses, whose deep technical expertise propelled them into management in the first place."

If an innovative, performance-based, data-driven company of engineers like Google tested its assumptions and found strong management skills and coaching ability to be a critical indicator of success, it has implications for the thousands of other managers and companies who want to tap into the best of their employees. To take this finding one step further, do you know how to be a good coach to everyone you manage? The new challenge is to understand the varying needs of those who bring a different lens to working in your environment. Make the connections, be proactive, and don't wait for your employees to close the gap with you. And whatever you do, don't leave your people "alone."

Fluent Leader Profile: Don Liu— Bridging the Gap through Generosity of Spirit

In life, there are givers and there are takers. Don is a giver.

For anyone who thinks leaders need be soft-spoken, mild-mannered, and conflict avoidant in order to be effective bridge builders, here's a rule breaker: the charismatic Don H. Liu—called "the Don" by many—senior vice president, general counsel, and secretary for Xerox. By any metric, Don is a strong-willed leader, intense, a man who moves at such a clip that his pace demands you keep up. Yet he couples that intensity with great self-awareness, an ability to communicate across barriers, and a selfless generosity of time and spirit. One lawyer who worked for him said Don gave her the most difficult job interview she ever had, but after she landed the job he involved her in everything, mentored her, and, overall, made her a better lawyer. "He can be a little intense," she said, laughing, "with a lot of energy. He's also a very focused worker and not the type who's going to stop and shoot the breeze that long." She remembered staring at her in-box when she received no fewer than twenty e-mails from him—on her first day in the office. "In the beginning I was intimidated because he was so well known for being tough," she admitted, "but he was also known for going to bat for you, and for being fair. He was patient with me, and he would explain why things had to be a certain way." With all his drive and success, Don has always made room for those just starting out in their careers or who needed mentoring or extra help to find their way.

Now a corporate senior vice president, Don was just a boy of ten when he moved from his native South Korea to a tough West Philly neighborhood. Plopped down into a new world, Don honed his ability to fight in an environment where survival depended on street savvy and knowing just how to play your hand. In elementary school, Don was relentlessly targeted by a much larger, tougher kid, until the day Don stood his ground and confronted him. "If you ever touch me again," he told his classmate, "I'll kill you." Don never did him harm, but the passion and intensity of his feeling came through. The bullying stopped.

It was perhaps this same drive that took Don through Haverford College on to Columbia Law School, then on to become one of the youngest general counsels ever hired at a Fortune 500 company. The one place Don never had to defend himself was at home. He describes his mother as the opposite of a "tiger mother"—she always bragged about him to her friends and peers, to the point that Don never wanted to let her down and instead drove himself to match the portrait she had painted of him. He felt, at his core, how much she genuinely believed in him and in his abilities, and she used words of praise to motivate her son to do his best. From these cumulative lessons Don grew to be a relentless, demanding boss who protects his team members the way his mother once stood up for him. He, too, genuinely believed in his team members and both modeled excellence and expected high performance from his team, which he, by all accounts, "fiercely protected." What made him a great manager? One former employee admitted Don "has a brilliant legal mind; he's one of the best GCs I've seen in my life," but it was his drive for excellence and belief they all could achieve it that made him stand out. "He wanted us all to be better." He's a tough boss, echoed another, "but he won't ask you to do things he won't do himself."

Don, like most fluent leader peers, excels in demonstrating this unconditional positive regard (UPR), the unconditional acceptance of those who've earned trust, even (or especially) in vulnerable and weakest moments. It is when an employee fails the team through a reckless act or even simple oversight that the mettle of a leader is tested the most. One former employee, a young female attorney, recounted a time when, as a new, overwhelmed, and very green lawyer, she delegated part of the duties for a report, then realized that the figures she got back were not 100 percent correct. It was Don who received the feedback that there was an error in a statement for the report once it had gone out. Don hadn't known that she had delegated the task in the first place; additionally, she hadn't proofread the document. While some managers would have screamed or yelled or offered the inexperienced lawyer up for sacrifice, Don offered acceptance and a learning opportunity. He took responsibility for the mistake with his peers, then approached her and asked her what had happened, and they worked the problem through. "Oh, what the hell," he said to her in the end. "It's not an SEC violation, it's just an error." His reassuring response to her closed the power gap and, after she had apologized for the mistake, allowed her to get back on her feet and focus on doing a better job going forward. He demonstrated his belief in her ability to learn and improve.

In fact, Don is very honest about his mistakes, sharing his more vulnerable moments, his background, and his lessons learned with new employees and colleagues alike. The executive director of a nonprofit on whose board Don sat came to him when she was in crisis. She was embroiled in some staffing challenges. Don was frank in his advice that the director focus on her own style and on her relationship with her staff, but he also shared some of his own failures, keeping her on track with lots of empathy and an investment in the time she needed to repair her important relationships and not get sidetracked by her problem.

Self-aware and engaged in the Korean communities and broader Asian community, Don is definitely proud of where he comes from. Known to spend countless hours mentoring young lawyers, he gives freely of his knowledge and time, speaks to organizations pro bono, and works on behalf of his community with a clear sense of respect and service. He is the vice chair of the Asian American diversity Advisory Council for Comcast Corporation, after serving as the National Asian Pacific American Bar Association's (NAPABA) In-House

Counsel Committee chair, and establishing their In-House Mentoring Program, among other contributions. NAPABA named Don the recipient of its first and only Icon Award, mean to recognize one "who, through outstanding and selfless dedication and leadership, serves as a catalyst for fundamental advancement of the ideals . . . of the Asian Pacific American legal community."

But what is perhaps most striking about Don, and what makes him a truly fluent leader, is his ability to bridge the gap with nearly everyone around him. "He doesn't get stuck in 'analysis paralysis,' " said one colleague. "He's not shy about his opinion, but he's able to avoid making situations personal, and focuses on what's good for the organization." He also offers a lot of himself to the people he works with, openly sharing his own personal background and inviting others to do the same. Recently, when he got wind of a group that met regularly for a "ladies' lunch," he announced he wanted to attend. Far from killing the spirit of the lunch with his presence, Don blended right in, talking about shoes and politics, taking his cues from the women, decreasing any gap between them, and enjoying their company. He knows when to be tough and when to sit down and listen and, perhaps most important of all, is able to translate legal concerns into a language that other departments can understand and use to the company's advantage. At one of his prior companies, he initiated dialogue with the publicity and marketing departments because he wanted to keep the company's core message straight. The collaboration worked because he was open to their ideas and was inclusive to a fault, instead of hinging the partnership on his ego or empire building. He is praised by nonlawyers for his ability to communicate ideas, concepts, and legal issues into day-to-day language, and also "really put himself out there to learn what he didn't know" from other departments, a move that earned him respect across the board.

In fact, many of Don's colleagues told us that he is reputed to work better with non-attorneys than with other lawyers, and can speak the business language as well as the guys who are doing the sales, marketing, and operations. This skill makes him effective at translating the business issues to zero in on legal challenges that the company cares most about. Not only can you bridge the gap and be tough at the same time, developing a variety of strategies to manage the gap with various stakeholders can be the very key to your success, a point Don Liu proves time and again.

CHAPTER 6

NAVIGATE THE POWER GAP WITH YOUR PEERS

All potential teams have hierarchical, functional, and individual differences that are at once a source of strength and a source of problems.
—JON KATZENBACH AND DOUGLAS K. SMITH, *THE WISDOM OF TEAMS*

Not all peer relationships are created equal. In fact, just like managers and their direct reports, peer dynamics have a built-in power gap that must be negotiated in order to get the information, resources, and attention that you need to get your work done. As a leader, you not only need to be able to close the gap with your superiors and those who work for you, you need to be particularly skillful at managing *sideways*, to flex to your peers and those who work in other functions of the organization to move your project forward. In fact, there are a number of direct benefits to applying flex principles in working with your peers, whether you are working on a large cross-functional project or seeking to enhance the quality of interpersonal relationships across your organization. The pros of effectively managing the gap with your peer colleagues include:

- Allowing you to maintain your status in the hierarchy
- Creating allies in the organization
- Fostering a stronger team relationship

- Building credibility and your own cultural capital
- Identifying you as a leader

Part of the art of closing the gap with your peers lies in identifying the precise dynamics of the power gap in a given situation. Some peer relationships might appear equal on the surface—two people share the same title, the same level, and perhaps report to the same boss, but display wildly different communication and cultural perspectives. Add in differences of culture, gender, or generation, and you have an even wider power gap to manage. In addition to this type of direct peer relationship, there are three additional peer subgroups where power gaps can occur:

Functional peers

You may work in the same functional team or department, and you have the same level of experience and expertise.

Dmitri and Wei-Ling are development managers at a multinational software company who have direct counterparts in the acceptance testing group of the company who engage with the software products after they complete the development stage of their product. Maneesh and Padma are principal test managers for the same company. Often they work on the same products, but at different stages of the process and with different goals and objectives. At times, conflicting priorities and deadlines imposed by the two groups' leadership chain create tension, and they begin to work at odds instead of working together toward a common goal.

Peers in your age group

These are the people who joined the firm at the same time you did and are in your general age bracket, though some may have risen faster in the organization since you were hired. You may share many of the same values and outside interests, yet work at many different levels in the company, with varying degrees of status.

Robert started at his company the same year as a coworker, Richard. They enjoyed a close relationship in the same cohort. However, as the years progressed, Robert moved up faster than Richard until the day that he was no longer colleagues with his friend—he was his boss. Though they began as peers, the change in status created differences in attitudes and expectations that each man needed to investigate before they could create a new, successful relationship.

Peers at the same level with different functional expertise

You have similar levels of experience and may share the same title (e.g., all managers, directors, or senior VPs), but you work in different departments or divisions, with different reporting structures and priorities.

Vu is a director of human resources at a large financial institution. He was tapped to be the co–project manager of a major corporate reorganization mandate where he was teamed up with Jennifer, director of administration in a different business line. Their directive was to colead an expense reduction and downsizing initiative. This involved working very closely with senior leadership to shepherd the people reduction process, and to ensure that this difficult process was handled with sensitivity and care. While Jennifer was

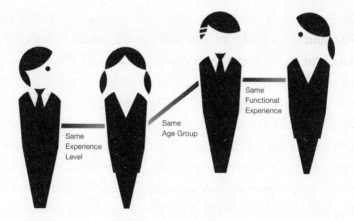

Closing the Gap with Different Peer Groups

recruited at the same time as Vu and thus functioned as a peer, she had more experience in managing reductions in force/layoffs (RIFs) due to her previous experiences working in employee relations and her legal training.

Throughout the duration of the project, Vu allowed Jennifer to report on the status of the downsizing initiative to management, as he assumed she already had those relationships and was keeping them informed of what they were doing collectively. At the end of the project, he was virtually an unknown to the senior business leaders. Why wasn't he more visible? "I felt that Jennifer always had a lot to teach me. So I focused on other aspects of the project, like the people planning analytics, and left the management interactions with the business heads to Jennifer," Vu said. "Looking back, she should have done a better job of giving me exposure to the business unit COOs whose businesses were impacted most by the employee reductions. But then again, I could have done a better job of taking more direct initiative with business unit COOs, and could have been more pro-active about driving those discussions, whether she brought me into them or not." Of his co–project manager, he told us, "Jennifer was the main person who interacted with the head of the largest business group because she'd worked with him before on a different project. She didn't bring me into those meetings, but in the end *I* got the flak. The business group head barely knew who I was, and he subsequently told my manager that I didn't contribute very much."

As a result, Vu lost credibility in the eyes of his manager, and he also lost an important opportunity to grow. Even if Jennifer, his "peer," was more seasoned with this type of project and knew exactly who the players were to get the information required to implement the initiative, he could have taken the initiative and called the business unit COOs directly to build the relationship with them. That way, regardless of whether she was guarding territory or simply working independently, Vu would have been brought on board. Looking back, he would have initiated the relationship with Jennifer as well as with all of the business unit COOs differently. But doing so went against his first instinct.

Vu's account serves as a cautionary tale for what it looks like when peers don't flex to meet each other partway to close the gap. Of course, as Vu mentioned, his co–project manager could have flexed toward Vu. She could have offered to mentor him in the process, or taken the lead but given him a bigger part to play so he'd be better prepared the next time. While we always tell our leaders to assume positive intent in others, at times your peers will try to win the spotlight for themselves, and will continue in that vein—unless you fight for your own voice. Because of this, as well as in the interest of more effective team cooperation, it's just as important to learn to flex to your peers—even those who are competing with you—as much as it is for managers to flex to their employees. Those who reach horizontally will be more successful in the long run. You will encounter less frustration, exhibit better communication to your superiors and those around you, and produce a better work product. Additionally, most large companies have instituted some form of peer review or 360-degree feedback process. That means your peers will also be evaluating you, and provide input about how you work with others on a team.

Reaching across the gap to your peers can prove as effective when you reach down to close the gap with your employees. Take the same flex principles you learned in the last chapter and apply them to peer relationships where you suspect there may be a power gap. If you stay open to different solutions, presume positive intent, and gently probe the underlying motivations behind your coworkers' behavior, it can lead to better working relationships.

Take Dmitri and Wei-Ling, the two principal development managers at the multinational software company. Not only do they need to work to close the gap with their counterparts in the testing group, they also found the need to flex toward each other in order to meet their own milestones. Working on a new software product slated to ship in six months, Wei-Ling's inability to meet her deadlines was frustrating Dmitri, whose work is dependent upon Wei-Ling finishing a portion of the code. Weeks would go by with Wei-Ling missing their milestones and not even acknowledging having dropped the ball. Finally, Dmitri couldn't stand it anymore.

A third team member advised him to send a "flame" mail to Wei-Ling, copying their boss. Then at least Dmitri won't be on the hook if the date slipped. But Dmitri opted for a different solution. Dmitri arranged to have a one-on-one with Wei-Ling, suspecting that he might get more information if he talked with Wei-Ling alone and not in the presence of their boss or team.

He explained he was worried about missing the ship date and wondered if there was anything he could do to help Wei-Ling with her portion of the project, since his work was interdependent with hers. He found out she had run across a big glitch in the existing code, a huge problem she didn't feel comfortable addressing in the team meetings. She told Dmitri she felt it was her job to figure it out and get the project back on track, which is why she didn't approach him or the others and explain the delay.

What Dmitri originally took as evasion of responsibility was actually Wei-Ling's deep-seated belief that the missed deadlines were her problem to solve, not an excuse. After learning more about the particulars, Dmitri was able to offer ideas about how Wei-Ling could solve the problem and continue her work. He also asked if they could have weekly status meetings, just the two of them, to keep things on track. With them working together, the product shipped on time.

PEER OR COMPETITOR?

It can be especially challenging when you and a peer work for the same boss and there is an unspoken or overt need to differentiate yourself as better performing than your colleague. People often wear multiple hats in a single role: While you are on the same team and expected to play well with others, there is still the expectation that you need to differentiate yourself from your peers. You are not only colleagues, you are competitors. Some companies assess performance through ranking or quintiling, processes where HR departments are charged with ensuring that the star employees are receiving promotions, bonuses, and stock offerings while the lowest-ranked employees or the bottom 20 percent are probably on their way out the door. In these systems, even if you do good work, you might find yourself in the bottom tier because you're not doing great work relative to those to whom you're being compared. Under that kind of pressure, where the competition from coworkers could literally mean your job, reaching out to close the gap with your peer might seem almost counterintuitive.

However, we believe it is important that you do set the tone for how a relationship can progress right from the start. If you can apply the pre-engagement questions before you begin working with your new peer, and commit early to bridging the power gap in proactive ways, there is a greater likelihood that your working relationships will survive the heat of corporate politics. Even if the relationship later experiences strain from the stress of competition or politics, it can be repaired.

Take the example of Robert and Richard mentioned earlier. After Robert became Richard's boss, Robert thought he knew Richard's feelings and motivations intimately since they had worked so long side by side. In fact, he expected Richard would play a foundational part on his team when he got the promotion to become Richard's superior. However, Robert soon realized he had underestimated how difficult the change in position would be for Richard, and he was initially caught off guard by how palpable the shift in their power dynamic was. The power gap that developed had drastically altered their relationship, despite the men having started at the company at the same time and having shared many experiences over the years. Robert began to notice signs of discomfort and a tension that hadn't been there before.

Robert was reticent to broach the subject with Richard—it was bound to be a hard conversation to have. Yet he also knew he couldn't pretend the issues weren't there and hope that Richard would come around. That would damage his credibility as a leader and hurt the whole team. He was honest with his colleague, and when he initiated the discussion, Richard was visibly relieved. "I thought I'd be okay with this," he confessed to Robert, "but the fact that it's been ten years and I'm still in the same spot I started in and you've gone up five levels is hard for me to stomach." They were no longer peers, Robert realized, and they would need to build a new relationship from scratch that took that into account. Robert spent a lot of time rebuilding that relationship, and Richard became a critical confidant to him on the team. In the end, the frank dialogue they shared, and the time they invested to flex to each other, paid off. The trust was rebuilt in their relationship, and Richard did end up becoming a cornerstone of Robert's team. At his retirement, he told Robert, "I thank you for giving me peace as to where I am ending my career."

Building new relationships and accumulating that kind of trust doesn't happen overnight. It's important to remember that just like becoming a fluent leader, establishing new paths of trust and communication with peers who feel jealous, betrayed, angry, or resentful requires powerful resiliency and humility, especially when you perceive you have done nothing to earn those feelings other than work hard and perform well. If you are able to commit, you may reap the rewards of a reconciled relationship. Flexing to your peers, especially those who are resentful of your position or authority, requires an empathic sensitivity to how the other person may be feeling, as well as emotional maturity and confidence in your abilities. Fluent leaders know that flexing doesn't show weakness but, rather, courage.

Especially in the case of flexing toward your peers, a leadership style that emphasizes skillful and fluent collaboration over blindly jockeying for power can reap better results. This can fly in the face of conventional wisdom, especially in highly competitive environments where colleagues are intentionally pitted against one another in order to coax the best from every employee. For women, who tend to favor a more collaborative style than their male counterparts, peer flexing offers a chance to turn that difference into an asset.

Lily, a young woman in marketing for an international beauty company, always experienced friction between marketing and creative at her workplace. Marketing would have an idea for a campaign, or maybe even have a big name attached, and creative would take the idea in its own direction, producing mock-ups that fell short of the marketing team's expectations. It was a scenario perfectly set up for fireworks, with marketing and creative both battling for control of the final campaign. But Lily told us her boss was an adept, hands-on problem solver. She called for a meeting with creative and couched the problem not as creative getting it wrong, but in terms of their all being in it together. There was a big celebrity attached to their campaign that needed to be featured—how could they make that happen together, she asked, and how could the creatives help that campaign to be successful? In the end, creative came over to see marketing's point of view, but the effect was one of collaborative effort rather than that of a battle won or lost. The VP's collaborative, team-based style was used in a very effective way to include its perspectives.

AGE CAN PLAY A ROLE IN THE POWER GAP DYNAMIC

Both age and generational differences can create a disparity and power gap between peers. Age, seniority, and title are used to differentiate between workers, and make up a critical part of high-context hierarchical cultures such as big multinational companies, or in local cultures around the world. In these environments, there is a natural progression since college on a clearly delineated ladder of advancement. You don't skip levels in these organizations; instead, respect accompanies age and seniority. As an example, in South Korea, respect is accorded based on when you graduate from college; and for men, your completion of compulsory military service and honorific titles that are used to refer to older colleagues or superiors.

Diane, the senior vice president for diversity and inclusion for a large financial services company, knows all too well the power gap that can exist between generational groups. The way her team approaches the distinctions in generational difference is not in terms of chronological age, but more as differences in their unique cultural perspectives and values. In her experience, Gen Y, Gen X, boomers, and traditionalists all have varied perspectives and different ways of doing things based on their own value systems. "We need intercultural competencies not just in Mumbai or Peru, but right here in the US," she said, adding that her organization looked at how they were operating in their global teams, then applied that lens to American diversity, including generational differences. Diane started out her career as a teller, then rose to management positions where she worked in the credit risk management group. Diane sees the power gap and generational "cultural" differences as a "business problem" to which she could bring her risk management background to bear. "In order to minimize risk, we need to better embrace and leverage the changes in demographics of our employees while fully understanding the needs of our clients." Diane's tale also offers an excellent insight into various generations and strategies for clearing the air and managing across to peers older or younger than you.

TRADITIONALISTS VS. MILLENNIALS: MULTIPLE GENERATIONS WORKING SIDE BY SIDE

Diane was faced with a deeply divided workforce in her region's retail branches. Over 71 percent of tellers in her banks are millennials, including lots of college students for whom a part-time job works perfectly with their academic schedules. Another demographic group that craves part-time work constitutes a small but vocal minority of the branch staff as well: retired traditionalist employees (she calls them veterans) seventy years old and older. In a typical hierarchy, the older employees manage the younger ones, but in this case, there were numerous instances where millennials would manage the boomers and the traditionalists, despite the significant age gap between them. They also functioned as peers working in the same branch. From the early days of their working together, both sides felt (and acted) as though they had zero in common. As time passed, the two generations of workers saw each other constantly, and over time, tensions ran high. Eventually, feedback from the branch managers and the millennial employees/traditionalists themselves pointed to increasing tensions that were deeply damaging their ability to work side by side in the branches.

THE TRADITIONALIST'S TAKE

The older workers complained that when no one was standing in the Gen Y tellers' lines, the young employees were always checking their phones or texting. They accused the young employees of lacking "common courtesy" since they rarely smiled at customers and didn't always make eye contact, which, to traditionalists, was violating the basic commandment of Customer Service 101. Despite that, the young workers would ask to be promoted quickly and be given more interesting job assignments. The bank branches had a policy of giving new employees a ninety-day review period to see if they would be kept or not, and before their trial period was up, some of these young employees would already be asking for a promotion!

THE GEN Y POINT OF VIEW

"The older workers have no idea how modern technology works!" the millennials retorted. They complained to their managers that their older colleagues spent *forever* with every customer, chitchatting about their grandchildren, asking about their spouse's health, or talking about the customer's dog. They didn't recognize talent when they saw it, the millennials said. When the younger workers pursued promotions or asked for increased responsibility in their job requirements, instead of explaining the rationale for why it couldn't be done, the older workers just told them to wait. They needed to pay their dues.

HOW THEY MET EACH OTHER PARTWAY

Interestingly, each group's preferences and values had both positive and negative impact on the customers. The Gen Y tellers were able to help solve many of the customer's banking needs through timely use of new online banking technology and being efficient about offering products. When a customer came to the teller window, they were also adept at pulling up their online banking history on the computer and at an instant offer customers more efficient ways to conduct their banking transactions. Not surprisingly, their transaction volumes and efficiency scores were high. The millennials' customer service scores, however, were lower. The older tellers used their personal, relationship-driven, get-to-know-you style to their advantage. Because they knew their network of repeat customers so intimately, they could gauge in advance if it was time for a boat or a car loan or other banking products. Their transaction volume numbers may have been lower, but their customer service ratings received consistently superior ratings.

These two groups of tellers were working side by side, but had become extremely critical of one another and were unable to see one another's strengths. Leadership had to intervene so that the two groups could be encouraged to work together to address the generational values, assumptions, and judgments, and keep the nuances of age differences right up front and center in the conversations. Diane's group created forums where members of both groups had a chance to talk openly with each other about the positive and negative traits each generation exhibited. Though the first step was not their own, they were able to begin closing the gap with one another when the groups were brought together. They were finally able to see and hear how they were perceived by others, then engaged in training to release their judgment and begin to learn ways to take advantage of one another's strengths as they worked side by side with each other in the retail branches.

Through the process, the following observations emerged that helped inform the value judgments each generation was making:

Baby boomers respect authority, even if they don't respect the person the authority is tied to. And Gen Xers want to be able to voice their opinion. As long as they are given that opportunity, they'll ultimately do what they've been directed to do by management.

For Gen Y, it is about keeping it real. They want to hear all the reasons behind a decision or judgment call. If the motivations seem authentic, they'll follow through; if it's just policy—the equivalent of "because I said so"—then that reads as inherently disrespectful and they push back.

Diane and her team's efforts helped to create a more inclusive work environment where tellers of any age could feel more comfortable working with others. It was the beginning of a learning process for the retail banking unit, and Diane was the first to say that there is certainly more to be done to build this "cultural awareness" of generational differences to new hires as well as throughout the culture of the organization. Her retail banking branches now have a platform where there is permission to continuously learn from one another, and a genuine appreciation for what tellers of every age have to offer their bank. Organizationally, they are making it easier for cross-generational colleagues to understand the motivations behind the differing behaviors of each generation, making it easier for the employees to reach across to one another and leverage their different skill sets to provide unified and comprehensive customer service.

ENTITLED

Job titles by their existence connote hierarchy. They were created in most companies to delineate the levels and years of experience of their employees, and to help leadership differentiate the mastery level of various job types/functions. For the most part, job titles exist in almost every Fortune 500 organization. Whether your title is analyst, manager, director, senior director, managing director, president, partner, or VP, each is meant to connote a hierarchal structure, authority, and power. A perceived power difference could exist simply based on the difference in your titles, regardless of the actual decision-making authority you wield.

Because of their power to impress and inform, titles are also no-cost perks or awards granted workers who have performed well. Even if they don't accompany a shift in responsibility or pay, a new title alone can be enough to create a power gap between former peers who still perform largely the same work. High power gap clients and coworkers may automatically confer greater respect and authority depending on that line below your name.

Our advice? Enjoy the honor of a powerful title—you earned it!—but take special note of any conflicted feelings and tension that exist in the peers you leave behind. As in the case of Richard earlier in this chapter, if you can find ways to bring them along and close the gap, your experience in the organization will be that much more productive.

ENGAGING PEER ALLIES

When Tracy, a Chinese Canadian with an MBA and international marketing experience in the UK, went to work in China, she was coolly received by other women who were in administrative and support roles. The senior leadership respected Tracy's work, but the women her age resented her because at twenty-nine, Tracy had already worked with major firms in both New York and Germany, had managed global projects, had an advanced degree, and spoke three languages. Tracy could have tried to ignore these women (or worse), and concentrated on the other managers who afforded her respect. After all, she hadn't done anything to hurt them personally. However, Tracy needed the support of these women with whom she worked in order to be effective in her position. She had to help them move past their feelings of jealousy and discomfort.

Tracy closed the gap by following these steps:

1. **Addressing the issue.** Just as flex leaders need to take the first step toward employees with whom they need to close the gap, it's up to you to reach out to your colleague. After you run through the three critical pre-engagement questions from the last chapter, decide on a plan of action and take the first move. In Tracy's case, she asked a group of these women to join her at an informal lunch. Moving the conversation out of the office helped mitigate the face to face, making it less of a formal meeting than a get-together. Once she broke through the initial discomfort, she was able to have better-quality conversations with a few of the women.

2. **Demonstrating intent to decrease the gap with a humble attitude and curiosity to learn from others.** Tracy's peers had begun to resent her for cross-cultural fluency as well as her direct access to the local senior leadership at such a young age. While on the surface she shared Chinese ethnicity with the women and even spoke their dialect, there was definitely an unspoken gap that needed to be bridged. An important key way to build trust with them was to show them how much help she really needed from this group, shifting the perceived authority graciously. Once she had them gathered, Tracy told them of her intent to build strong working relationships with them, proceeded to explain her role, and followed through by explaining specifically how they could help. Later, she continued to offer her assistance as they worked on projects together.

3. **Enlisting allies and sharing power.** Once Tracy had explained how these other women were vital to her accomplishing her work, she began to recruit allies and bring the women over to her team. She asked a few of the women to support an upcoming project she was tasked to lead. She also used her educational background and experience to help her female peers. She began to mentor them in their desire to improve their communications skills with dealing with management in other offices outside of China, and later wrote a recommendation letter for one of the women who showed great promise and who demonstrated marked improvement in her performance.

PLAYING WITH THE BOYS

Kate is a partner at a boutique investment bank. She has a petite frame, looks young for her age, and works primarily with men, creating even more layers of difference and widening the perceived power gap between them. This often meant that Kate needed to be very strategic in reaching across to flex her style toward that of her peers, even if it meant going out of her comfort zone. Over the years, she has figured out ways to work with her male colleagues and established ways to flex in order to be heard and hold her own in various interactions. "I don't talk about sports and I don't play golf," she lamented, adding that she doesn't even swear, a common bonding communication lingo among the men of her firm. In order to make up for these style differences, she needed to doubly prepare for every meeting. When she was younger in her career, if she couldn't connect on the soft issues, she made sure she made up for it by being whip-smart about zeroing in on the key information about a client, and demonstrating confidence about her numbers. Over time, Kate also had to adapt her communication style in order to seem more on par with her peers, highlighting her accomplishments more openly and strategically, and being more direct in her communication.

It wasn't just inside the organization. When they had initial meetings with clients, because Kate was often mistaken as a subordinate to those who worked *for* her, based on her youthful appearance and stature, she had to develop a more direct communication style to compensate for those perceived differences and send a clear signal to clients that she was as capable as her peers. Because she had to be attuned to these perceptions and manage how she was received both internally with her peers and externally with clients, Kate developed a fluency that helped her manage the gap with colleagues and also close the gap with clients. She leveraged her difference from her peers in way that improved outcomes on both sides.

In general, Kate has become quite adept at picking up on peripheral, unspoken cues about a client in the first one or two meetings. One day, she and a senior partner in her firm, an older, very charismatic man, were going to meet with a client. Before the meeting she did her research and found out the client had a style very different from that of her partner. Unlike her loquacious partner, the client held a PhD and appeared in a recent media interview to be cerebral and reserved, and spoke in a very slow, deliberate pace. Kate's experiential understanding about different styles worked well for her in this case. She intuitively knew how to approach the client; her senior partner would have taken the wrong tack with his hard-driving sales approach.

First, she closed the gap with her senior partner by sharing what she knew before the meeting took place. With hard evidence in hand, she took her insight to him and advised that he flex his style to the client—she explained the importance of toning it down for the meeting in order to make the client feel more at ease. By doing her research ahead of time and presenting her partner with data rather than just a gut feeling, she was able to convince him of the best approach. He followed her advice, and they got the client.

Truly fluent leaders will find ways to flex across to peers, across differences, and even in the face of resentment and friction. Relationships become complicated when those who were once peers are then divided by the gap between boss and employee, compounded by cultural, gender, or generational differences. Managing across can sometimes morph into a managing-down situation.

When Jackie McNab was promoted, a former peer who'd also had his eye on the job was furious. He was openly disrespectful, and even told Jackie she got the job only because she was a woman. At the same time, he wasn't owning his job responsibilities. She told us, "I had to say, 'I'm sorry you feel that way, but my qualifications are the reason I got it. I expect you to do your job and these are the responsibilities.'" As they continued to work together she would ask him in her one-on-ones, What do you want to do? What are your goals? He still wanted her position—that desire never left him and he was honest about that. She kept her cool and was able to give him feedback about his strengths and weaknesses that helped him grow into the qualifications of a position similar to hers. Eventually, when she moved on, he was ready to replace her. Jackie moved through different relationships with him, from peer to boss to mentor. She wasn't defensive and she didn't try to get him fired, and eventually, as a mentor, she was able to emphasize that he needed some more skills and tied his growth to specific actions and steps.

PROVEN STRATEGIES TO REACH ACROSS THE GAP

Befriend your peers.

Initiating a cross-cultural dialogue with someone who is a peer can be sensitive conversation. Extending a heartfelt "I can learn a lot from you" can go a long way toward eradicating animosity and getting you on the same team, literally and figuratively. Let them know that you need their support, and ask in return how you might help.

Extend yourself and offer your own skills and help.

Especially if you're the senior person, by offering help and aid for a peer learning the ropes, you can communicate clearly how you like to get things done.

If you have risen faster in the ranks, stem jealousy and competition by sharing ideas about how you can share power in your new position. But don't just say it; go beyond the talk. Give credit to those who have supported your ideas, and reciprocate often.

 TAKE STOCK OF YOUR +'S AND -'S: QUESTIONS FOR SELF-EXAMINATION

- What will you do differently to communicate more effectively with your peers? (Use a broad definition of peers—peers in age, peers in title, etc.)
- As you consider your past peer relationships, what type(s) of peer relationships have been challenging to you? Are there patterns to these relationship dynamics?
- How can you build goodwill in peer relationships and reach out, even in conflict situations?
- Which peer relationships are challenging for you right now?
- How can you build allies with your different peer groups?
- What steps can you take to demonstrate your support for others in your peer group?

CHAPTER 7

GO THE DISTANCE WITH YOUR SUPERIORS

I f you happen to work in a start-up or small office, it might be hard to spot who's in charge. Everyone's wearing casual gear and works in the same open layout. They eat lunch together, might work out at the gym together, and drop by each other's desks spontaneously to ask a question. And everyone appears to enjoy easy access to the boss. But though they may not show it through closed-off corner offices or executive boardrooms, even start-ups or small firms with flatter organizational structures have a hierarchy or command chain through which decisions get made.

In most other corporate settings, there is a corporate ladder with both explicit and hidden power structures. In order to work your way up the organization, you build relationships with people who have more power than you and are several levels above you in the organization. If you are the CEO, it could be your corporate board that you're accountable to. We all have someone to whom we report, someone responsible for evaluating our performance, granting us promotions, advocating for our next position, or navigating the growth of the business. Not reaching up can severely limit your future career options. When you ignore closing the power gap with your boss (or don't know how to do so), you may get passed over for promotion or have your opinions discounted.

OBSTACLES TO CLOSING THE GAP FROM THE BOTTOM UP

Fluent leaders with a good sense of awareness of their own style and preferences employ relationship-building skills to manage up and work to close the power gap from the other side. They do not wait to have their leadership reach down to them. At times, this can be difficult to do if your superiors exhibit very different styles from you or operate by values that you're not familiar with. Some employees report feeling uncomfortable with this task—and don't feel it is their responsibility to "manage" their boss. Individuals range from believing reaching out to higher-ups is inappropriate or disrespectful to thinking the act signifies extreme submission, a move detrimental to his or her long-term career. Others don't want to reach up because their boss simply seems so different and distant from them and they don't feel they have an "in" or a natural way to engage. When we discuss the importance of building rapport with senior leadership, they ask, "What do I talk about with him? We have very little in common." Still others might be fighting the perception that they are trying to kiss up to the boss.

No matter your reasons for not wanting to bridge the gap before, let us tell you now that it remains a critical skill in the workplace. Reaching up is not only acceptable, it's critical, especially in situations where the superior isn't making an effort to reach down. Contrary to popular thought, reaching up is not only about trying to win favor or brownnosing to get what you want. Your goal is to build a more authentic relationship with the people above you so that you can achieve mutually beneficial goals.

American executives want their employees to take the initiative. Employees who do so become visible and are most readily identified for key projects, get good press, and are generally well thought of. But the accommodation has to go both ways. The first step toward closing the gap with your superiors may be harder for those of you accustomed to more of a distance between you and your manager(s). All the same, it is possible to respect and even revere your boss without viewing him as an infallible authority who can't be approached.

OVERCOMING THE "FREEZE" WITH AUTHORITY FIGURES

Tom, a Korean American attorney who now works as in-house counsel in the hospitality industry, remembers very clearly how his cultural perspective played out in the law school classroom, and even in his early days as a practicing attorney. "In my first year of law school, I did this thing I called 'the freeze.' I tended to get this deer-in-the-headlights moment whenever the professor called on me, a pattern I started to notice in my fellow Asian students as well. Most of the others appeared to be comfortable with the Socratic method where your point of view is constantly questioned and analyzed, and responded in a way that engaged healthy discourse. I definitely had respect for the professor, and the professor was merely doing his job: to test you and to poke you so that you are ready when you're inside that real courtroom. After this happened a few times, I resolved that I would work on this and fight this instinct to shrink back when I got called on. Before going to class, I practiced speaking up and stating my opinions. I made sure I knew my material well enough and that I could express my thoughts confidently enough so that I could think quickly on my feet. It made a big difference in how my peers and professors saw me.

"As I look back on it, it goes back to whenever I would speak to my dad's friends and family members. I would lower my head, bow slightly, and say '*Neh*' ('yes' in Korean). It would never occur to me to answer back to them or look at them directly in the eye—it would be disrespectful. So it's ironic. To my family, acting that way meant I was brought up well by my parents: respectful. But in American culture, to be submissive is weak! Today, as in-house counsel, I see this in a few of the Asian outside-law-firm attorneys that come to visit us for meetings. They do the same 'freeze' when they are challenged by us, and these are graduates of the best law schools. Most of the time, it's not their lack of capability or smarts; there are definitely some cultural factors at play here. From the in-house counsel side, it really hurts to watch this, as it erodes the confidence level we feel from the other side."

Gearing Up to Be Challenged

"Having made the same mistake, it's only after many years of practice, many of my own 'freeze' moments, and with more practical experience, that I feel more confident with people. So now, whenever I feel like I'm being challenged by a superior, by an internal client, or the CEO, I get prepared to 'bring it.' I can anticipate cases and business transactions that might cause a headache early on, and I prepare to respond in a confident way in the formal meetings. Looking back, I realize it took time and practice to grow into this job. I get now the importance of managing your superiors, no matter how senior they may be—your CEO, your partner, your client. You've got to understand that they need to feel that they can send you out there and feel confident about your abilities. Every day at the office, you have to 'bring it.'"

DON'T PUT AUTHORITY FIGURES ON A PEDESTAL

Realizing that your boss is human may help to close the gap, allowing you the space and objectivity to more accurately gauge how he or she wants to be approached and "managed." Holding the boss up as a figure beyond your reach can have the opposite effect: not only does it guarantee you won't approach her and take the initiative, it can give too much weight to every word she utters. In those times when it's most important that you think on your feet, instead of thinking rationally in your discussions, you're more apt to freeze up. You won't be able to come up with a quick solution, or know how to respond to criticism because it's too loaded. As you consider how to close the power gap with your manager, it would help to identify how you want to get yourself heard in ways that are respectful yet convey a strength of conviction that your manager needs to hear.

Jackie McNab, a technology executive, had found a position where her manager also became her mentor. They enjoyed a close working relationship until Jackie noticed a disturbing pattern. During quarterly review meetings, she felt on the same level with other members of his staff even though she was the only woman when they were in the boardroom. Inevitably, they would take a break. As the men headed into the restroom together they kept talking shop, and when they emerged, Jackie would discover they had made progress on the agenda or made some decision without her. Jackie approached her boss and described the situation she'd noticed and said, "I think that's unfair. You can do one of two things: either I come into the bathroom with you all, or you refrain from having those discussions in there when I'm not present!" Her boss loved her candor and her bold solutions got her boss's attention. He made a rule that no business was to be discussed once the group left the boardroom and Jackie was once more fully included.

Jackie closed the gap with her boss by being bold and using a bit of humor, a technique that Kelley, an MBA applying for a job at a stock-broker firm, applied with aplomb. Ushered into the manager's office, Kelley was told to have a seat while he finished up a meeting in the conference room. She got up from her chair and looked at the photos on his wall—action shots of the Chicago Blackhawks. Kelley knew absolutely nothing about ice hockey; she only surmised that this guy was a fan. When the manager returned, she tapped into his passion and asked who his favorite player was to get the conversation rolling.

Now, some of you might be thinking, What if I'm not genuinely interested in sports, or don't know anything about my coworkers or superiors? Might this come off as fake or self-serving? It all depends on your strategy in asking questions. Even if you don't know anything about hockey or care about your boss's favorite charity, you can demonstrate curiosity because he or she is excited about it. It can be infectious to be around passionate people and to examine why they are into . . . whatever that might be. You don't have to feign interest in their hobbies or the object of their interest; rather, be interested in them. This focus on the person will naturally beget questions like, What attracts them? What/who do they like or admire? What drives them? And give you a point of entry in order to break through the initial discomfort and get to know them over time.

Kelley's strategy was to make her potential boss "feel comfortable while he was interviewing me. I realized that it wasn't just his job to make me feel at home. It was mine to reach up to him as well." It worked. After fifteen minutes of hockey talk and banter, the hiring manager was already feeling good about the prospect of hiring her. He pointed to the trading floor outside of his glassed-in office and asked, "So what do you think about our company?" The inviting mood was already set: she smiled and observed jokingly, "Well, I don't see a lot of women there." To which the manager replied, "That's why we need you!"

Remember the research we cited in chapter 1 that shows that hiring managers tend to hire and promote people like them? In this case, by closing the gap with her interviewer Kelley was able to establish rapport even though hockey was not a passion they shared. The resulting easy conversation flow gave her the space to talk about her strengths, while making the hiring manager more at ease with his interactions with Kelley.

REVEAL AND OFFER YOUR UNIQUE VALUE

It is optimal when the person above you in the command chain is willing to flex down to you, especially if you have talents and skills that fall outside the norm. However, you can't always wait for your boss to reach down to you to single you out for that unique leadership opportunity or decipher how you might best contribute to the organization. If you have hidden skills and talents, or recognize that there is a power gap between you and your boss, you will accelerate the forging of a productive working relationship when you can reach up and close the gap. In any workplace interaction, you'll remember, the only thing you can control for certain is your own behavior and responses. Your ability to even influence the behavior of others may decrease as the power gap widens between you. This means you might need to stretch out of your comfort zone to manage up, and it might seem daunting at first. However, you need only devise an effective method of communicating your value that ensures recognition and appreciation for your contribution.

CHOOSING THE RIGHT FRAME FOR YOUR MASTERPIECE

We explain it to our clients as "framing" themselves, or giving their superiors a frame through which to view them. If you don't do that for them, how will they know who you are or recognize your unique gifts and attributes? Joshua Bell, a violin virtuoso who has played to standing-room-only audiences around the world, in elegant venues including the Library of Congress, agreed to change his "frame" in order to participate in an experiment for the *Washington Post*. One cold January day in 2007, Bell planted himself outside a DC Metro station and played some of the most stirring pieces Bach ever wrote on a 3.5-million-dollar violin. He didn't draw a crowd—he barely got anyone to stop and listen, though he earned $32 given him by passersby who considered him nothing more than an average busker trying to hustle a living from the busy commuters. As with Bell, you need to position yourself correctly in order for your superiors to realize what a valuable piece of art you are; tell them what they are looking at. Especially if you are part of a minority culture, others don't know how to recognize what they are looking at when they see you. Help them understand and better position you by choosing the right frame for your talents.

STEPS TO CLOSE THE GAP

1. Approach your superiors and be ready to volunteer something about yourself the next time you connect with your manager. Acknowledge that you have distinct aspects about yourself and that there are differences (external networks in the community, nonprofits or social causes that you care about, language skills, family or cultural practices) that may not be public knowledge.

2. Communicate your value to your manager by linking how you might use some of the external knowledge, skills, and insights that you have acquired to enhance your contribution to the benefit of your team, business, or company objectives. Describe how you might use your cultural capital or what makes you unique, then connect the dots for them as it relates to their goals for growing the business.

3. Take the first step to initiate the dialogue with your superior (it is unlikely that your manager will unearth these unique experiences in your personal history if you don't share them) and incorporate it into a broader conversation about your career development.

To take these steps toward closing the gap with a superior you need to be a little more forthcoming than you might be comfortable with. You should prepare for the actual conversation, just as you would any critical business meeting for which you prep. Your initiative, if positioned correctly, should help remove the discomfort that your manager might feel about the discussion of differences. As you prepare to take this initiative, arm yourself with the mind-set of an entrepreneur with a brand-new discovery. How would an entrepreneur disclose his unique qualities? With this risk comes reward. By naming the difference between you and bringing it up yourself, you give your superiors an easier way "in" for talking about what they may have already started to notice—that there's something about you that's not like all the people on your team. You will all feel more at ease, and it sets the stage for the next step, where you describe for them how you may be of use to the team, to the product, or to the client. By closing the gap with your superior, you have taken control and framed your differences as attributes, not detractions.

Even if no one is talking about your unique value or asking you about it, you can close the gap by offering up the information yourself.

For example, "I'm involved in an active women's group that might make a good sounding board for our new marketing initiatives," or "There's a new software program that can accomplish the task in half the time." Remember, what makes you different from others in your workplace might also make you a special conduit. You might be the voice of a customer, a link to an outside market, an "in" into a larger group, or even the unexpected perspective of a competitor. Perhaps you could even help with recruitment in areas where more diversity is needed if you have ties to a different community.

The *HBR* "Leadership in Your Midst" study conducted by the Center for Talent Innovation found that much more frequently than their white counterparts, minority executives led "hidden" volunteer lives outside of work that demonstrated not only an ethical commitment to their communities but also served to develop valuable skills transferable to the workplace. Of the Latino, African American, and Asian executives surveyed:

- 26 percent served as leaders in their religious communities
- 41 percent engaged in social outreach activities
- 28 percent acted as mentors to needy young people

As an example, African American women reported spending a great deal of time mentoring young people and having excellent connections with nonprofit organizations and boards, but didn't feel comfortable bringing up their volunteer duties at work. Some felt because they weren't on the board of an orchestra or other major mainstream nonprofit recognized by their company that their volunteer time didn't have the same weight. On the contrary; your hidden talents, passions, or unique service might prove very impressive in terms of character and even useful to your superiors. Don't be afraid to share these things with your boss to build and strengthen your connection. The key point here is to identify aspects about you that are distinct and that can add value to your organization's mission and values, its core business direction, or add to the bottom line.

THE GENERALLY ACCEPTED RULES FOR PROMOTION (GARP)

In chapter 5 we identified the six principles of GARP (Generally Accepted Rules for Promotion) and talked about how you could bridge the gap with subordinates who might have a more difficult time understanding and following through on these time-tested ways for getting ahead. These principles also provide a framework for managing up and bridging the gap with your superiors.

Take the initiative.

Step up and ask questions, pitch new ideas, and identify ways to promote your concepts to senior leaders. Taking the initiative in this manner may feel uncomfortable to you at first if you are more hierarchical, but if the expectation is for you to take the first step, you should consider what active role you can play to close the gap with your superior.

Demonstrate confidence in your communication style.

Speak with conviction. Tell your boss and your coworkers what you think, and how you make business decisions. Communicating well refers also to how well you advocate for your (or your team's) position. Make sure that you communicate in the manner your boss prefers and give him (or her) the information needed to do the job most effectively. A good example of how not to communicate well in this situation came from Youssef, who asked a member of his technical team to describe to him the possible impacts for the client related to a server failure. What she gave him was an incredibly detailed blow-by-blow of the code she was trying to implement to fix it. "What I wanted was two bullet points. Not only did her report lack the information I needed," he said, "but it invited me to micromanage her response to the problem because of the level of detail she provided me."

Be aggressive about building your own network.

Build relationships up, across, down, and outside of the organization that will help you connect with superiors. It often takes a village to get both the resources and information that you need to do a given project, to get support about an important initiative, and to find your next move inside the organization. (Practical ideas for finding and connecting with a mentor can be found in chapter 10.) It's important to know not only your immediate boss, but also those one to two levels above, as well as cross-functional group leaders.

Javier, a vice president with a large insurance company, first got exposure to the upper levels of management in his organization on the advice of his mentor. Early on in his career a manger told him that the United Way campaign was a big deal to the CEO. There was a program for officers, and there was a certain level at which you had to contribute to get on the CEO's radar. At that donor level you got invited to a special event filled with upper-level management. Javier followed the advice and later enjoyed a new relationship with the CEO and other critical sponsors. When building your network, don't overlook creative opportunities like Javier's or forget that those people may control access to your superiors, including mentors but also assistants and others in supporting roles.

Manage your boss and showcase your accomplishments.

As pleasing as it is to have your boss slap you on the back for a job well done, you may see more progress more quickly if you learn to walk into the boss's domain, gracefully point out your latest accomplishments, and discuss your career agenda. Due to the nature of American business culture, there is an expectation that the employee connects back to the boss regularly and looks for the best way to manage him or her.

Take charge of your own career development.

On some level, you need to act as your own boss. Think strategically; target and work toward your next assignment in the organization. Don't depend on your superiors to hand you that next dream job, or even to know what your dream job would be.

Say "yes" to stretch assignments.

It's an unspoken rule that if you want to move ahead in the organization, you're going to need to have demonstrated the ability to be successful in more than one function. Look to broaden your skill set, and at significant points in your career, seek out job assignments that take you outside of your existing area of expertise. That might mean taking on a special project, a global role, or perhaps a cross-functional assignment. It might mean learning additional skills through school or training classes. Make sure that you are able to define your new learnings and added expertise and, when possible, take on projects that have an impact on the business and high visibility. Keep a constant eye on what is on your manager's (or your manager's manager) top-priority list, as these items may change over the course of the year.

David Howse joined the staff of Boston Children's Chorus in 2004. Only five years later, this young leader assumed the role of executive director, in which he leads the development of strategies, policies, and programmatic priorities, and oversees operations of the organization. Surprisingly, his role as ED is the first time he's held a formal leadership position. He credits his nontraditional route and great advancement to saying yes when his founder/mentor pushed him to succeed. "When I was new to the nonprofit, he reached out to me and offered to help me. He saw something in me that said I was a leader. I took him up on his offer." Lots of people wanted to be in David's position as his manager's mentee. "I might have reached out, but he is a huge figure; I would have built credibility first before approaching him. But he asked me to lunch and made it easy for me. He suggested that I not surround myself with yes men, but with people who would speak with honesty and candor. David took his cues from his manager and learned at his side, eventually climbing the ladder to the top.

David could see the hesitation of another promising employee in his organization whom he hoped to encourage and advance as his manager did for him. His experiences as an African American formally trained as a musician meant he had grown up attuned to the impacts of difference when you're immersed in a dominant culture different from your own. When a Korean American employee had difficulty acting on David's encouragement to reach for a bigger role, he encouraged him to get a coach and tried to help him understand his leadership possibilities. "He was so reserved—self-effacing. I told him being a leader is about who you are as a person, not just skills or work output. It surprised him because he sees helping himself as too selfish."

 ## GET IN POSITION TO ENGAGE: PRINCIPLES FOR CLOSING THE POWER GAP WITH SUPERIORS

- Create a relational link with your superior by initiating informal check-ins to discuss work and personal career-development-related topics.
- Inform your superior about challenges that you are facing on the job. Tell them what you're doing to address them. Highlight a way for you to be a resource and part of the solution.
- Avoid complaining—you can be written off as a whiner, and negativity without solutions doesn't go very far.
- If you encounter a serious problem and are not getting an adequate response, don't have enough resources, or are running against a deadline you can't make, let someone know about it.
- Listen. Be attuned to the needs of your leadership and their

changing priorities, and be sensitive to their needs/concerns/ fears, and respond with how you might add value. Offer to help in areas outside of your written job description.

WORKING WITH BOSSES WHO MAINTAIN THEIR POWER GAP

There will be superiors who expect subordinates to just listen and follow through on directives. Some may prefer providing you with very clear direction/structure about your job tasks and may not be as comfortable with your initiative taking. Whether they choose to keep their distance because they feel threatened and vulnerable or because they just do business that way, you will need to find a way to close the gap if you want to get results. Increasing your level of formality can read as more respectful and may afford you the "in" you need. In being more formal, you may want to request meetings ahead of time, work around his calendar instead of relying on ad-hoc check-ins and spontaneous communication, and work intentionally to respect and acknowledge your superior's authority.

The level of formality can play into the power gap, especially for bosses of millennial subordinates. Reaching up might pose special challenges for millennial workers who want access to high-impact assignments quickly upon hire and simultaneously don't feel the same sense of adherence as their superiors to hierarchical models. You feel ready, so why can't you take on the responsibility? If you want to stay in the organization, you may have to refine your plan for advancement. Remember, while bosses value initiative, they don't enjoy employees hovering in their doorway every five minutes asking when they'll get their next promotion. We're not saying you must sit around and not take action, but the power gap between you calls for some artfulness in your delivery. According to Gen Y guru Lindsey Pollak, Gen Y employees should recognize that "they are new to the workforce and haven't developed the professional 'language' and communication style more prevalent in the workplace. Since our culture has gotten more casual over the years, they have never known anything else. But using 'hey' even in e-mails, or calling people by their first name, especially when they're older or expect to be addressed as 'Mr.,' 'Ms.,' or 'Dr.,' hurts the relationship." Younger workers need to recognize what respect looks like to different generations and adjust accordingly.

While it is true that the first rule of GARP is to take initiative, especially with superiors, millennials need to be careful with this, as they are often perceived as "too strong, too fast" in their organization. If that is the perception about you, we would advise you to soften the pitch and attitude so that your expectations and timelines are not overwhelming to your manager. Instead of leading with the "ask" at the beginning of your first meeting, begin with illuminating your accomplishments, step by step, and asking about the possibility of adding to your responsibilities over the year. Offering to take on an extracurricular assignment that has become top priority for your department apart from your immediate job description is a proactive way of solving a potential problem for the boss while allowing your boss to see how you communicate, make decisions, and exercise judgment. It provides more opportunity to build a natural rapport with your boss outside of your day-to-day responsibilities. Alternatively, you may need to have a senior-level sponsor in the organization who has the ability to pull you into a role that you are targeting. Until you see evidence to the contrary, presume good intent from your superior. Often it's all in the how (and the timing) of the ask and your willingness to do your part in contributing to the organization.

So how informal can you be? Closing the gap is imperative to your success, but a fluent leader knows the degree of initiative you can take is limited by the degree of formality that your boss prefers in daily interactions. If you're new, you may have no idea what's considered the norm in your group until you get asked to do a specific task. Be attuned to such factors as culture, gender, and generation when determining the level of formality you should employ.

David Cross, who provides services to a diverse mix of multicultural students and faculty at Houston Community College, varies his approach depending on his audience and is able to flex down and up as the situation warrants, using the level of formality, structure, and his own gregarious demeanor to help set the tone. With the students, he finds that sitting with them in an informal setting and getting them to open up and talk is the way to close the gap. "If you don't walk into these situations with openness and humility with students, you're not working in the best interest of the college. I listen and to try to meet the student's needs." However, he's frequently called upon to meet with administrators and with the chancellor. In those meetings David is much more formal as a means to close the gap with his superiors. He always wears a suit and prepares a set agenda for the meetings. As part of his job, David is also called upon to soothe frustrated constituents or hear complaints. David flexes to meet this group, too. "You set the tone when you walk in. You can't walk into a room of angry folks with a sense of weakness."

Sometimes, a show of strength is warranted. Retired lieutenant general Ron Coleman was the second African American man in the US Marine Corps to reach the three-star rank. And he didn't do it without having to challenge some of his superiors. "When I was stationed in Okinawa, Japan, I was a major working for a colonel. It wasn't working out well. I tried to respect him, but it just wasn't working. I asked to talk to him privately and said, 'Here's what I think. I don't like you. You don't like me. I need to be reassigned.' He pretended to be surprised. 'I do like you,' he told me. I took lots of risk to clear the air—that could have ended my career." In the end, the colonel respected Lieutenant Coleman for bringing up the bad nature of their relationship. "It ended up on an okay note. We talked openly. Weren't friends after that, but we worked it out. We focused on the Marine Corps and its objectives."

If you're unsure of the right approach to take with your manager, listen, observe, and let your manager set the tone. Careful observation is required before you offer criticism, too. Managers in small, loose-knit organizations may say, "If you see me headed in the wrong direction, call it out!" On the other hand, if you work in an organization with a very strict pecking order, it may be career suicide to contradict your superiors in a group meeting or question a project direction. Use the following questions to help guide your development in managing up to your superiors and to reflect on past experiences to spark ideas and directions.

 ## QUESTIONS FOR ASSESSING YOURSELF AND YOUR TEAM

- Whose responsibility is it to build trust in your working relationship?
- Are you comfortable initiating a conversation and confronting difficult issues with a superior?
- Do you easily present ideas and questions with your superiors and feel comfortable with giving and receiving feedback?
- What steps can you take to establish more trust with your superiors? What gestures or overtures can you make that will help you to begin the effort?
- What are you doing now to build a relationship with your boss/ superior?

 ## EXAMINING OTHERS' ACTIONS CAN INFORM YOUR STYLE AND PRACTICES

- Are there people around your boss who have built a strong trust relationship with him or her? How have they gained his or her trust?
- What does your superior value most in a professional

relationship? How can you show respect to this person in a way that would be best received?

- What situation(s) have you had that was an opportunity to close a significant power gap with a superior? How did they respond to your efforts? What did you learn from that situation?

Reaching up should be empowering, rather than intimidating, to those who think they have to wait or that this is not their role. Even in very hierarchical organizations, taking the initiative to reach up to superiors often allows for greater learning and open communications. Some companies have instituted reverse mentoring programs to provide a forum for such mutual learning. Senior leaders are matched up with younger, or more junior-level, employees. In these pairings, each party is encouraged to ask questions about how they (as a demographic) are perceived by the younger generation, and vice versa. The senior leader obtains a valuable, often unseen peek into what new hires in the organization are looking for in the company, and areas to work on.

Toni Riccardi, now senior fellow at the Conference Board and formerly the first chief diversity officer at PricewaterhouseCoopers, once held a seat on PWC's thirteen-member management committee, responsible for the company's day-to-day operations across the country. Throughout her career she's had to work to close the gap, especially in relation to gender. "When I have had to address senior men about a difficult topic, the most important thing to do was to be as direct and honest as possible. It is not always easy, but leaders often have a hard time getting honesty from others. If you are able to be gracefully honest, you will be of value to the relationship." She was a manager at PWC when a new head of human relations asked all the managers to provide him with their résumés, but did not share his with the people he would be managing. At the holiday party, Toni asked him why he did that and he replied, "Because I wanted to get to know you." She replied, "Didn't you think we would want the same opportunity to get to know you? Did you consider sending us your résumé when you requested ours?"

He got the point, and from that moment on Toni became his go-to person. Toni was able to bridge the gap in a manner that gave him valuable feedback while offering him a clear sense of her style and who she was. He went on to become a valuable coach to Toni.

Fluent Leader Profile: Erby L. Foster Jr.— The Fluent "Agent" and Champion

The power of diversity shines in a culture of inclusion, where differences are valued and encouraged. Common values are the foundation, but different perspectives and behaviors lead to new understanding, ideas, and growth.
—ERBY FOSTER

We've met many fluent leaders who are excellent mentors, coaches, and sponsors, skilled at advancing the company's objectives in part by bringing their people along. But Erby Foster, director of diversity and inclusion at the Clorox Company, might be one of the best we've seen, flexing up, down, and across with incredible ease and a natural grace. His stated role is to advise senior management and the board of directors on the company's diversity strategy, employment-branding initiatives, external partnerships with professional organizations, and manage the company's employee resource groups (ERGs).

But Erby clearly goes above and beyond his job, showing his true passion for people. Every discussion about his job goes back to the work he does connecting individuals and helping them advance in their careers. To that end, he challenges his mentees to think of him as their "agent" instead of as a mentor, seeing his role to be their biggest supporter in public and their toughest critic behind closed doors. For Erby, these relationships aren't an additional responsibility that comes attached to a director-level position—they are the entire reason he is there. "I'm just a vehicle that can help others succeed," he said. "When I see people, I think, How can I help them be successful? I stretch people outside their and my comfort zone." Upon meeting someone new, Erby kicks into connection and influencer mode immediately: first, how can he connect them with the right people and opportunities, and second, how can he influence them to do something that would be good for them or for their careers that they might not try on their own?

One year, Erby accompanied CEO Don Knauss, then the senior VP of sales, and four other white executives to a meeting with the national Hispanic grocery owner association. The next year, Erby didn't go to the meeting, on purpose. Instead, he sent three Latinos, mid-level managers who flew out on the corporate jet. Not only did they have a better connection to the group and to the market, they got rare face time with the CEO. "I told them, 'Don't be intimidated. Give your insights!' " said Erby, and the connection proved fruitful. In a similar vein, Erby found a way for ERG leaders to attend a conference when there was no money in the budget. He submitted Clorox to be recognized for an award. When they won, it not only raised the profile of Clorox, but the conference also flew out the chief marketing officer, who was able to bring the leaders with him. Erby is always looking for opportunity, for the company and for the people around him.

LEVERAGING HIS NETWORK TO GIVE TO OTHERS

It was this extraordinary fluency that Bill Ingham, now global human resources director for Gap, noticed when he hired Erby at Clorox. "He is exceptional and navigates across all boundaries, levels, and geographies. Best connector I've ever known. He has a genuine desire to see people succeed and uses his personal network to do that. He uses the little things—he writes notes and adds personal touches; he uses a different font in his e-mail. His communication is very specific and personal, and he's complimentary in his comments. By the end of the e-mail, you want to pick up the phone and connect with him right away! And he doesn't let his network die. He knows hundreds of people he can reference right away. I know him well, and he reaches out to me on occasion. But when he does, it's not to get, it's to give."

For a person with such innate skills for managing the power gap and fluency, it is surprising that diversity and inclusion are not where Erby began his career. Instead, Erby was a finance guy. A math whiz in high school who took college classes as a teenager, Erby also read up on black history, played on baseball team, ran cross-country, and loved nature. Not like every other kid in school, "I started celebrating myself with these differences," Erby said. "I embraced it and people respected me for it. That foundation put me on this path of understanding that I was capable of doing many things." He studied engineering in college, one of only three African American students at Harvey Mudd, the prestigious Claremont College devoted to mathematics, sciences, and engineering. Erby went on to study business at USC before landing in an accounting position at Arthur Andersen, where Erby was one of only ten black employees out of one thousand professionals in the Los Angeles office. Through various stints as the CFO of several large corporations, Erby became used to seeing few black faces around him, especially in financial roles. But it was through membership with the National Association of Black Accountants (NABA) that he also discovered a hidden talent for building the business case for diversity. It was also through NABA that he met Dan Heinrich, former Clorox EVP and CFO, which led to his current role at Clorox.

The recognition of Erby's ability to connect his finance position to the area of diversity and inclusion came when Erby served in a senior-level position at the McDonald's Corporation. In 1998, CEO Jack Greenberg was speaking to the black employee network group when participants raised significant issues during the Q&A. They said they saw significant issues in that there were no senior-level role models: there were no black VPs in the Finance function and they felt that when blacks got to the director's level, they were directed toward a franchisee relationship role, instead of considered for controller or for another finance-role track. "The next day, the CEO called me into the office and I was asked to lead minority recruiting." Astutely, and with some risk, Erby went on to ask if minority recruitment was a real business goal or more of a public relations goal in order to ascertain just how he could play his connector role in the best possible way for the company. "I asked because that answer will change my strategy. If it's a public image goal, I know all the organizations and can introduce you. But if you really want to hire minorities, I'll put together a strategy for you," he told them. They were committed and one year later, Erby saw his opportunity. The National Association of Black Accountants conference came to Chicago in 1999, and he recommended that McDonald's take a dominant role in participation. Erby set up meetings with all the execs and senior-level African American leaders, and walked away with the largest amount of sponsorship money. He bought up convention marketing opportunities and did employment branding to move McDonald's beyond restaurant prospects and reposition the company as a potential employer with the NABA conference attendees.

KNITTING IT ALL TOGETHER

As his efforts at McDonald's demonstrate, Erby is extraordinarily talented at making connections for individual careers at the micro level that also positively influence the organization at a macro level. One former employee was thinking of leaving the company, and told Erby the reason was that she was interested in pursuing international opportunities. "He asked me to stay and went to help me find those opportunities in the accounting area." While she was initially shortsighted in her career prospects, "Erby taught me the value of a diversity background. He showed me that accounting was more than numbers—you have to understand business. Erby developed training for young high-potentials and created opportunities for exposure." Though Erby is in a diversity role, he is unusual in how much he coaches people and in the level of investment he demonstrates. In his former employee's case, this meant not only helping seek out opportunities for international experience, it meant encouraging her to follow her best career path after she gained that experience— regardless of whether it led back to the company where Erby had helped her grow. While many others in his role work with ERGs and deal with diversity in a more tactical or event-focused way with initiatives and programs, it's personal with him, and he is committed to helping individuals as one part of his greater strategy.

Whether it's connecting accounting with diversity goals, or individual careers to company growth, Erby really shines. He fluently ties diversity to business outcomes, then moves seamlessly from an individual level to further tie in employee resource groups and outside associations, then knits it all together until it makes sense for everyone involved at the company level, often employing inventive and adaptive methods to accomplish business goals.

USING INCLUSION TO DRIVE INNOVATION

Because a big part of his job is about building relationships with diversity organizations and encouraging ERG engagement, he is constantly looking for opportunities to make a business connection, from the individual level on up. One Asian employee credits Erby with broadening his view of diversity and helping him understand how to use the ERGs strategically while connecting with them on a personal level. "When I attended an event and talked to him it became clear that his vision isn't just an Asian initiative, or Hispanic, or LGBT. It's more about how do you bring your self to work and use that to grow the business initiative. That was a new view for me." The employee went on to assume the chief of staff role for his employee resource group at Clorox, interacting with Erby as a key stakeholder and learning how to lead and interact with other ERG leaders. "In 2010, our ERG wrote a vision statement and mission, then strategy and tactics. We got the idea from Erby, then took the challenge to grow and focus and run the ERG like a business."

As a fluent leader, Erby is able to see to the ABC's of employee resource groups (advancement, business connection, and culture of inclusion) and connect them to larger growth opportunities. "In just a few years, our ERGs have quickly moved from promoting cultural awareness, to developing talent, to becoming trusted advisers, to being recognized as business advocates," he said. "Today's global marketplace is very different from the one many of us grew up in, requiring new approaches and a diverse leadership team in terms of worldviews, experiences, and thought processes." As an outgrowth of Erby's work with the ERGs at Clorox, in July of 2010, CEO Don Knauss challenged the Asian ERG to think about how its members could help target Asians—one of the fastest-growing consumer groups in the United States, with $600 billion in annual buying power. They immediately went to work, brainstorming business challenges resulting in a top three: targeted marketing for Clorox's Green Works brand; food mergers and acquisitions; and gaining market entry into India. These three initiatives paired with business coleads to develop their ideas and perform the necessary research. What they found was that a country increasingly comfortable with Asian flavors still needed a little prepackaged help to get dinner on the table. The end result: Clorox acquired Soy Vay Enterprises, a small California company known for its tasty, kosher Asian sauces.

FLUENT LEADERSHIP CONTRIBUTES TO NEW BUSINESS OPPORTUNITY

The acquisition didn't happen by accident; instead, a fluent leader worked to put into place an institutional and organizational culture of inclusion tightly integrated with business activities, yet another example of the synergistic effects of Erby's connecting and networking abilities. "Diversity without inclusion is like adding a few drops of vinegar to oil and calling it a great dressing!" Erby muses. "How can new people be expected to fit into old models and drive new value? The power of diversity shines in a culture of inclusion, where differences are valued and encouraged, leading to new understanding, ideas, and growth."

CHAPTER 8

CONNECTING WITH CUSTOMERS AND PARTNERS

Putting people first and embracing differences has always been the cornerstone to our success.
—ARNE SORENSON, PRESIDENT AND CEO, MARRIOTT INTERNATIONAL

Your customers and clients are a critical part of your business agenda—you couldn't exist without them. You wouldn't grow your market share without a solid base of customers who believe in your value proposition. A satisfied customer can serve as a sincere advocate for your services or products in today's competitive marketplace. Numerous studies have shown time and again that people do business with, and select business partners with, those they know and trust. And yet business leaders sometimes focus on internal relationships and processes to the exclusion of extending those lessons learned to their clients and engaging with customers in ways that build trust and establish productive, long-term relationships.

We've spent a good portion of this book showing you how building relationships and leveraging difference with employees across cultural, gender, and generational lines helps your bottom line. The same holds true with your customers and vendors, whether you are a Fortune 500 company, have offices around the globe, or are a small, local, nonprofit organization. After all, does a nonprofit have any less investment in connecting with its stakeholders? All organizations, for-profit or not, want to grow, increase market share, or increase visibility for their mission. It is just as critical for organizations to think of how they can connect best to customers. In today's business climate, you need to connect more authentically and more quickly with your customers than your competitors do. It's a matter of survival.

FLEXING YOUR RELATIONSHIP-BUILDING STYLE TO SELL TO CUSTOMERS

Even if you're already skilled at working with the different styles, cultures, genders, and generations that make up your team, there is still room to grow your skills. Business success is not just about flexing your management style to better reach people who are different from you inside your organization. It's also directly tied to your relationship building, the underlying foundation to all selling, negotiating, and client-development practices. Global and globally minded organizations need to understand and play to their customers' diverse needs, both in the United States and in overseas markets, and skillfully bridging the power gap enables that. If you are able to notice, appreciate, and ultimately leverage the difference between you and your global clients, as well as build trust and communication with your external vendors, your business will thrive.

A few years ago, when we were speaking at a conference in Hong Kong, we noticed that the audience was very engaged throughout the presentation, but that there were very few questions during the public Q&A. However, when we went out into the crowd afterward there were no fewer than thirty-five people waiting in line wanting to ask questions. Clearly uncomfortable asking the questions in an open forum, they were very direct and inquisitive in the one-on-one setting immediately following the talk. This time we were the ones who needed to flex to the client culture and alter our style to meet them partway! Since then, we make sure that we add thirty minutes to every presentation that we make in the region to accommodate the Q&A, as well as creating multiple avenues for our audience to react to our presentations throughout our programs. It was up to us to analyze the experience, choose the appropriate forum for each group, then reach out to them individually. Doing so enabled us to reach a greater audience and be able to connect more fully with our clients in attendance.

As with flexing toward your internal employees, bridging the power gap with clients, customers, and vendors begins with an honest evaluation of the power dynamic between you and them. As the saying goes, the client is king, and in most business relationships the client enjoys a power advantage over the service provider. Most sales and customer-facing staff are trained on the motto "the customer is always right" when managing customer inquiries and complaints. However, if you are contracting with external vendors the power gap might tilt in the other direction as you are now the client.

As an example, the more egalitarian cultures and organizations deemphasize the power and authority that come with senior positions, which may come off as confusing or even insulting to some of their clients who are presented with a young, junior-level account manager to manage the client relationship. Whether you are negotiating a contract or asking for delivery of a product, the power gap will affect every aspect of your business.

ALIGNING THE INSIDE AND THE OUTSIDE OF YOUR ORGANIZATION

So what do we mean when we talk about aligning your internal and external business culture? Say your company is trying to target a new customer segment. Your ads and marketing campaigns are increasingly diverse, and you are participating in community initiatives in the countries you are serving as well as at home. Perhaps you've even increased the number of multiculturals in your workforce, as well as women, but if none of their perspectives are represented in the sales process, or if their opinions are completely missing in your business strategy, then your multicultural campaigns and targeted advertising may be missing their mark. As one of our clients confessed to us, "We sell a lot of products to women, who happen to make more than three-quarters of the purchasing decisions in the country. But their voices are not heard in this company. They are less represented in the P&L functions as well as in senior management ranks. They often have to leave for other opportunities at other companies to attain the senior posts that they seek. By losing them, we are losing out on not just talent, but our reputation among customers." Chances are that you, too, have talent right inside your organization that reflects your marketplace. It might be good timing to tap into their perspectives and knowledge and leverage your talent's cultural capital to access new markets and more customers.

IBM knew this back in the mid-1990s when CEO Lou Gerstner tackled the imbalance between his diverse workforce and market and his senior management. Under the direction of Gerstner and Ted Childs, IBM's vice president for workplace diversity at the time, the company created eight task forces organized by differences such as gender, ethnicity, sexual orientation, or ability, and charged the groups with exploring not only what it would take for them to feel more valued and increase their constituency's productivity, but also what it would take to influence that constituency's buying habits. Gerstner credits the success behind IBM's diversity initiative to its direct link to a concrete and imperative business opportunity: how could IBM better tap into its markets and understand its customers' needs better? Because, while a diversity group focused on the needs of women employees can help women rise in the ranks at IBM, it can also help connect them to female customers, who made up 30 percent of the company's customer base. Understanding the needs of multicultural employees helped bridge the workforce and the global marketplace (and over 170 countries) in which IBM operates and helps identify latent business opportunities and strategies to reach those customers.

One tangible example of reaching external markets through internal leadership is IBM's creation of its Market Development group, tasked with growing the company's market share with minority and women-owned business. It does so by various strategies, including partnering with external vendors to provide sales and service to the many small- to medium-size businesses run by minorities and women. It leveraged its internal cultural capital to reach into underutilized markets to great effect, understanding that, as David Thomas, dean of Georgetown's McDonough Business School, put it, "diversity was an untapped business resource."

Was it easy? Not always. Sometimes the company had to go to extraordinary lengths to build those bridges effectively, including penning equal-opportunity legislation for countries in which it wanted to do business, aligning its internal company goals with external practices because, as Childs has said, "workforce diversity is a global topic—a global workplace topic and a global marketplace topic." If a portion of IBM's sales force wanted to do business in a third-world country and that was tied to its business expansion strategy, then it led with its diversity strategy and by investigating the differences. We don't know how to open up businesses in these countries; how can we do that? We don't know how to break through government restrictions to do business there; how can we accomplish our goals? But the company had a long way to go before it broke open those global markets. Even though it was tied to market expansion, shifting the focus from minimizing differences to promoting them made many people uneasy. Some felt the formation of the group was nothing but lip service; others felt it was disrespectful; still others worried that by highlighting the ways in which they were different from the norm, they would be penalized or thought of as nonexecutive material or needing extra help to succeed in the workplace. But Childs persevered with this shift, which he termed "constructive disruption" in the usual way of doing business. He also carefully structured the groups, partnering each with a sponsor from a different area to facilitate dialogue and encourage the deconstruction of stereotypes and bias or help another area gain specialized knowledge that could aid its business development.

You don't have to be a company as large as IBM to use a similar strategy, though many of the world's leading businesses do. Smaller companies and organizations across the country also have affinity groups or employee resource groups (ERGs) already in place. If leadership commits to the power and possibility of these groups, and invests in their ability to leverage their cultural capital to the company's and the constituency's benefit, ERGs can function as an excellent bridge to connect your organization with your partners and customers.

HOW EMPLOYEE RESOURCE NETWORKS CAN CLOSE THE GAP WITH CUSTOMERS

The marketplace has become increasingly diverse and is in a constant state of change. To stay on top of customers' needs and preferences, leaders in forward-thinking organizations have learned to leverage their internal employee populations to spur creativity in connecting to external customers' tastes. Internal networks called employee resource groups (ERGs) are networks of employees who form together around a common social interest, heritage, or affinity. Common examples might include a women's, Gen Y, veterans', or Latino employee group. And these internal groups, when facilitated well, provide an effective way for employees to reach beyond their current job descriptions to advance the business as well as accomplish other strategic organizational goals. Hence, even if you work in a back-office research function, through your involvement in an ERG, you might have access to working on an initiative to provide input to marketers and sales strategy. Consumer products companies and retailers have an opportunity to leverage these valuable internal resources right in their backyard.

Indeed, innovative companies are approaching their ERGs and asking them to provide insight into the different worldviews, cultural touchpoints, experiences, thought processes, and lifestyles of the customer segment they represent. When diversity and inclusion efforts are integrated into the system of R&D, marketing, operations, HR, and sales, everyone wins. Leveraging the ERGs in this way becomes increasingly important in today's global marketplace, where multinational companies are finding much of the incremental growth coming from untapped and underdeveloped markets.

PEPSICO ASIAN NETWORK CREATES MARKET OPPORTUNITY WITH CUSTOMERS

One notable example of this type of collaborative effort was with PepsiCo, a global food and beverage company with brands that include Quaker, Tropicana, Gatorade, Frito-Lay, and Pepsi-Cola. Recognizing the incredible purchasing power among Asian Americans, the company established PepsiCo Asian Network (PAN), one of the many employee-led groups within PepsiCo working to meet the needs of various consumer and interest groups.

In this instance, the PAN employee group created a special promotion intended for the fastest-growing ethnic group in the United States by collaborating with the PepsiCo sales division and marketing group. They chose an external retail partner popular with the Indian American community for a special promotion centered on Diwali, the popular Indian holiday known as the "festival of lights," highlighting traditional Indian flavors in PepsiCo's drinks as well as chips. They created a similar promotion with different products to celebrate the Lunar New Year, an important holiday for engaging Asian customers, who celebrate both the Western calendar's New Year as well as

Lunar New Year. The group also connected the company with the Korean-American Grocers Association, understanding the powerful place that community-oriented mom-and-pop stores occupy in more urban environments that are not conducive to big-box stores or large supermarket chains. By leveraging their cultural knowledge, language abilities, and their employees' broad networks, the ERG was able to support PepsiCo with new external partners and customers to tap into this important consumer group.

CLOSING THE GAP TO CREATE BUSINESS OPPORTUNITY AND BOTTOM-LINE IMPACT

Fluent leaders who understand how to navigate inside and outside the organization can close the gaps with various levels of management inside while also closing the gap with customers. But that doesn't happen overnight.

Starting in 2004, PAN senior leadership began to build a relationship with the Asian American Hotel Owners Association (AAHOA), given the complementary nature of the hotel and food and beverage industries, and the business opportunity that could be realized through partnership. Early on, PAN began to work with Mehul (Mike) Patel, who became the chairman of the organization in 2013. And over the years, PAN members continued to strengthen ties between PAN and AAHOA, with PepsiCo's Kuntesh Chokshi being especially focused on nurturing the relationship with Patel.

In 2013, PepsiCo was able to help fulfill a long-standing wish of AAHOA, which was to have Indra Nooyi, the chairman and CEO of PepsiCo, speak at their national conference. When it was announced that she would be the keynote speaker at their 2013 conference, it cemented the relationship between the company and the professional organization and opened the doors to new collaborations and opportunities for greater marketshare in the hospitality industry. For PepsiCo, the potential return on investment was huge: the organization represented 3.5 million hotel rooms and 20,000 properties in their 11,000 membership.

It also presented PepsiCo with the opportunity to connect with AAHOA's 4,000 independent franchise owners of hotels, restaurants, and more who attend the convention—a huge potential customer base for the company.

SPONSORS WHO ADVOCATED FOR THE INITIATIVE TO MOVE FORWARD

PAN and its leadership would not have been able to perform this incredible accomplishment on their own. It took the critical organizational senior-executive sponsorship by two key people: Tom Greco, president of Frito-Lay, who served as an active executive-level sponsor for PAN for the previous seven years, and Al Carey, CEO of PepsiCo Americas Beverages, also an active executive-level sponsor for PAN prior to Tom. Also both Al Carey and Tom Greco, along with Tim Trant (SVP, FoodService) and Kuntesh, had Top2Top preconvention meetings with Mr. Patel. These preconvention meetings helped our partnership and alignment on driving revenue between the two organizations. PAN would not have continued to attend the national AAHOA conventions without both their support and advocacy. Not only did Tom provide sponsorship to AAHOA, he supported other leadership initiatives as well as community outreach events and access to leadership training, and he provided air cover to the group when needed. He placed his faith in Kuntesh's efforts and allowed him the latitude to continue building the relationship in the style he thought best, saying, "Kuntesh, I trust that you are taking this in the right direction." Equally critical were three other active mentors to Kuntesh: Michael Crouse, VP and general manager of sales at Pepsi Co; Sri Rajagopalan, the second PAN president and a PepsiCo director whose leadership was essential in the success of PAN as an organization; and Deepak Aurora, the first PAN president and a retired

PepsiCo director, who was the initial liaison to AAHOA and Mike Patel. Michael was a strong advocate and took initiative to quickly get up to speed on PAN accomplishments. He dedicated his personal time to focus on business-development activities with PAN, coaching Kuntesh and other PAN leaders during after-hour calls regularly with real-time advice about how to skillfully navigate the organization. Through the process of cementing the business relationship with AAHOA, all these leaders demonstrated fluent leader characteristics required to flex up, down, and across the organization.

PASSION, PATIENCE, PERSISTENCE, AND THE RIGHT TIMING

This story reveals the complexity of connecting with customers and the necessity of securing sponsors at the highest levels by working up and across to close the gap. There were many pieces to this accomplishment. Getting to the "right moment" required the platform of PAN, the unequivocal support and mentoring from Tom Greco, and the perseverance of Kuntesh Chokshi and other PAN members. Employing flex principles and giving organizational support to groups like ERGs or affinity groups can yield the same results for your organization. In designing or building an employee group network, our experience shows that an affinity group or ERG is most successful when it:

- Opens its membership to any employee interested in its target focus. While these groups should strongly focus on a certain population, others should have an opportunity to be interested and supportive in their work.
- Has a strategic mission connected to the organization's mission and growth strategies.
- Has both internal goals (networking, professional development,

and mentoring opportunities) and external goals (outreach to customers and communities, better serving the client).

- Provides employees with exposure to senior management (and possible sponsors) and allows management to connect with employees on core business communications.
- Provides company leaders with well-managed access to the ideas and initiatives of different types and levels of employees.
- Unlocks pathways to untapped business opportunities by connecting disparate parts of the company to spur partnership and innovation (such as linking marketing and operations).

Remember, too, that the marketplace is broad. ERGs should reflect that. Extend your own thinking about diversity and constituencies. As one example, PepsiCo and other companies have also created ERGs meant to support and connect veterans, military personnel, and their families.

WHEN THE PATIENT IS YOUR CUSTOMER

Sometimes it's easy to forget that the doctor-patient relationship is really one between a provider and a customer. The health-care system is poised to add 5.6 million new staff by the year 2020 and is an industry in which Americans spent $2.8 trillion in 2012. When there is that kind of revenue at stake, and with the growth expected in this country alone, it's incredibly important the health-care system is able to understand the needs and wants of its customers and be able to serve an increasingly diverse population, including patients of all ages, multiculturals, and women as well as men.

Adina Kalet, professor of medicine and surgery at NYU Langone Medical Center, NYU School of Medicine, teaches cultural competence to medical students in order to help them better manage the power gap between them and their patients. Adina has great self-awareness about the relationship between doctors and patients, the inherent power gap there, and how that gap is shifting. "It used to be that the doctor spoke and he was the expert or brought 'the truth' to the conversation. Now there is more of a shared decision-making view and it's more a true dialogue." Patients have their own health resources for information (especially online) and they can ask a lot of questions. "There is a convergence of the way physicians care for patients. It is becoming less hierarchical, and cultural competence is becoming more important. That said, self-awareness is a huge element of cultural competence. After all, it has been a while since doctors have been a homogeneous group of white men from middle- and upper-class backgrounds. We are, as a profession, diverse in terms of gender, race, and ethnicity, and therefore as individuals have our own value systems and sets of beliefs we bring to the equation. Sometimes medical students have a lot more to teach the professors about diversity because the younger generations are more experienced with diverse environments and know a lot more and are more sophisticated than their seniors in this area." Similarly, nearly half of all applicants to medical school are now women. Several studies have shown that women provide slightly different care than men, asking more questions, spending more time, and behaving in somewhat more empathetic ways. Studies also show that the gender of the patient might matter more, with female patients discussing their illness in more personal and experiential ways, a style female physicians seem more responsive to. In a recent *New York Times* article, Klea D. Bertakis, professor of family and community medicine at the University of California, Davis, offered that for male physicians, "it's not about trying to become a woman. It's about learning behaviors." In short, learning to flex.

Because while physicians bring their own experiences and styles with them to medical school, they don't always know how to apply their knowledge and attitudes to their patients. In their courses, students cover the basic principles of effective communication skills and culture, and they even use actors to put together cases and examples so they can role-play different issues. In her medical school, Adina says they see cultural competency "as part of the health-care system." In order to flex toward their customers, physicians must take into account a wide variety of belief systems and values, including cultural differences, all compounded by the fear and confusion that can surround illness. Adina gave an example her colleagues use in helping students practice cultural-competence skills. They train an actor to play the role of an American-born Chinese woman who moved to New York. The patient reports that she hadn't had asthma since she was a child. The student needs to explain to her why it's back after so many years. The answer: the woman's more traditional grandmother now lives with her and doesn't want her inhaling steroids. Instead of allowing her to use her inhaler, the grandmother treats her with herbal teas and other natural remedies. In order to ensure the patient gets better, the students need to engage her in a dialogue and help her negotiate a respectful and satisfying path forward. In a second case the students engage with a Caucasian woman who refuses to vaccinate her two-year-old child. Knowing that vaccines are the most safe and effective way to protect children from life-threatening illnesses, the students struggle to understand the reasons behind her refusal. If she deeply believes the vaccines meant to protect will instead hurt the child, how do you go forward and have this conversation? These are typical, everyday conversations between physician and patient.

Differences even extend generationally, an especially relevant topic as the aging boomer population explodes as a client base for health care. "Older patients can tolerate the paternalistic model more so than younger patients in the health-care arena," Adina says. "And when people get sick, their response gets exaggerated." If a doctor has bad news, she needs to assess how that should be communicated and through what channels. "I need to ask each individual, How do you want me to communicate this information? Do you want to have your son here with you? Do you want your spouse to be here with you? Or should we have this conversation privately first? As a physician, you may have your own inclination about how this conversation should go, but you need to put that aside and seek to understand the patient's preference as separate from yours." This is difficult to remember, especially when you are busy or things are very emotionally charged or complex.

In the boardroom as well as in the exam room, flex principles can help bridge the gap between health-care providers and their consumers, improving outcomes on both sides.

WORKING WITH OVERSEAS PARTNERS

Many of our clients have not only diverse American consumer markets to appeal to, but also international markets. Whether you have a customer base in another country or have operations in another country for global distribution, it's critical that you bridge the gap between you and your vendors, even if you have the upper hand in the relationship. Simply expecting your vendors to communicate in the same way you do and operate with the same set of values will probably open you up to disappointment and missed opportunity. Using flex skills to close the gap with external partners and vendors, however, can turn even difficult situations into win-wins. Based on a common scenario we hear often from companies with overseas operations, here's an example of what can go wrong—and how much you have to lose if you're unaware of the power gap.

When Melissa and Ed launched a new tech company in Seattle, Melissa had already produced a number of software projects, often working with teams in India, but Ed had never worked with international colleagues. Approaching an important release date for a new product, both Ed and Melissa knew that the timing on this project was crucial—and tight. When he contacted their partners in India, Ed demanded they put the product on a crash schedule, saying, "We really needed this yesterday. You have to get us the product on this date." The manager on the other end of the line agreed, and Ed was satisfied. However, Melissa overheard the conversation. "That time-line is awfully unrealistic," she cautioned Ed. "You've set a deadline they're not going to make."

"Don't worry," Ed said. "Why would you doubt them? They are the experts. If they couldn't pull it off, they'd have just said so."

The Bombay-based manager called a few days later with a prog-ress report, noting, "Yes, we are doing your work. Though we are very busy now."

Melissa started to read between the lines. "They are just telling you they can make our deadline because they know what's what you want to hear," she told him. She understood what qualifiers such as "we are very busy now" meant: it was unlikely that they would make the date Ed asked for.

Ed refused to listen, and even became angry at Melissa. Three weeks later, there was no product, and the company missed its delivery date.

What can we learn from stories like this? Often the overseas vendor can't say no for fear of losing face, or they rely on subtle voice cues or qualifiers to communicate their inability to give the client what they asked for instead of coming out and saying no. While Me-lissa was attuned to how the India-based engineers communicate, Ed minimized the difference between the way Americans and Indians do business. With all the best intentions, he assumed that culture was not going to be an issue. But he didn't think through how basic cultural assumptions could affect his delivery date. The most effective way to work with overseas partners and vendors is to share the power up front. The fluent manager, instead of laying down strict deadlines, could consult the partner, saying, "You're the expert. You have full knowledge of this process. I am looking to you to guide me. What is a realistic deadline, based on our resources for the project?" We in the West tend to assume that you can make a demand and that if the other party says yes, that it will happen. In countries like India, it doesn't really happen until you define what it has to be.

Suresh, an Indian engineer, hears Ed say, "We need this yesterday." He understands what they want, but indicates that there may be a problem with the schedule by focusing on his enthusiasm for the project rather than on the due date. "We would very much like to do this for you by September." Suresh may even note it is going to be very hard to make that deadline with the resources he has. To Ed, it still sounds as if he has promised to deliver. Reviewing specs with Ang, who works for Ed, Suresh lets him know that it may not work out, believing that Ang will share the message with his team in a face-saving way for Ed. As the deadline approaches, Suresh grows more worried and asks Ed what contingency plans he has if they do not make the delivery date. In Suresh's mind he has been very clear in his communication with Ed. Ed's anger over the missed date seems misplaced.

Given the amount of outsourcing American companies have done in the past fifteen years, misunderstandings like the ones we describe are commonplace. Many of them can be diffused by discussion procedures and deciding to share authority with partners overseas, rather than expecting other cultures to intuitively abide by distinctly American practices.

If you work in an egalitarian environment, hierarchical behavior, such as when your client wants to work only with someone who's at the same level (e.g., president to president, VP to VP) will require intentionality in order to manage effectively. In hierarchical cultures, even if a mid-level person is the lead on a certain account or initiative, they'll manage it through that person's superior (with a higher title). Some customers may insist on working only with senior-level staff, and in those situations the businesses may have to cater to the customer or risk losing the account.

It can be helpful to use the pre-engagement question technique to get a different perspective on behavior that seems at first dismissive or counterintuitive. Your clients may conduct business this way because of a hierarchical culture or other deeply rooted tradition, or they may just want their problem solved and feel they won't get what they need by dealing with someone right out of college. Depending on their motivation, you may simply need to adapt to their style or be able to do some education to allay their fears and meet them partway. Methods for doing so might include pairing up a senior-level person with a more junior associate and working on the project as a team, or acting to help facilitate the client's comfort level with more junior staff.

GETTING EXPOSURE TO THE CLIENT

We know of a partner in a professional services firm who was sitting in an engagement meeting with three subordinate members of his team, including a senior manager. The client, a CTO of a major Fortune 500 company, turned to the partner he'd worked with for eight years and posed the question, "So how are these acquisitions going to make an impact on our business processes?" Instead of answering the question, the partner turned to his manager and asked, "Jean, how would you handle that?" giving her the floor to answer, which she did. A few minutes later, the client again turned to the partner and asked a follow-up question, "What other issues do we need to look at?" The partner responded, "Jean's done the analysis. What do you think, Jean?" By the third time, his glance was enough to have her respond to the question, and his unspoken support was enough for the CTO to begin dealing with Jean directly.

Others look for middle ground. Quentin Roach is chief procurement officer and senior VP of Global Supplier Management Group at Merck. It works with a number of global partners and tries to ensure its suppliers have a voice. It had an experience in Germany where its supplier was having difficulty meeting requirements, so it asked the supplier to make some changes. The supplier came back and turned the issue back on Merck, asking it to send a number of reports and charts and, in the eyes of some of the employees, jump through a lot of hoops. Responding to a request with a request can come across as defensive, and the Merck employees working with the supplier were a bit put off. "This is so unresponsive," they said about the German supplier. Quentin made a very fluent move and asked the team to consider another option. "They may be more analytical than we are. Maybe they don't need all of those materials, but instead, want us to talk them through the data." Quentin's openness to other styles and issues enabled him to smooth over frustrations on all sides and allowed Merck to help them put a good product together—the ultimate goal.

HOLDING FAST TO YOUR PRINCIPLES

While flexing is important for business success, companies must also maintain their integrity when working with customers and partners and stay true to the internal values of the company. Back in the 1970s, before she was the deputy mayor of Los Angeles, Linda Griego was a telephone installer at a phone company. She hired a female installer who really knew her stuff. When the installer went to put in a line at a client's home, the owner wouldn't even let her in the front door. Instead, he asked for a "real installer"—a man. Linda drove over and had a discussion with the client in person. He wouldn't budge, and neither would she, even when he threatened to call the president of the company. When the boss asked her why she wouldn't send another installer she said, "If I sent a black man, and he rejected him, would the phone company send out a white man? Is that the policy?" Under continued pressure Linda held her ground. In the end, the female installer did the job and the customer apologized. "In a lot of ways, you just have to know when to fight. Here, I couldn't take the easy way out. I couldn't live with myself. In this case, I knew she had the right experience and I had absolute confidence in her abilities."

TAKE THE TIME TO BUILD RELATIONSHIPS

We can sometimes undervalue the importance of building relationships with customers and partners before getting down to business; it's not just about the transaction. American business culture is often so focused on efficiency and results that we can easily forget that when building overseas relationships, presence is as important as power sharing.

We once did a 360-degree evaluation of an American company doing business across Asia. One of the service providers in Singapore was extremely critical of his American manager, Susan, and felt that she didn't show any appreciation for his team. Susan had great technical skills and was clear about assignments but she never thanked people for their work. She was also inconsiderate when she set up meetings across time zones, always at the convenience of the New York office. By the time we were finished with our evaluation, we had learned that, like so many American managers, Susan relied primarily on e-mail and online communication, and there was very little personal interaction between her and the top executives in Singapore.

Most overseas companies we've worked with complain that American managers rarely show up and take the time to get know their partners, or feel that they always have one foot out the door. When there is no solid, ongoing relationship, these people will not go the extra mile for you. This is particularly true in "being"-oriented relationship cultures that believe building trust comes first, before discussing the parameters of the work they've just been hired to perform. It takes hard work and repeated effort to draw out the opinions of others in a high-power-gap environment; you need to focus on building relationships built for the long haul, whether you are dealing with a vendor in Bangladesh or employees inside your own company. Though conventional wisdom may say efficient and immediate is best, sometimes the quickest solution will not earn you the trust and support so essential to connecting authentically with your clients or customers, or getting your vendors firmly on your side.

PREPARING FOR WIN-WIN: TIPS FOR IMPROVED COMMUNICATION WITH PARTNERS AND CUSTOMERS

Some of the most effective ways we have found to overcome differences in communication styles and culture, especially with global partners and customers, include the following:

- Give the partner or customer explicit ownership over their own expertise.
- Provide a platform for open discussion, giving them permission to speak honestly about their needs.
- Establish expectations in a way that honors their contribution.
- Clearly explain your requirements as well as the reasons behind them (including project overviews, scopes, resources, budgets, and schedules).
- Close with questions.

These closing questions can prove key. Offering humility on your part ("I don't work in your environment, so does it seem reasonable?") and offering your help to meet shared goals ("What do you need from me as your partner to make this happen?") are a few ways to share power and get great results. Other closing questions might include:

"Is this timeline reasonable for what we've proposed?"
"Do you need more people or more resources to help you do this better?"
"How can we help make these deadlines?"
"How can we make this process run more smoothly, efficiently, and/or economically? I want to help."

Profile: Memorial Hermann Southwest Hospital—Health-care System Identifies Innovative Solutions for Patient Needs

You don't want to be afraid to be the first.
—GEORGE GASTON, CEO, MEMORIAL HERMANN SOUTHWEST HOSPITAL

No one enjoys a trip to the hospital. Now, imagine how much more frightening and stressful your experience is if you can't understand the doctors or nurses or accurately communicate your level of pain. Or if you are served strange, unfamiliar food and your family is unable to stay near you in your room. When you leave, you don't receive clear instructions from the doctor or other caregivers on follow-up care, or understand what to do next. There might also be cultural barriers to communication that supersede mere language barriers. These are just some of the constraints expressed by patients from other cultures in the hospital's primary service area. Inherent in the doctor-patient relationship is a power and knowledge gap, and there once was a time when physicians had a strictly hierarchical approach, creating a dynamic of one-way communication: patients were supposed to simply follow "doctor's orders." This dynamic still exists and is compounded when, due to cultural value differences, some patients may feel uncomfortable discussing their issues with a physician. Given that the doctor is the clear expert and authority who is supposed to deliver any and all information, whom are they to challenge or ask questions of any relevance?

When George Gaston took the reins as CEO from interim CEO Rod Brace of Memorial Hermann Southwest Hospital in 2010, all these concerns and more were faced by growing Vietnamese and Chinese populations who lived just north of the hospital in southwest Houston and made up a growing portion of the hospital's patient demographic. Additionally, MHSW's senior population, another of the surrounding community's fastest-growing

demographics, were experiencing increased stress during emergency-room visits. The ER was often loud and full of unruly patients
and chaos that made them feel anxious and unsafe. Geriatric patients also often presented with complex histories and diagnoses
that needed extra time and expertise to untangle, a process that
challenged the staff and was made more stressful by the tempo of
the emergency-room setting. It all added up to a serious mismatch
between the hospital's services and style and those of its major consumers. This mismatch was adding up to more than lost revenue and
a sliding market share for the hospital—it was affecting the quality
of life and care of people who really needed help.

The patients were not the only ones in decline. After being in
business for thirty-five years, the hospital was hurting financially.
Once the flagship of the Memorial Hermann Healthcare System,
MHSW saw a dramatic decline in volume. Morale was bottoming
out, including among the physicians also challenged by the gap
between the needs of the changing patient population and the care
they were able to provide. When a proposed sale of the facility to
another hospital group fell through, George saw a second chance.
The community rallied around the institution, realizing that Memorial Hermann was its community hospital and that it was there for
the long haul. However, it was clear that if George wanted to keep
his job and the community its long-treasured hospital, they would
need to turn the tide.

So what type of fluent leader traits did it take to turn around the
fortunes of Memorial Hermann Southwest and its patients' experiences? George picked up the initial efforts of his predecessor and
reached across and down the hierarchy to obtain feedback from
others. He and his team sought to close the power gap between his
Asian patients and the hospital system by listening to their concerns.
In doing so, he demonstrated the simple notion of humility. George
credits "servant leadership" as critical to his and the hospital's
success; for him, leaders are supposed to roll up their sleeves and

work hard to lift up their employees and to serve the community and the patients who rely on and trust them. Their patients and their families were their clients, yes, but more than that, they were human beings whose emotional and physical needs deserved focused attention. "You've got to put yourself in the shoes of the patients," George says, demonstrating the kind of empathy that fluent leaders regularly exhibit. Practical business sense says that if they didn't focus on the needs of the community closest to the hospital they wouldn't be viable. But this other-centered approach allowed them to move past any type of defensiveness in a time of crisis to implement a process that changed how they responded to the community's needs.

In George's case, this was not a simple academic exercise. After being diagnosed with a serious condition, he himself underwent several lifesaving brain surgeries at another of the Memorial Hermann facilities. While he still needed to explore the root difficulties for these patients that differed from him in age or culture, he understood all too well the basic needs for comfort, respect, and communication that he himself desired as a patient.

A DISCIPLINED APPROACH TO PROBLEM SOLVING

Before George Gaston took over as CEO, the hospital and his predecessor had already been soliciting customer opinions and feedback on their quality of service. In fact, they had collected detailed information on how dissatisfied certain patients were and their concerns. The hospital utilized patient-satisfaction surveys translated into various languages and employed an outside company to conduct the analysis. The survey asked a broad range of questions related to the patient's overall experience, from questions related to the décor of the hospital rooms to how well the hospital staff provided pain management. They asked the patient to rate his physician's care and how well the hospital teams communicated, both in frequency and style. More important, they listened to the answers and made the patients' responses count. They aligned their leadership team with key metrics in patient satisfaction. They even held brainstorming sessions with former patients, their family members, and physicians in an effort to get to the heart of the issue.

While tough to hear at times, the information yielded useful insights for how they could move away from their traditional model to a more culturally adaptive approach to providing care. With patient satisfaction being a core value of their leadership development, when they encountered areas that were not running well, they decided to take action. As they analyzed the data, the administrators found trends that clearly signaled that business as usual was not working for the Asian patients and their families. Additionally, physicians approached senior leadership to express the concerns of this growing community. The community comments reflected that many patients didn't understand their physicians' plans for their care. They couldn't communicate pain effectively. Bilingual language lines were not effective. The food was not always appealing, especially for those who followed a more traditional, non-Western diet. For these close-knit and extended clans where family members were often counted on to act as interpreters, the rooms weren't providing an environment for a loved one and advocate (such as a son or daughter) to stay. In the most difficult times, families reported, the hospital's practices for handling patients who had passed away were at odds with Buddhist rituals surrounding death and dying. Ideally, a Buddhist priest should be present at the time of a patient's passing to perform chants and help ease the transition. More important, Buddhist tradition also dictates the body not be moved for a number of hours following death, as the loved one's spirit is believed to linger for some time after separating from the body.

THE BIRTH OF THE SENIOR CARE WING AND THE ASIAN CARE UNIT

With these problems identified, George and his team carried on the work begun by his predecessor, Rod Brace, to implement concrete, innovative solutions for changing their practices and providing targeted care. As the first step, they hired an Asian service line manager to help bridge the gap. They made sure that the person who filled the position was fluent in either Vietnamese or Chinese to better communicate with patients, their families, and Asian physicians. The new Asian service line manager was in charge of facilitating meetings with former patients, family members, and physicians to solicit feedback and help devise solutions.

Instead of hospital staff behaving defensively and explaining its way of doing things, or patients and families rehashing past complaints, as a group they were able to wipe the slate clean and hold productive, solution-oriented brainstorming sessions. Critical to this process was the fact that the hospital knew what the patients wanted; it listened without judgment, asked for help from members of its team and from the outside community, and then took advantage of all the feedback in crafting innovative solutions that flexed to the needs of specific patient populations. By considering all of the ideas that people brought to the table, the hospital demonstrated a great deal of respect for its health-care providers and empathy for its patients. "Never forget the people you are there to serve in health care," says George. "We cannot lose sight of the true customer . . . the patient." In the end, the hospital decided to implement a two-pronged strategy to serve its two fastest-growing populations, and created special inpatient units and care wings that cater to the specific needs of Asian and also elderly patients.

What does it look like for a Texas hospital to flex to the needs and comforts of an Asian population? It may surprise you how simple and even mundane some of the changes seem, until you reflect on what matters most to you when you are ill. So much about feeling and getting better is about comfort and familiarity. Local Asian chefs were brought in to teach the hospital kitchen staff how to create meals that were more in tune with an Asian palate. In the

Asian patient care unit, televisions featured programs in Vietnamese and Chinese. The revamped rooms feature space for extended family to linger in or stay comfortably. Patients and families alike are greeted by a décor featuring bamboo materials and lots of red, an auspicious color in many Asian cultures. The unit is staffed with bilingual nurses and in-house interpreters seven days per week. And for those families facing the greatest difficulty of all, a patient's death, Buddhist rituals and customs are allowed to be practiced in place to aid the grieving family. Soon, the hospital plans to build an onsite pagoda funded by a gracious donor.

Though some at the hospital were initially skeptical about the changes, there was no arguing with the overwhelming response to the new unit. The community felt so respected, listened to, and cared for that the hospital received an avalanche of free, unsolicited PR. Memorial Hermann Southwest received community involvement awards and was highlighted on Vietnamese TV and in the Asian print media. There was a groundswell in the community and that base, in turn, helped with recruiting new physicians and attracting top talent. Now Memorial Hermann Southwest is also more integrated with this segment of its customer base, offering free health fairs in the community semiannually and other types of preventive outreach specific to the Asian population.

Similarly, George carried on the work begun by Rod Brace to implement an ER dedicated solely to elderly patients who often felt unsafe or stressed in the frenetic pace of the typical emergency room setting. The hospital now also offers a geriatric psychiatric unit, the Senior Treatment and Recovery Unit for Behavioral Care, where seniors suffering from dementia or acute psychosis can receive care tailored to their conditions. In addition, a senior-care inpatient unit allows physicians and staff the space and time to address multilayered, complex health issues often faced in the geriatric population. As with the Asian inpatient unit, the hospital addresses even small details that emphasize comfort and peace of mind, from beds having thicker mattresses to a quieter, more peaceful environment that speeds healing by lowering patient stress.

THE FLUENT ORGANIZATION

George didn't stop at simply listening to the patients; he paid just as much attention to his staff, as well as to the doctors who served them. Initially, in May 2010, morale was plummeting at Memorial Hermann Southwest, with physician satisfaction at the hospital scoring in the abysmal twenty-ninth percentile for physicians nation-wide. Happier, more fulfilled patients and improved resources make physicians' jobs easier, but additionally Gaston created a physicians' council to help give voice to the ongoing concerns and issues of doctors at MHSW. In a study conducted by HealthStream Research, his physicians' satisfaction rating soared to the ninety-second percentile by May 2011 following the establishment of the council and a culture of physician involvement in hospital decision making.

Memorial Hermann Southwest took one of the most challenging and often-debated issues of the modern age—health care for an increasingly diverse and aging population—and illustrates beautifully how fundamental fluent leader principles like humility, adaptability, and innovative thinking can make a profound difference to the bottom line and to people's lives. It took very deliberate steps to close the power gap between the hospital system and its patients and their community by initiating steps to better listen to and address the difficulties that different constituencies had with their hospital experience. Its actions yielded solutions that were of benefit to both groups. The hospital became profitable once again, and patients and physicians found the kind of care that made them feel truly cared for and valued.

George Gaston and the staff of Memorial Hermann Southwest were able to translate miscommunication and unmet needs into an opportunity for incremental growth and financial success for the hospital while improving health outcomes for their patients. Employing these principles in the workplace not only improved communication and morale for both patients and health practitioners, but also boosted Memorial Hermann Southwest into a top-fifty-ranked hospital out of five thousand in the United States by HealthGrades in 2011, 2012, and 2013.

PART III

MULTIPLYING YOUR SUCCESS

CHAPTER 9

ONBOARDING YOUR EMPLOYEES— GETTING IT RIGHT FROM DAY ONE

When Jane Hyun used to conduct new-hire orientation sessions during her days in HR, they were held early on Monday morning, and scheduled at a time immediately preceding the time when the new hires started their first day of work. The session itself was an organized forty-five-minute presentation that provided an overview of policies, benefits, company history, and the business's core values. Given that it was their first entrée into the company, the new hires were on their best behavior, looking to make a favorable impression. After the orientation, they went on to their first day of their jobs, and HR could only hope that their leadership would do their best to develop these new employees and provide them with a good introductory week after their initial welcome to the firm.

Even today, when new employees receive an orientation, it is typically a single event that takes an hour or two to complete. To be sure, companies have become more high tech and are beginning to use Web-based interactive platforms to deliver their orientation programs instead of using an in-person HR director. For the most part, these sessions deliver static data such as benefits, processing information, and official company policy. Moreover, these short orientation sessions don't provide the forum for the new hires to ask the really hard questions about what it's really like to work at the company.

Whether it comes through a person or through a computer screen, this onboarding process is a new hire's first introduction to your team. In this chapter we'd like to invite you to rethink how you bring new hires and new team members into the fold, particularly to reflect the vast array of cultural, generational, and gender perspectives that your incoming hires will bring. For many, the first few weeks of work provide the best and most fertile opportunity to bridge the gap and create immediate trust and enhance communication with your incoming talent.

ORIENTATION VS. ONBOARDING

While most people tend to use the terms *orientation* and *onboarding* interchangeably, we believe that there are a few important differences between the two. In some ways, *onboarding* is the updated term that organizations have come up with to replace *orientation*. One important distinction is that onboarding is seen as more of a process rather than a single event like those Monday-morning new-hire sessions. We see onboarding as a company-initiated talent development process whereby the hiring manager, with the support of HR leadership, designs the most appropriate and useful entrée for new employees to be enfolded into the team. Proper onboarding conveys much more than just how to sign in to the company database and the location of the nearest restroom. During this onboarding period, the new employee will gain new insights about the company culture even as she is going through it, meeting her new colleagues, and integrating herself into the fabric of the team. Additionally, there might be guidance provided throughout the first few months to introduce employees to critical people in the organization, connecting them to a "buddy" or insider who could help integrate the new hire into the group.

Though this is how we define the term, often when we ask managers to tell us what onboarding means to them, we still receive answers that resonate much more with that brief introduction to the company than with a robust process of integration. They think of paperwork, binders, videos, and even fingerprinting or the drug tests that are part of the orientation process many new hires receive. Remember, too, that most companies, regardless of size, don't do much of either an orientation or onboarding in any form for their new hires. In fact, some company cultures may intentionally make it harder for employees to get comfortable! In these ruthless, cutthroat work environments, colleagues even use an informal hazing process, forcing their new employees to "walk through fire" to figure out the unwritten rules and decipher who will help them get around the organization during their first few weeks. Their thinking is that only the most skilled and savvy will survive. Unfortunately, the most common outcome is that management blames the employee, not their own actions (or lack thereof), four or five months down the road when the new hire isn't hitting his sales targets, appears unable to get the right resources, or isn't contributing in the way his manager envisioned.

The good news? Mindful onboarding can prevent this from happening by engaging the new hire right away and greatly increasing the chances for success.

THE IMPORTANCE OF ONBOARDING YOUR EMPLOYEES

Why bother? You might be thinking that as long as the new person figures out how to do the important aspects of his job, he's going to be fine. You might have never had the experience of being onboarded formally in your own organization, and perhaps things turned out okay for you. But there are real risks to not giving adequate time and attention to this process. Employees in the United States and the UK cost businesses an estimated $37 billion each year because they do not fully understand their jobs, according to IDC, a global market intelligence firm. Their white paper, "$37 Billion: Counting the Cost of Employee Misunderstanding," quantifies the losses that occur as a result of actions taken by employees who have been misunderstood or misinterpreted. Additionally, we hear of many cases of early attrition from new hires who felt that they had a hard time assimilating into the corporate "insider" network. Further research from human resource experts shows that an average of 25 percent of new employees leave within the first year.

MEANINGFUL ENGAGEMENT BEGINS WITH CLOSING THE GAP

If you are an organization that values your talent, developing a thoughtful onboarding process helps ensure that you capture the rich insights they bring into your company by fully engaging them from the beginning. This early engagement process is a powerful mechanism for flexing up, down, and across the entire hierarchy and sets the tone for these new working relationships. Remember, good onboarding is more holistic and more intentional than just taking care of administrative details. Broadly speaking, it defines the intentional way you introduce new people to how things get done inside your organization, and provides a true insider's perspective on:

- Who the players are
- What the company culture is really like from the inside and how things get done
- Developing your personal career objectives
- GARP (Generally Accepted Rules for Promotion) specific to the organization
- Understanding the internal power dynamics

While each company might set a unique period of time for onboarding, from a week to sometimes six months or more, how long it takes to orient oneself to a new position or a team also depends on the complexity of the job, as well as on the complexity of the processes a new hire needs to understand. The time and energy devoted to onboarding largely depends on how much your organization values socializing new employees to your organizational style and culture.

When done properly, orienting your employees provides an excellent and immediate opportunity to close any gaps that might exist, establish great communication foundations between you and your employees, and deliver more positive outcomes along with accelerated and increased performance. Not only will you help develop a connection to broader communities and access to diverse talents you may not otherwise have inroads to, but you'll help ensure your employees reap the benefits as well, including a reduction in new employee stress as well as increased job satisfaction and retention.

For those still doubting onboarding's efficacy, consider the demonstrated improvements of 40 percent in productivity and a return on investment inside of three months for onboarding initiatives in sales departments, according to one AT&T Mobility director. Moreover, by decreasing the power gap that exists and flexing toward your employee in the beginning, you will remove the chances of your new employees feeling alienated from the existing team. This holds true both for new hires and new team members who have made an internal transfer into your group. By closing the gap with your new hires from the moment they set foot inside the door, you, too, will see the benefits of increased productivity and better results, and faster.

ONBOARDING SERVES AS A MECHANISM FOR INSTILLING CORE VALUES AT LIVEPERSON

In 2010, during a time of rapid growth, LivePerson's CEO Robert LoCascio took measures to ensure that his company was growing in a way that preserved its core values of Be an Owner and Help Others. But what does being an owner and helping others mean? Later that year, under the leadership of Steve Schloss, global head of people, and Edie Mitchell, head of talent management, the Global Welcome Program, a three-day in-person onboarding experience for new hires, was launched. A Global Welcome occurs every eight weeks in either New York or Israel. Regardless of position or location, employees are flown in to attend this important experience. As part of the three-day onboarding requirement, every employee must go out into the community to help others. One particular group chose to knock on the door of the Ronald McDonald House, learned about their missions and practices, and ended up donating toys to the organization. Others delivered meals to homebound patients. Employees then come back together to debrief the experience and the impact that it had on themselves, one another, and the community. While this might seem like a pricey proposition, the long-term impact that it had on the employees' engagement with the organization was priceless. Says Schloss, "The return is personal and provides validation: that saying yes to LivePerson was the right decision for the employee."

ONBOARDING INTERNAL TRANSFERS AND EXTERNAL HIRES

When Regina was tapped to handle campus recruiting at her company, a large financial services organization, it was her third assignment. Though she wasn't a new employee, she had rotated in from one of the operating units, so she was new to recruiting and new to the human resources function. Knowing this, for Regina's first week her manager prescheduled a full five days of meetings and lunches. Her manager made a list of everyone Regina would need to connect with in order to be successful in her new job, from administrative support to employee relations to HR systems—no part of her department was overlooked.

By setting up these meetings and introducing her to all the key players, this onboarding process accomplished two things: Regina's boss made her feel welcome and connected, and Regina was able to dive into the recruiting calendar almost immediately, as she had all the resources at hand to kick off the recruiting season. Unlike so many new employees who feel like they're imposing on others because everyone is too busy to acculturate them properly, Regina took notice that everyone she met with was ready for her and well prepared. This set the tone that Regina's role was important and that it was important, too, that she function well—not just at her job duties but as part of a team. By the end of the week Regina knew where to go and of whom to ask questions. Regina's manager made a concerted effort to close the gap and connect Regina throughout the hierarchical chain with people on whom Regina would need to depend. In doing so, she set Regina up for success and accelerated her ability to contribute.

Compare Regina's experience to that of Josie, who moved to a new organization after working at a much larger and more hierarchical company. At her old job, Josie had had an executive assistant who handled everything from taking care of her car service to ordering dinner if she worked late. In addition to handling all those details, every assistant held a college degree. Each was able to write excellent memos and handle overflow work; her assistant was almost an extension of Josie's role. However, when Josie moved to a flatter organization that was more DIY, she wasn't clued in to how the various team members worked together. When she approached her administrative assistant with a request in the same manner as she had in her old job, the woman looked at her like she had horns! At her new company, administrative assistants had very set duties. Josie was seen as overreaching and rude when she assumed the processes operated the same way in the new organization. Proper onboarding, and maybe even an internal buddy, would have given Josie the information and skills for working most effectively with the assistants in their defined roles. Josie, too, could have taken the initiative to investigate the internal processes and learn how best to work with other team members instead of making assumptions.

CONNECTING

A Gallup study found that a mere 30 percent of employees report having a best friend at work. People without a best friend at work have only a one in twelve chance of being engaged in their job, while those who do are seven times as likely to be more engaged in their jobs. That's seven times more likely. Proper prehire preparation and carefully designed onboarding strategy will help new employees meet others in the organization, enabling such relationships to develop more naturally.

WELCOMING MILLENNIALS INTO THE FOLD

Research shows that successful and mindful onboarding can be especially critical for retaining those new Generation Y college graduates. While one study found that a stunning 46 percent of new hires fail in their first eighteen months on the job, companies that paid special attention to the different ways millennials learn and operate in today's business world saw an increase in the success and retention of new hires in that age group. Successful onboarding programs for millennials could include opportunities for them to contribute right off the bat or suggest new initiatives, satisfying their need for meaningful challenges at work. Millennials also benefit from a clear introduction into the business culture of each organization, especially regarding business goals that are tied to doing well in the company, the broader community, and perhaps globally. Millennials enjoy working in teams and prefer to work in a collaborative environment. Doing a careful job of connecting millennials with their peer groups and allowing for collaborative work projects and environments helps set the stage for success for younger workers and helps them commit fully to your organization. Your Gen Y employees want to connect with one another and create and leverage networks inside and outside the organization. Onboarding that doesn't address this type of human relationship-building won't work well to integrate your new hire into your team, and might cause frustration and anxiety.

Innovative New York start-ups like eyeglass company Warby

Parker, menswear outfit Bonobos, and beauty-supply subscription platform Birchbox are also stressing the importance of this type of interaction and relationship-building, sometimes with a humorous touch. Their approaches range from a computer program created by a Warby Parker developer that randomly assigns lunch dates with different employees, to a company-wide version of the game Two Truths and a Lie facilitated by Bonobos's hiring manager, wherein a new employee's colleagues have to guess which of the facts about the new hire isn't actually true. These companies recognize that in addition to giving people information, access, expectations, and direction, connecting people with one another can prove the best way to build a team.

BARRIERS TO SUCCESSFUL ONBOARDING

If onboarding is such a win-win for companies and employees alike, why do so many companies choose to skip this step? We see several pervasive attitudes and processes that seem to get in the way of acculturating new hires properly. The first is when new hires aren't made aware of the proper channels to go through, or when there are simply too many levels of hierarchy or a slow-moving bureaucracy in place. When it takes too long to get things done internally, you stifle the energy and creativity that new hires can bring to your organization. As you design your onboarding programs, consider how you might best capitalize on the fresh ideas your new recruit is bringing in and make sure there are avenues for them to channel their newcomer's lens and innovative ideas.

Employees confess that their learning process can be stifled by a company culture best defined as "no holds barred." When the culture is too aggressive, it forces employees to "show up" and show what they know rather than demonstrating humility and showing what they can learn. This often discourages a team approach and instead favors a singular person's individual achievement, regardless of the style and preference of the team members. Additionally, this sink-or-swim mentality simply doesn't reflect the real needs of even the most aggressive self-starters. It can be especially difficult for people from other cultures, particularly those who prefer more indirect communication–style cultures, to learn the unwritten rules. Your new, diverse hires may not be used to the informal network that facilitates how their jobs fit into the big picture. Younger employees may reach to broaden their scope immediately even before becoming grounded in their position. It's true that some people don't need a lot of help navigating a new culture, but it's also true that new employees don't always know what they need. They don't know what they don't know! It's far better to put processes in place to help all new employees acculturate to your organization.

We have already referenced perhaps the largest impediment to proper onboarding: a lack of investment in the process. We hear from countless workers, "I don't even know how to do my job well," or "I don't know how to get my ideas heard," and, most commonly, "My manager is too busy and I don't know where to go to ask questions." As all managers know, it costs a lot of money to train an employee, both in time and resources, as well as dollars spent on recruitment. Don't be pennywise and poundfoolish by skimping on the onboarding

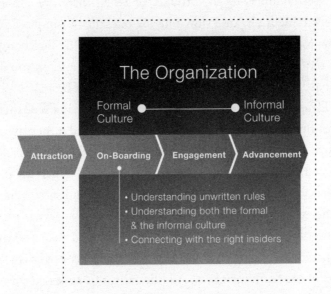

The Importance of Onboarding in the Talent Management Process

once you've recruited top talent. Not only will you have wasted that time and money, but you will also have missed out on building a culture of innovation in your organization. Consider this: new recruits to your team allow you to gather new perspectives as well as competitor intelligence. Every onboarding process is an opportunity to learn a new approach and to evaluate your positioning in your industry. You can get the best out of fresh talent eager to prove themselves if you take the time and commit to onboarding in a thoughtful manner. After all, they want to show you their best by demonstrating something positive. Don't throw away that opportunity by turning them loose without direction, guidance, and support.

With proper onboarding there is a greater likelihood of increased engagement. The acculturated team member is ready to participate fully, able to accelerate her work, and perform at or above expectations.

BRIDGING THE GAP WITH EMPLOYEES NEW TO THE COMPANY

For employees new to the company, the onboarding process is a rich opportunity not only to express clearly to them your mission, company values, and internal processes, but also to bridge the gap and understand the values that shape their interactions as well as their preferred communication style. Instead of forcing new hires to fully assimilate into the status quo, look at points of difference as an opportunity. You might begin with the three questions we reviewed on pages 78 and 79 to set the tone for how you'd like to grow the relationship. When you notice moments of disconnection or that you don't understand, we can apply these additional pre-engagement questions to ask yourself about your new hire, tailoring them to a new hire:

- What are they thinking? What's behind the action?
- How might their experience in their previous job affect their

behavior here? What don't they know about our company culture that's causing a disconnect?

- How do I connect with this person?
- How do I integrate her more fully into the organization?
- How will I pass on both formal expectations and explain the unwritten rules?
- How will I put myself in her shoes and demonstrate positive intent?
- What and who would I need to know before starting at this organization?
- Can I connect this person with other stakeholders or an internal buddy to help her find her way?

As a new manager, the onboarding process can be a powerful place to address different aspects of your job expertise at a more micro level. You can use the questions and communicate your intent to get to know that person.

Phil, a manager new to his senior VP role, sat down with every-one in his newly inherited team and was clear, right from the get-go. "I'm a talker," he told each of them. "I like to be direct—have face-to-face communication." He then asked each team member, "How do you prefer to work?" By offering his own preference first he put himself out there and bridged the gap, allowing other team mem-bers an opportunity to express their own preferences. Even without differences related to culture, gender, and generation, people of sim-ilar backgrounds can communicate in wildly different ways! Some people think you can never overcommunicate. They prefer it when you repeat certain messages over and over again. Others only want the summary version of the report, or a two-minute headline update and none of the details. They use one word when others use thirty. For the people who embody these two very distinct communication styles to get along well, they're going to have to notice this difference and learn a way to work with each other that is successful. Make your preferences known and then ask how others work best instead of assuming they operate as you do.

As a manager introducing a new hire to your team, it is critical that you create a culture of mentoring for your new recruit, both from you and from the team at large. For example, set the expectation with your team to be inclusive, and discuss at length the place your new hire will occupy in your team structure. Don't make the same mistake as Phil did when he added a new sales associate, Matt, to his team. The new sales associate had incredible potential; Phil's problem was that he didn't prepare his team to receive Matt. Phil had a global reach. He was a busy manager who traveled 90 percent of the time, part of the reason he was excited to have Matt in place to handle the day-to-day management of the business. However, Phil didn't take the time to create an inclusive team culture back at the home office. The result was that Phil's sales team, already competitive by the nature of the sales function, perceived Matt to be a favorite of Phil and worked against him, rather than helping him acclimate to their team processes. Left to fend for himself, Matt didn't have the skills to notice and correct their misconceptions about his place on the team. Although talented, Matt was finding he was not successful in his new role, especially because he was not able to reach down to those who were the building blocks of the organization, such as those in the junior sales–support roles. Six months into Matt's tenure, the great new hire Phil had been so excited about was on the verge of leaving.

ONBOARDING YOURSELF

If you are the new employee or transfer to a new team, you should bring to bear all your skills in reaching up and across to bridge the gap with your managers and your new peers, as well as reaching down to those in support roles. If you're hired into a management role with significant responsibility, in addition to observing and asking questions, you will find that demonstrating humility and not "knowing it all" can earn the respect from those around you. There are variations in how individuals respond. Nancy, a program manager in a large nonprofit organization, was excited about her new position. However, since this new position meant a career change from her previous job in an insurance company, she knew very little about the sector and decided that she would take a more "observe and see-as-you-go" approach. For the first few weeks of her job, she remained quiet in meetings and didn't push her way into building new relationships, wanting to get an idea of how the internal politics of the organization played out. However, this had a negative impact on how people perceived her, including her manager, who had high expectations of Nancy. Given her level of experience, he wanted her to step up right away, and take much more ownership with her lead projects in meetings, and build relationships with various departments of the organization. Once Nancy realized that there was a disconnect in expectations, she was able to shift gears fairly quickly. However, the initial perceptions about her willingness to connect, her initiative, and her commitment were already formed, and she had to work that much harder to gain the credibility that she sought from others.

Others experience the opposite problem. For many, it's hard sometimes to pull back; there's a strong temptation to show what you've got and prove to the company that they made the right decision to bring you onboard. However, depending on the relationships of the existing team, know that your desire to strut your stuff may backfire and even alienate you from those around you. Many of the power gap masters we interviewed took the time to figure out the nuances of the new company culture and how best to communicate with those around them before plunging in.

In the absence of a formal onboarding process, you may need to be very direct in closing the gap with your new peers and superiors. When Audrey Lee was hired into a marketing position early in her career, she was personally escorted around the company and introduced by the president of the company as her protégée. That was where the process ended. Because she reported to the president, who had little time for her, she took a coworker's advice to get on a list of people's calendars. The position involved working with customers and internal teams including finance, sales, and engineering. Audrey had no choice but to pick up the phone, make the appointments, and wander the halls saying hello to people, trying to sort out who was relevant to her work and who her stakeholders were. In a way, she closed the gap by not having any clear sense that there was one—she assumed she could go talk to anyone and that it was her responsibility to do so. Though it was trial by fire through self-onboarding, she integrated very quickly and developed trust and relationships in a short period of time.

GREAT ONBOARDING MODELS

There are great examples of companies that do onboarding right, connecting new hires with stakeholders and mentors, integrating them into their teams, setting clear performance expectations, and helping them develop a plan on how to achieve their goals, giving them actual rule books that explain processes and team functions and transfer crucial institutional knowledge on to new hires. We have learned, too, from our clients and the leaders we have interviewed how to react in environments where onboarding isn't done as well as it can be, and where people have helped onboard themselves by closing the power gap and flexing to their new colleagues in order to succeed.

Ten years ago, Virginia-based Capital One invested heavily in recruiting top talent to fuel an ambitious growth plan. Yet once the company had all these new executives and managers in place, it found that the expected output fell short of expectations. The anticipated creative and innovative boost hadn't happened. The new recruits weren't plugged into their team network and hadn't connected with their employees. It was so dire that some new hires left within the first year citing displeasure with the lack of an onboarding process. Others were asked to leave.

To help turn things around, the company's training and development team created a new process called the New Leader Assimilation Program meant to get new executives and managers up to speed in a rapid yet holistic process aimed at creating productive, innovative leaders. The process begins with giving new leaders a complete picture of the work environment they are stepping into, from existing challenges within the team to performance expectations. It ensures that the new leaders engage their team members as well as encourages communication, and it puts in place set milestones so that the new leader is given 360-degree feedback after six months, allowing for a revision of goals and an evaluation of areas of strength and challenge for each individual.

Many of us have stepped into positions where we wished someone could have handed us a map that showed us where all the mines were buried so that we could have avoided them! Perhaps there was an internal candidate for a job you received whose reception of you into the team is markedly chilly. Maybe you notice a peer is able to work incredibly effectively with the admins in your team while you haven't yet figured out the right way to engage them. Capital One produced this map in the form of the "Customized New Leader Transition Guide," a report that culls information both practical and personal from all the new recruits' stakeholders to give the leader every advantage in integrating seamlessly into the team. Not only does the leader have each stakeholder's honest assessment of the team before she begins, she knows more about the critical history of the team within the organization as well as of each team member, providing some of that institutional memory lacking in poor transitions. The new hire's manager also uses the "Transition Guide" to identify potential trouble spots and create a three-month development plan for the new hire.

Some power gap masters are readily able to bridge the gap with their new team members and direct reports, while others need a bit more help. At Capital One, their onboarding process includes a facilitated team meeting during the first week where employees get to learn everything about their new manager, from her personal goals to her educational background to her preferred communication style. Here the facilitator helps bridge the distance between the new hires and the employees, giving them access and opportunity to their new boss. To help new managers reach across to their peers, each new leader is assigned a "buddy" or peer mentor for the first ninety days who helps the leader navigate the new company culture and often becomes a close colleague beyond the initial onboarding period.

Beyond the ninety days of rapid or accelerated onboarding Capital One delivers, new leaders are still given feedback and held accountable to their performance plan and goals. At six months each new executive and manager receives a 360-degree performance evaluation, and is able to compare how well they think they are doing with the perspectives of their direct reports as well as their colleagues. This helps new leaders stay on track and even shift strategies as necessary. In all, Capital One devoted a substantial amount of time, commitment, and resources to ensuring that its new execs and managers were onboarded quickly and effectively, and it realized tremendous results for its efforts.

This type of rapid or accelerated onboarding is similar to the model used successfully by Marie's new employer after she left her conservative banking institution and moved to a company with a very different way of getting things done. Her new firm was decentralized and the units were more independent of one another than she was used to, and she credits good onboarding with helping her realize how things got done. Marie had worked in lots of different places and contexts, and knew that several critical functions for her position depended on knowing the internal processes and unwritten rules for each organization. For example, she would need to know how to get money from the budget for her team. Maybe one person is in charge of budgeting but another has the purse strings, and knowing how to negotiate the interplay between the two would prove crucial to the success of her team. She is adamant about the importance of learning not only tasks but about how to relate to one another as we step into new positions. "It's amazing we have taught our computers to talk to each other but we still don't understand how to connect as people and communicate across differences. We still mess that one up!"

Marie had a peer mentor assigned to her during her ninety-day onboarding process. However, Marie did not receive a clear and transparent written guide, and the lack of information transition caused difficulty for her. In the first ten weeks she was there, one of Marie's direct reports quit. Losing someone that quickly from your team is never a morale-booster for a manager in a new position. However, it turned out that the woman who quit had applied for Marie's position and was not happy at all that she was coming onto the team. Yet no one had told Marie about the situation and explained the crucial backstory about what was going on in the team before she started. Frustrated that she hadn't been apprised of the situation so that she could help mitigate the consequences, she thought about going to a senior person to complain, but then changed her mind and went to the peer mentor instead. By taking the lateral approach and using her peer mentor, Marie avoided looking whiny to the boss, and also got her question answered and registered her desire to get all the information up front. Because her peer mentor felt badly about how things had turned out, Marie said, "he sort of 'owed' me from that point on and it bonded us together." They stayed close and he kept her informed going forward.

More than just understanding the unwritten rules, Marie says, "it is during the onboarding process that you will determine whether people want to help you or not as you go forward in your career." When Marie was hired, there was actually a hiring freeze in place in her organization. To get the new hires necessary for the performance of her department she had to go through lots of layers to get approval, and the decisions were all clad in an aura of secrecy. Even the people in HR didn't know all the jobs that were open! Only two weeks after she started in her new position, Marie learned that the deadline for submitting for new positions was coming up, and still the chief of staff and the head of the business hadn't told her what the numbers were looking like. She was not being given the information she needed, so Marie chose to close the gap and flex up to her superior. One day she saw the top brass were having a meeting in the boardroom. She interrupted them to get the numbers she needed, a bold move for a woman new to her position. Her moxie worked, however. "Boy, you're tenacious!" the chief of staff commented before giving her the numbers. Not only could Marie now do her job better, but she had already set the tone early with her internal client. From that point on they saw her as a business partner and recognized the value she added to the team.

"It is during the onboarding process that you will determine whether people want to help you or not as you go forward in your career."

One of the final and often overlooked points to remember about the onboarding process is that the informal connections are often some of the most crucial. Folding an employee into the team in a real way, where they have people they understand and on whom they can rely, can make all the difference in a new hire's success. Don't overlook the importance of relationship building in this early and critical stage. It's every bit as important for a new hire to focus on building trust as it is for companies seeking to form new relationships with global partners. The relationships form the basis for all future interactions.

Giving each one of your employees a fair chance to succeed and give his best can be directly enhanced by taking a more strategic approach to welcoming your new hires. The companies that do it right employ a set process that spans a few months with regular check-ins after the initial period is over. The process should connect an employee with your team, introduce her to the company culture, and give her the key to the unwritten rules of your organization. You should provide clear performance expectations of your new hires and work with them to create a career development plan to achieve it. Check in frequently, give constructive feedback, and make sure to celebrate early successes. This process constitutes your first chance to flex toward your employee. One clear benefit of your efforts will be your employee knowing she's made the right choice in choosing your organization. She'll also feel a sense of ownership over her work, and begin fully engaged and ready to contribute to her company.

Fluent Leader Profile: Steve Miola and Ray Bain, Merck Research Laboratories—Creating a Fluent Company Culture

To be a good manager, I learned don't expect others to do the things the way I do them. It would be easier if I could manage everyone the same, but it wouldn't work. And it wouldn't be innovation if it wasn't diverse.
—RAY BAIN

We first met Merck Research Laboratories' Steve Miola, director of training and professional development, and Ray Bain, VP of its Biostatistics and Research Decision Sciences (BARDS) group, when the two wanted an innovative solution to a talent "problem." As we got to know them better, we were continually impressed by the fluency exhibited by both Steve and Ray at not only the individual level but at an organizational one, creating a truly sustainable fluency model within the company. In looking to bridge differences between a group of culturally outlying scientists and their managers, the two focused not just on the scientists but on their managers, recognizing there was work to do on everyone's part to increase understanding and success. Ray's work at Merck created a department that was conducive to this kind of growth, creating a company cultural DNA that valued the mutual investigation of difference with an eye toward leveraging it instead of eliminating it.

A TALENT "PROBLEM" IS A TWO-WAY STREET

Due to the nature of its work, Merck Research Laboratories employs a large number of scientists, including statisticians. Candidates are PhDs with strong academic credentials, basic research experience, and the motivation to apply their skills inside a global pharmaceutical corporation. Over the past few years, they hired a large group of PhDs from China, resulting in a research team that was predominantly Asian. The company had acquired a world-class team of scientific talent, and yet it discovered after the fact that the scientists had some profoundly different styles of interacting to which their overwhelmingly non-Asian managers were unaccustomed. And they recognized that other teammates and managers overemphasized the need to get people to "fit in" rather than work together to acknowledge and mutually understand and leverage their differences.

Ray decided that needed to change—and committed to retooling how the entire department understood and processed difference, especially relating to culture. They sought to close the gap in a powerful way through the program, and they were not afraid to take risks in order to do it. In the process they created a program that was bidirectional; it wasn't just about helping the scientists understand how they could develop their leadership skills and gain a renewed understanding about cultural differences, but also about helping the managers and management understand the dynamic of culture, and how they might actively do something to improve work relationships and foster the scientists' development.

The BARDS group of highly qualified and scientifically diverse professionals offered critical value to the organization. "But we needed to get our whole group to understand a need for a style shift if we were to be effective with the increase in the current and incoming scientists from Asia, for the scientists as well as management," said Ray. "For the management, I shared what I learned: don't expect others to do things the way you do them. Not everyone is the same. It would be easier if I could manage everyone the same way, but it wouldn't work. And there wouldn't be innovation if everyone was the same."

From the beginning, they knew there was a disconnect but they didn't understand all the dynamics. What they did have was an insatiable curiosity to find out the root of the issue and figure out the best way to learn and grow from it. Steve and Ray showed genuine concern when they told us, "We are hiring these people and managing these people. We're noticing when they're leaving, and we're noticing when they're disengaged, but we can't figure out why." We were struck by how Steve and Ray's fluency had created this unique culture, an environment that allowed for this kind of conversation. Together, we created a program that allowed Merck to engage both the Asian scientists and the management. The program featured an intensive training program for the scientists that helped them better understand how their cultural values came to bear in the workplace and helped them build their leadership skills. The training included discussions with senior leaders of the division and was complemented by roundtables for the managers that enabled rigorous and—more importantly—candid conversations about differences between the managers and the scientists. This resulted in deeper understanding of other cultures on the part of the managers, and helped them formulate action plans for team development and interactions.

SETTING THE TONE: EXTENDING THE REACH TO ALL LEVELS

It's important to note that these solutions didn't take place in a vacuum. We brought expertise and helped the participants work through the program. But our invitation to do the work, as well as the openness of the participants to having those difficult conversations and flexing toward one another, was made possible by the company culture. An organization that sees difference as opportunity makes it the responsibility of all parties to look for solutions within themselves, and sees how value in every individual sets a powerful stage for individual transformation.

That company culture was created by fluent leadership. The unconditional positive regard Ray and Steve extend toward employees, their curiosity about difference, and their comfort with the ambiguity of differing cultures prove a potent example of what leadership can do when flexing is a key management strategy. Not only do Steve and Ray support and leverage one another's abilities and innovative thinking, their beliefs and behaviors have multiplied the effect, creating a company culture that helps inspire, values, and rewards fluency in day-to-day behaviors.

THE FLUENT ROLE MODEL

One researcher who joined the group back in the 1990s still remembers being part of Ray's group. He admired the ability of the senior management to not only help the individual but also the organization with diversity. "I see Ray and his team as role models," the researcher said. "They are respected within and outside of the company. He was always good to me in providing opportunities for me to develop external and internal leadership." The researcher felt that the BARDS leadership shared noticeable traits—an ability to be candid but still respectful with direct reports, and a willingness to elicit ideas and opinions from their staff. "When people come to brainstorm ideas, Ray sets the example. He doesn't talk about his ideas at that time. If his ideas conflict with the flow of the brainstorm, he listens and supports rather than taking the stage. He doesn't impose his ideas in the process. He offers if people are really off, but encourages them to innovate and discuss. Most managers try to copy his style! I'm one of them."

Ray's fluency is exhibited in the trust he places in individuals at all levels of the organization and his ability to recognize their potential. When we went into Merck to work with the research labs, the administrative assistants expressed a strong desire to understand cultural differences in dealing with various levels of management, and asked to be included in the trainings. As critical mediators between the scientists and management, they, too, wanted a better understanding of cross-cultural skills and improved relationships with the researchers. Ray immediately responded to that need by including them in the conversation and providing the training they needed.

Not tethered or constrained by the limits of a job title, Ray gives the administrative staff freedom to pursue other interests and strengths and learn new skills. As one example, led by Linda, an administrative assistant, the admin team built an internal Web site on its own, completely owning the project. None of them had any type of experience with Web site design or coding, but they saw the need for a central communication hub and were empowered by Ray to solve the problem. They learned the software, did the design, and controlled the content and communications. Now it's the centerpiece of their group. "Admins are often considered the lowest on the totem pole," Linda told us. "But when I sit in on Ray's meetings, I always feel important and heard. I have a voice and my opinion is valued. That is the tone that Ray sets in the meetings. All the admins are treated as part of a team. The lowest-level statistician is not made to feel intimidated by a room full of superiors."

Because Ray recognizes the value of all the people in his group, he is able to use them for significant projects that are critical to the organization. Being given respect, trust, and autonomy changed the administrative staff's outlook and capability. "Admins aren't just people behind the desk and phone," said Linda. "We are people with knowledge and power."

PERPETUATING A FLUENT CULTURE

When people in BARDS talk about the mentors who have made their mark, the conversation often turns to Steve. As a scientist him-self, Steve was perfectly positioned to pick up the mantle and work tirelessly to promote and mentor individual scientists, looking in un-expected places for input and value. Profoundly influenced by Ray's approach, he is now part of this consistently fluent fabric where he looks at individuals and is able to ask all the right questions to unearth potential. "The guy who hired me into marketing took a chance on me. I had a PhD in science—no marketing experience. But he hired me into his group. It was so challenging but such an opportunity. I thanked him when he retired, and he told me, 'Don't thank me. Just hire someone like you!' I always remember that when I find the right people with potential." Even, and especially, when those people aren't like everyone else.

In this work, Steve finds consistent opportunities to apply this approach and help shape and mentor countless protégés. In one memorable example, he was approached by a scientist of Asian descent who had just been appointed as a manager. She wanted to do well and didn't know what was expected. "She attended the course for new managers, and asked me to be her mentor. I gave her a clear picture of processes and support and guidance. In doing this, I got to understand firsthand her challenges in being a first-time manager as well as how growing up Chinese had affected her culturally." As an example, when his new mentee was preparing to make a case to promote someone in her group, she had to defend that decision to senior management and present a credible case. She was so intimidated by the whole process that Steve helped her prep and, through his coaching, she gained confidence. Steve walked her through how she might conduct herself in presentation and approach. "She was successful in that presentation and I later received unsolicited feedback from management in how well she did in those meetings," Steve says with pride in her accomplishment.

Coaching this manager was not in Steve's job description. But Steve proved to be an excellent mentor and displays fluency in his approach in that he is able to give advice and guidance while paying attention to what he doesn't know so as to learn from experiences unlike his own. That manager had lessons to teach him, too. "You have to sit down with the person and understand the obstacles. It was challenging for me to look at the world with her eyes, but it helped me understand. Then I worked to gain her confidence by being really honest and spending the time. I let down my guard and shared my stories and experience, both failures and successes."

In scientific settings such as these, the conflict arises between the "research personality"—people who like to work by themselves and work with theory—and the general expectations and rules that govern business success. For the former, success is measured by the frequency of your publications, the accuracy and depth of your documentation analysis, and the thoroughness of your reports. Collaboration is not seen as the obvious problem-solving technique, and yet it's absolutely necessary in a business environment. Steve himself is a quiet thinker with great observation skills and an insatiable curiosity—so he understands many scientists' more reserved styles. From Ray he learned to ask the critical questions—How can they do even better in their jobs? How can they advance further inside the organization?—and helped them overcome barriers to their success.

In a presentation he gave, "Being Smart Isn't Enough," Steve talked about how scientists "have to communicate your specialty to others so they understand. These skills aren't readily honed in a researcher's life. On top of that, you have cultural differences that impact communication. . . . You can have all the talent in the world, all bottled up, and it can't get across the barriers. 'You got the job, congratulations! Now the real work begins.'" When Steve talks about the mentors and leaders who have made their mark on him, he quickly points to his colleague who has championed work regarding cultural competency and understands the issues. "Speaking at government and academic institutions, Ray is asked, 'What kind of people do you look for?,' and we try to get across that we don't look just for tech competency. That may get you interviewed or hired, but to move ahead, the skill set you need is broader. You also have to communicate effectively and work collaboratively in teams. That's what gets you to stay. Then to advance, you also have to be a good critical thinker, and you have to be a visionary."

LOOKING TO THE FUTURE

One year, at the end of our annual leadership program, a senior leader pulled us aside and said, "I just want to tell you that I don't know exactly what's going on yet, but there's a change in the halls.

There is a difference in a way the Asians are talking about their work and I can't put my finger on it, but there's a definite shift." This is what happens when, organizationally, you reach out to your talent and bridge that gap. Steve and Ray understood the current and future value of their extended team members, and were committed to helping them build their skills to help them get to the next level. Consequently, there was a lot of investment in this group of people because they recognized their value.

This culture of curiosity has continued to flourish with individuals who continue to grow. It has gifted the company with the opportunity to innovate and expand the business. Six years ago BARDS started with a tiny group in China, and now it's accelerated its reach in the Asia/Pacific region. Today, in a country where multinationals are competing for talent, it is a growing organization. The effort of building an organization characterized by unconditional positive regard, support, and sponsorship paid off. We remember our first conversation with Ray and Steve. They anticipated working more and more with Asians globally, and years later they can take pride that not only has their prediction come true, but they are getting it right from day one!

CHAPTER 10

MENTORS, SPONSORS, COACHES, AND THE GIFT OF FEEDBACK

In certain cultures, it wouldn't be unusual for a new hire to look to a more seasoned coworker on his first day at work and say, "I depend on you to show me how to succeed," and then expect that the more senior person will guide him and teach him to do his job well. The newcomer is acknowledging his need for help, saying, "Because you are more experienced I need your advice," as well as asserting his junior status in the work relationship. There is a very clear acknowledgment of the power gap. Indeed, in strong, hierarchical, Confucian cultures like South Korea or Japan, you might even address someone one or two years older than you as "older brother" or "older sister," even colleagues at the office.

From an individualistic North American perspective, this may sound like you are coddling your junior employees. But if you are working in one of the countries in the Asia/Pacific region, there is an expectation that the senior person will take an active role in looking out for the junior person who joins the organization, and there is a continuous cycle of teaching and mentoring. The boss acts as the mentor in the reporting relationship, and the older, more experienced person is expected to initiate the relationship with the younger person. If that doesn't happen in that cultural context, the junior employee may have a difficult time advancing in that organization.

In the United States, this hands-on responsibility isn't as deeply ingrained as in some other cultures. We expect that after the first day and initial introductions, new employees, regardless of age or rank, will take it upon themselves to figure out who the important players are, and learn the rules of the road.

As managers encounter interactions with employees across a range of differences with greater frequency, we see more challenges to establishing productive mentoring relationships, right when the need for them is more important than ever! Being effective at establishing mentor or sponsor relationships requires the flex skills that we described in part 2, in order to break through any barriers that exist to forging those relationships. There is plenty of data that shows the importance of mentoring and sponsorship as success factors, and we are seeing the organizations slowly come to value formal programs for mentoring, especially for women and multicultural professionals.

As with effective onboarding techniques, proper mentoring allows you to multiply the effect of your newfound flexing skills by passing on what you have learned to your circle of influence. Through these relationships, you can help individuals learn and practice their flex skills, which in turn ripple out broadly into your organization. The difference is that while onboarding is based on an organizational process, mentoring is a rich opportunity to close the power gap by investing one-to-one in your employees.

MULTIPLE WAYS TO SUPPORT, GUIDE, AND GROW YOUR EMPLOYEES

Before we get to best practices, it may be helpful to define and differentiate the roles a manager might play in supporting the career of an individual employee. The role of a mentor is to give hands-on career guidance, lend emotional support leading to success, and teach the mentee the unwritten rules of his or her job. It's a close relationship wherein the mentor becomes an employee's go-to person when he or she has questions. A mentor offers her personal experiences and influences to enlighten and guide. A good mentor not only listens to the mentee and understands where he wants to go, but anticipates developmental needs and options to explore. "I know you need to be increasing your management skills; how can I help? How can I help you think through your next steps?" Often, he or she also has the influence and involvement to provide developmental opportunities and visibility. It's important to note that a mentor doesn't have to be an employee's manager; people can benefit and learn from mentors at all levels, inside and outside of the organization. As a manager, you may serve not only as a mentor but benefit from mentorship relationships with peers, more senior-level managers, or well-matched leaders in the community.

Distinct from a mentor in several important ways, a sponsor is someone who advocates for an employee and is able to do so because he or she is in an influential position to make high stakes moves inside the organization. Often very senior in the corporate hierarchy, a sponsor may even be positioned outside a protégé's department but is still able to put him or her forward for opportunities. Protégés may not interact frequently with a sponsor, and the relationship is likely to be far less intimate than with a mentor. Because of a sponsor's high-ranking position, the power gap between employee and sponsor is apt to be quite wide, so protégés need to work consistently and over a long period to develop connections to set this foundation for success.

That said, we have heard from protégés who didn't even know they had a sponsor until they were nominated for a critical job assignment! So as your visibility increases, you may organically attract leaders who are interested in sponsoring you. But this should be less of a happy coincidence and more of a strategic effort on your part to build the relationship. It's critical you do so—sponsors are key people to have at the table on your behalf, especially at the top levels and in those C-suite positions. You need someone with influence and authority saying, "I want her to get that job" or "I want to see her promoted to the next level."

In addition to being a mentor and sponsor, a manager might also function as a coach, who possesses the skills that help employees get to the bottom of issues and guides them toward self-awareness. Instead of handing over a rule book, coaches help employees assess their SWOT (strengths, weaknesses, opportunities, and threats) and find their own solutions to their problems. Coaches should be equipped with formal tools and frameworks to help employees analyze situations, leverage strengths, and overcome and minimize weaknesses. The best coaches help tease out complex issues and lead individuals toward the sustainable self-awareness that is a hallmark of fluent leadership.

A coach can be your direct manager, your mentor, or someone who operates more formally in that role. A few Fortune 500 companies have internal coaches who are there to support the career development of junior to mid-level staff. External coaches are professionally trained experts hired by an organization to help a leader develop certain leadership skills, improve his leadership communication skills, develop global management skills, or to accelerate his development in a new position.

Not only can a mentoring or coaching relationship make a difference in whether an individual reaches his potential in a given position, it can make the difference in whether or not he keeps his job at all. External coaches are engaged when there's a leader who might be put on formal probation if he does not effect a 180-degree change in behavior or results. This type of coaching carries the highest of stakes: someone's job is on the line.

MODEL MENTORSHIP

Most of us can point to one or many mentors who play, or have played, a pivotal role in our leadership development. For us, one of those people is Frances Hesselbein, the courageous woman who rose from being a Girl Scout troop leader in Johnstown, Pennsylvania, to becoming CEO of the Girl Scouts of the USA in 1976, a position she held for thirteen years before becoming the founding CEO of the Peter F. Drucker Foundation for Nonprofit Management, recently renamed the Frances Hesselbein Leadership Institute in her honor. We have found Frances's leadership example and advice to be invaluable, and she lifted us all up by breaking hierarchical barriers and demonstrating the special dimension women bring to any role. As CEO of Girl Scouts of the USA, she built relationships with diverse cultural groups that the Girl Scouts had not yet reached, and taught collaboration through her active engagement and outreach. Her leadership had a tremendous impact on broadening the involvement of diverse communities in the United States, and consistently closed the power gap, thereby improving the organization and increasing the reach of its mission. Proving her incredible ability to connect with people across diverse groups, she also recently served for two years as the Class of 1951 Chair for the Study of Leadership in the Department of Behavioral Studies and Leadership at the US Military Academy at West Point, where she helped advance the same leadership principles she instilled during her leadership tenure with the Girl Scouts.

Frances continues to travel around the country, and around the world via global webinars, mentoring and inspiring others. Her work is grounded in "the passion to serve, the discipline to listen, the courage to question, and the spirit to include." We will always remember the incredibly important leadership lesson taught by Frances: as leaders, we have a responsibility to mentor across genders, generations, and cultures. The potential for payoff is immeasurable . . . for leadership in Frances's eyes is circular. Not only might you create an incredible difference in someone's career, but you will also grow and develop as a leader along the way.

We also remember Rosabeth Moss Kanter's research, concluding that in a high-risk, high-reward environment, senior leadership tends to hire and promote people who are most like themselves. As the diversity of our workforce increases, the ability to seek out a mentor with our exact values, style, and mind-set, or choose a mentee that's like looking in a mirror, may need to shift, providing us all with an opportunity for growth outside of our comfort zones. The need is clear to learn how to reach out and teach people whose values and drivers of success may not be the same.

The best managers and mentors are great coaches, though they wouldn't necessarily see themselves in that light. Still, they help their subordinates come to important realizations about their strengths and areas for development, and help them think through issues and problem-solving instead of simply providing them with answers: "I noticed you volunteered for the new assignment today when I know you're already pulling all-nighters. What's behind you doing that? Let's talk about what's on your plate these days."

Sometimes, if you're lucky, you may work for someone who can play all these roles: mentor, sponsor, and coach. While this is rare, there are fluent leaders like Steve Raymond, the president of Raymond Handling Concepts, who has invested organizationally in developing leaders by supporting a formal leadership program in his business. He also personally backs the program and, even though he is president of the company, is directly involved as a mentor. "Having a mentoring relationship as part of a leadership program—it has been something I've never been involved with previously," said one of Steve's mentees. "It's eye-opening, especially with the economic downturn, and the company still invests in leadership and shows commitment in bettering their employees." Steve is able to bridge the gap with him, even though he has a quiet and thoughtful style and the mentee is expressive in communication. "As a sales guy, I'm very reactive and, sometimes, my guys are afraid to address things with me, because I am reactive. Steve gave me advice: 'Sometimes people call you to vent, not to react. Ask them what they want from you.' That has had a profound effect on my relationship with the team." Steve and his mentee talk on a regular basis, with both of them bringing up topics. Steve models a fluent leader style to his mentee but also reaches down and across to employees apart from his mentee, even down to his team. "All of my guys know they can call him," affirmed one of Steve's executives, "and they know he'll call back."

OVERCOMING BARRIERS TO MENTORING

In a mentoring or coaching relationship, you might suspect that the power gap is experienced differently than in other workplace relationships. Since the goal is guidance, it's not really about who has the upper hand. Yet some people might still experience that dynamic in the relationship. When we work with clients, because we are coming from outside their organization, sometimes we see tension if they perceive they are in a subordinate position. Even if they don't call it by the same name, they are sensing a power gap that we must work to decrease in order to earn their trust and support. The same dynamic can exist for coaches or mentors outside an individual's department or area of expertise. If the potential coach or mentor doesn't work to decrease the gap, that tension can prove a barrier for people looking to get into a mentoring relationship that really serves and guides them. Just as you learned how to flex down, across, and up in part 2, you need to learn how to reach across differences to relationships that inspire, support, and empower—whether you provide mentorship or coaching to an individual or are seeking a mentor or a sponsor of your own.

Interestingly, we often find that people don't feel the need to establish mentor-mentee relationships. They don't feel like they need help, and are invested in proving their strength by not reaching out. This mind-set provides an obvious barrier to someone recognizing the need for and then taking the steps to reach out for mentorship or coaching. Some business environments exhibit a friendlier coaching culture than others. If your boss is a coach then it doesn't seem weak or remedial to seek out a coach or mentor yourself. Some organizations have even established mentoring programs. We appreciate the spirit of these programs and think they can help us, to a certain point. In our experience, the best mentoring relationships happen organically, but it is always good if the organization provides structures in place where potential mentors and protégés from different parts of the organization can meet one another in a more informal, relaxed setting.

How can management help make that happen? We worked with one large company that took an innovative approach to a common problem: there was no link with the C-level executives with influence to shape careers and the people who worked on the line. Their solution was to recruit over thirty-five executives, VP level and above, who wanted to establish connections with people in subordinate positions across the company. They held twelve separate "What's On Your Mind?" sessions, with two to three executives per group who facilitated discussions and helped people connect across levels and across departments. Lots of mentoring relationships were formed after those sessions, since the more junior-level employees had a chance to informally meet various people in executive-level management, and then followed up with the one or two with whom they felt the most connection.

A SPONSORSHIP PROGRAM BRINGS RESULTS

Organizational initiatives that facilitate sponsor-protégé relationships can help tackle lingering disparities in who has access to the most powerful roles within the company. "Women tend to do our jobs and wait for people to notice us, so connecting in this way to more senior-level people is still a little uncomfortable," said Jackie Krese, a managing director at Credit Suisse. "However, if you haven't had an opportunity to work with the most senior executives at the bank you haven't had a chance to see how these relationships play out."

When Michelle Gadsden-Williams took the helm as chief diversity officer of Credit Suisse in 2010, she was tasked with putting in place an initiative that could help identify a strong pipeline of female talent for future leadership roles. With the support of senior leadership, she helped create a group of cross-divisional executives called the Mentor Advisory Group. Thirty high-potential women managing directors, each nominated by her own manager, were selected to take part. The women worked across the bank's functions, across North America, EMEA (Europe, the Middle East, and Africa), Asia/Pacific, and Latin America and represented a variety of cultural and racial perspectives including European, Caucasian American, Middle Eastern, black, Hispanic, and Asian backgrounds. The MAG program matched these high-performing women with opportunities for future growth, combining classroom sessions aimed at understanding yourself, others, and the business with exposure to in-depth business challenges and simulations. Through the course of the yearlong program, the women were provided sponsorship and mentoring by a member of the Executive Board. Working in collaborative teams, the women identified a business challenge to tackle, and at the end of the year presented their findings and action steps to the Executive Board. The team with the best idea then escalated its findings to the board of directors.

Keys to Success of the Mentor Advisory Group

- Cross-functional teams highlight and explore difference
- An ability to openly discuss the challenges of being women leaders
- Direct feedback on the importance of influence, communication style, and executive presence
- A high-trust atmosphere
- One-on-one sponsorship and mentorship with executive team members and access to the highest levels in the company

Jackie Krese, who runs a corporate sales team for the foreign exchange and commodities businesses, was one of the women selected for the MAG program. "I was honored and excited to be chosen for it," she said. She felt there was a clear need for the program because it's not easy for women to develop strong mentorship relationships and get exposure to the executive board. As Jackie reflects, "Few of the women in this sponsorship program are what you might call shrinking violets, but unless you reach out on your own or through a structured program like this, you don't get that sponsorship. When a senior-level woman reaches out to a senior-level man, the effect can be a little uncomfortable on both sides. Structured programs normalize the interaction." However it happens, it is critical that women receive the same exposure to the executive suite and receive mentorship at that level. Jackie's sponsor was Credit Suisse CEO Brady Dougan. Throughout this program, Jackie met with Brady for quarterly one-on-one meetings, offering time for her to discuss her projects and precious time with the bank's CEO.

"When a senior-level woman reaches out to a senior-level man, the effect can be a little uncomfortable on both sides. Structured programs normalize the interaction."

The success and impact of this program was far-reaching, for Jackie and the others. At the end of this program, close to 50 percent of the thirty women that participated have either been promoted or have moved into different roles with an expanded scope of responsibilities. The program also had a tremendous positive impact on the younger generation of women at the company; due to the success of the program, a second cohort of women is being chosen as we go to press.

BUILDING A MENTOR RELATIONSHIP

It will come as no surprise that some of the traits exhibited by good mentors mirror those of the fluent leaders we covered in part 1. One of those traits is an overriding curiosity, which drives an ongoing investigation of difference. Jim Wilson, CTO at Frito-Lay North America, came to one of our roundtable discussions because he was interested in learning more about Asian culture and better understanding the culture's impact on global business. He demonstrated curiosity with his depth of questioning and appreciated the fact that his employees have different ways of doing things, and saw connections between their insight and cultural capital and the potential positive impact on growth markets.

Tom Greco, president of Frito-Lay North America, takes that curiosity about people and puts it into practice with a great method for really getting to know people upon meeting them for the first time. This is how he does it: Whenever he attends a meeting, he asks each person to introduce themselves in a round robin, and as he does so, he jots down their name and business unit and function on a piece of paper. He is fastidious about remembering those important personal details about people, and can recall them in future conversation. Because he manages down so well and is invested in connecting with his employees, he is able to be a strong sponsor.

Once you have the right mind-set, you need to take deliberate steps to establish a mentor relationship with people who are different from you. You need to lay the foundation and be prepared to spend time investing in building a relationship.

1. First, ask yourself if you are ready to understand how the power gap works with this person. (Please go to www.flextheplaybook. com to take the Fluent Leader Inventory.) Are you ready and prepared to ask the right questions to help guide this individual?
2. Notice the differences between you and the other individual and accept those differences. Determine how the differences between you are impacting your behavior. Are they putting up barriers? Help your protégés apply these discoveries to the mentor-mentee relationship as well as their workplace interactions.
3. Close the power gap by flexing to those differences. If both the mentor and the mentee are made to feel comfortable about those differences and about being in that space, it allows for real disclosure and growth.

Good mentors act like coaches: they don't force any issues where there isn't readiness to explore them. Ask instead, "Do you feel comfortable talking about this?" and if you receive permission, proceed.

Here's an example of what a dialogue about projecting confidence and authority with a female mentee might look like, whether you are a man or a woman: You say to your mentee that you've noticed in big meetings she doesn't initiate new ideas on the table. You then add, "I've also noticed that we're a rowdy team talking over each other all the time. As your mentor, how can I help you work through that dynamic?" If you're her boss, let her practice developing that skill. Have your mentee seek out more meetings where she is the only woman and practice. Don't try to solve the problem for her—help her seek out appropriate action.

In all mentor situations, it's important that you are not doing the work for the mentee. The mentee is there to gain advice and guidance. In remedial situations this becomes even more important, as it is the inherent nature of someone in jeopardy to get defensive. Before you begin working together, it's critical to determine, by asking your mentee if she is in a fix-it place or in a development place.

A good mentor can flex to difference, but also knows when barriers to development mean he is not the right person for the job. Even the best mentor can't help someone who isn't ready to make changes. Women who feel like there is too much of a gender power gap may not be able to get everything they need from a male mentor. While good coaches or mentors will do their part to close the power gap, there may simply not be the right fit. For example, a male employee may be initially uncomfortable seeing a woman as someone who can help him, but a woman may still be able to mentor him and help him challenge and change that position. However, if the man persists in being unable to receive direction and guidance from a woman, a male mentor would be a better fit. He might be able to guide this employee toward greater awareness more effectively. The objective is for the coach or mentor not to judge the behavior or difference. It's to determine if he or she can build a safe, trusting relationship with this person where he can be helped.

KNOW YOUR AUDIENCE

A great mentor can also help others understand how they need to flex in order to meet success. Many people make the mistake of getting trapped in handing out good generic advice and wisdom, but don't go outside those roles to see how nuance operates on an individual level. Someone might give the general advice to a woman to read a well-received leadership book that advocates being more assertive in meetings, to speak up loudly in order to appear more confident and gain respect. Well, if your mentee is an African American woman, and she already operates in a world where she might have been cast by previous colleagues as the "angry black woman," then advising her to walk into the room and be more assertive won't resonate the same way. If your mentee is a recent college graduate, she may already be predisposed to be perceived as disrespectful or even audacious if she takes an assertive role in a meeting, especially with people from older generations. The best advice for that young woman might be to close the gap by defying expectations. If she walks into the room and acts in a manner contrary to their assumptions, showing more deference for authority and respect for people who have been with the organization longer, she may change their perceptions. Once she creates this positive impression, she could put her difference to good use and show them what she brings to the table—a new, innovative approach to an existing problem.

A good mentor can also help mentees navigate the difference appropriately to help them promote their unique offerings and perspectives and turn difference into real cultural capital. In order to navigate the difference, a mentor can help mentees understand how their behaviors and style might be perceived by others so the mentees can work effectively to reach up and close the gap. Sample conversations and role-playing can be effective when getting people to understand and work through different behaviors. Coaches take an involved facilitator role in helping others identify and understand their own "pain spots"—it is their job to pull this out of their protégés so that they can then change their own behavior to elicit a new response.

FLEXING TO YOUR MENTORS AND SPONSORS

We coached a technical subject matter expert in an accounting firm who was on the brink of rising to a new level, but felt stuck. She wanted to make partner but she was locked away in a position with no exposure. She added great value to the company—and was adept at handling critical accounts—but the accounts weren't high-profile clients, so only two people in her group knew she was a rock star. One of them was her boss, with whom she had built up a great relationship. One day, she approached him in an effort to communicate her desire to make partner and ask for his help in getting there. Her approach to closing the gap with him, however, was all wrong. She spent most of the time in the meeting talking to him about her desire to get married and have a family, which to her were additional, personal goals on which she had her sights set. They were all equal signifiers to her of success—making partner while also having a relationship and children. However, what he heard was her focus on the family part instead of her career, and was left with the opposite impression she intended to give: that because she wanted a relationship and children, she would not have the time or investment to serve as a partner in the firm.

As coaches our job was to help her understand the results of her approach to building a great relationship with her boss. By being completely open and sharing all her thoughts and feelings about her personal goals, she made it hard for anyone (including us) to believe that that was not her number one goal. In talking to her boss as though he was her best friend she was making assumptions about how he would filter and receive her message. Perhaps a female boss would have recognized this particular struggle of a young woman who wanted to get married and have a career; regardless, the protégé needed to realize the difference between men's and women's experiences and understand how he, as a man, was receiving her messages. While he was sympathetic, his main takeaway was that career advancement was not a top priority for her.

Our job was to help her see that she needed to reset her relationship with her boss and treat him not as a best friend but rather as a true sponsor who could put her forward only if he understood her objective clearly. She needed to flex to close the gap between their different expectations about the relationship and the boundaries between personal and professional. By communicating her own struggles regarding potentially conflicting personal and professional goals, she had muddied the waters. She needed to reach out to him and communicate that she was serious about her career. Outside her group, she needed to identify her stakeholders, meet with them to build relationships, discuss her current successes and challenges, and articulate her professional goals in order to get help reaching them.

THE PROTÉGÉ'S PART TO PLAY

The most frequent mistake mentees make is that of expecting their coach or mentor to do all the work. There are definitive actions that the protégé can and should take in a healthy mentor-protégé relationship. Many individuals think that once they have found the right person, their job is just to sit back and wait to be told what to do. This could not be more wrong! The individual is not in a passive role with his mentor or coach—he needs to actively direct his own behaviors and growth, asking for guidance along the way. In *Lean In*, Sheryl Sandberg offers that she believes women are being taught to depend too much on others and often wait around for Prince Charming to create the happily ever after. We would offer the same advice, not only to women, but for all employees looking to advance in their careers and excel. For mentors who encounter a mentee who doesn't seem to want to do any heavy lifting, we encourage simple, positive redirection: "This is your time. I'm guiding and setting the framework for you, but you will need to do the work." Both parties need to flex across the gap and play their parts.

In order for the relationship to build and grow, it's ideal if your mentor has followed the three steps listed above—assessing her own power gap preferences, assessing the differences between you and pinpointing how those differences might affect your dynamic, then flexing to help you as an individual. However, even if the mentor doesn't take these steps and prepare to play her role, you can take steps to close the gap with her.

One way of doing this is to share information about your background and your values in order to frame your behavior clearly, using your own self-awareness about your power gap preferences. Then you can talk about your style as it relates to that background. Let's refer back to Audrey Lee's example in the introduction, where she shares how her Confucian Chinese upbringing taught her it was undesirable and even unseemly to promote her own accomplishments, a trait that we learned runs counter to the Generally Accepted Rules for Promotion. In trying to address that issue, she might choose to share that personal history with a potential mentor, highlighting the differences and laying plain the motivations behind some of her behaviors: "There are a lot of reasons I feel uncomfortable highlighting my accomplishments. My style is generally assertive, but in this specific area it's not, and these are some of the reasons why. . . ."

Bringing up differences and asking your mentor's or coach's level of comfort in discussing those issues can relieve your mentor, especially if she's a manager, of potential discomfort, embarrassment, or even trepidation over talking about the differences between you, especially if she comes from a more dominant culture. By demonstrating humility, vulnerability, and a willingness to learn, you will earn the trust and respect of your mentor and motivate her to engage you and help you navigate those differences. There are countless individual variations in how to mentor across the cultural, gender, and generational gap, but we would like to share with you a few insights that we have discovered from our own work:

CONNECTING WITH YOUR WHOLE TEAM

Mentoring Multiculturals
- Provide them with detailed, "unwritten" knowledge as to how the company works.
- Give them the big picture about the organization and describe the corporate culture.
- Don't shy away from delving into their background and experiences (prepare with the three pre-engagement questions and five steps to productive dialogue).
- Demonstrate genuine interest by taking initiative in the relationship.

Mentoring Women
- Instill confidence, reliability, and trust.
- Empower her to take risks and push beyond her comfort zones.
- Recognize that her life experience and career trajectory may be different from yours. Don't make assumptions.
- Help her clarify their objectives and leverage their strengths.

Mentoring Younger Professionals
- Provide feedback that is real-time and continuous.
- Acknowledge the importance of technology and the social network tools (Facebook, Twitter, LinkedIn, Instagram, Pinterest) and level the communications playing field.
- Explain to them the role that their individual job assignments play in the broader mission/overall business context.
- If you are also the boss, think beyond money in terms of rewards—engage them in the dialogue and consider rewarding

them with time off, access to community outreach projects, and work/life integration.

- Especially with younger mentees, guide them to opportunities for showcasing their work to enhance their visibility in the organization.
- Model how they can more effectively communicate their value to the organization so that their viewpoints might be heard.

"HOW AM I DOING?": THE ART OF GIVING FEEDBACK

Honest criticism is hard to take, particularly from a relative, a friend, an acquaintance, or a stranger.
—FRANKLIN P. JONES

Reality TV shows like *The Voice* and *Chopped* show contestants receiving brutally honest, direct feedback from famous experts about their singing talent or their culinary expertise. For the most part, the contestants appear to be quite gracious in receiving these sometimes cutting remarks. In the corporate world, however, feedback is not always easy to deliver and not always easy to take, as one of our favorite quotes, above, makes clear. Yet in order to be effective, mentors and coaches must develop the skills to deliver timely, constructive feedback if they are to help their protégés hone their skills. Remember that a trait of fluent leadership is an ability to admit one's mistakes and learn from the experience in order to experience career growth and development. If you are not providing direct feedback in a manner your mentee can understand, you aren't protecting him— you are keeping him from addressing obstacles that could derail him from his career aspirations.

Still, it is with regular frequency that we have experiences that reflect how reticent managers can be with constructive feedback. We provided external coaching to an employee who needed to work on her presentation and communication skills. After an extensive conversation with her boss, we discovered the specific issues he wanted to address. We encouraged the boss to take part in the program and deliver his specific feedback during and after the coaching engagement. What opportunities did the employee have to improve? What behaviors were starting to change? Were team members and clients taking note? The boss agreed, but throughout the program, he delivered only vague comments. And when the employee tried to reach up and ask for specific and constructive feedback, what did he tell her? "Do whatever your coach tells you." Well, the boss blew an incredible opportunity to provide helpful insight and point out errors in the specific context of the employee's day-to-day interactions.

MANAGERS HAVE A LEGAL responsibility to give feedback, but, as you can see, the truth is they are uncomfortable doing so. And they grow even more anxious and distressed when it comes to talking across cultures, generations, and gender. Add to that a lingering concern over potential litigation if they do it poorly, and the stage is set for flawed feedback loops with no opportunity for change or growth.

As an example, Bill has six direct reports. Four are men who generally share Bill's communication style, as well as his cultural background. The other two are women. "I know how the men think," Bill says, "so I tell them like it is: 'You messed up on that deal, your numbers aren't right. Go fix it.' But I'm nervous with the women. I'm afraid one of them might get upset if I give her the hard news. So I tend to waffle in those evaluations."

This is how it starts; this is how feedback gets watered down. As a result, managers fail to be fully honest with their employees. At the same time employees, who don't get a chance to address their mistakes, wonder why they can't move up the ladder.

Esther, a nurse in a large teaching hospital, learned quite a bit from the feedback skills employed by her recently retired director. She was able to communicate her needs and observations while still expressing respect. "She really understood nonverbal communication and listening skills. Whether she was speaking to a housekeeper in the hallway or to a surgeon in a boardroom, she adjusted herself to some extent; she expressed kindness and gratefulness, lots of thank-yous, but provided you with both the boundaries and freedom to figure it out for yourself. She'd ask why something had happened and let you come up with the answer. She rarely used *you* when addressing problems, but instead focused on *I* statements: 'Maybe I misunderstood, but this is what I expected. . . . Tell me where we are on this project. My understanding was that it was due?' "

WINNING PLAYS FOR COACHING AND GIVING FEEDBACK

In order for feedback to be effective, it needs to be delivered appropriately and in the right format. If you take the time to hone the content of the feedback you give your employees and deliver it in the right way, you will notice a clear difference in how much of an impact that feedback makes on an employee's performance and outlook. As a first rule, don't water it down. Good feedback is direct. While you don't need to be harsh in your delivery, you need to be clear about what is going well and what is not. Helpful feedback is also value added: "You did very well on the overall presentation of the piece and you sounded confident about your content. Where you can improve the next time is by zeroing in on the client's concern over efficiency and productivity. . . ." Effective feedback is very specific—it doesn't backtrack and recount an employee's problem behavior over the last five years but directs her attention to her specific behavior in the meeting you just came out of with a client. And, while this may seem intuitive, feedback has to be understood by the person receiving it. Even if delivered indirectly or through a third party, the person has to understand your message and intent.

In contrast, unhelpful feedback is untimely, lost in the delivery, or vague. Even positive feedback can be unhelpful in this manner. Recognize any of these?

- "You're doing just fine."
- "Keep it up! Whatever you're doing, it's working, so keep it going!"
- "Good job!"

Even when offering praise for work done well, it's helpful to be as specific as possible. This gives your mentee a map for directing future efforts and provides real opportunity for growth.

Meanwhile, all employees need to learn how to receive feedback from their mentors, managers, and peers. Instead of becoming defensive, each of us should adopt a healthy mind-set for receiving constructive criticism and managing objections. Treat it as an opportunity and get ready to listen. As we'll cover more in the next chapter, being able to receive and address criticism about behaviors and ideas not only help you reach your desired goals, it can spur you on to greater creativity and help you reach for the most innovative solutions out there.

- Adopt a mind-set for continuous improvement.
- Any feedback is valuable; it's up to you to validate and understand what to do about it.
- Feedback is a snapshot, not the definitive verdict on you.
- Don't agree or disagree too quickly.
- Treat each objection as a question or a request for further information, not a closed-case scenario. Ask questions to clarify vague feedback.

SOLICITING FEEDBACK

Seek out opportunities for growth by soliciting and inviting feedback. These are some examples of phrasing you can use to get the answers you need.

- "How did that go?" "How did I do?"
- "What does an ideal answer to that challenge look like? And how did my response stack up to that?"
- "Where else should I be looking to learn more about the project?"
- "This is how I read the meeting. Does this make sense?"
- "How can I do it better the next time around?"

Fluent Leader Profile: Rich Hille— From the Baseball Fields to the Corporate Boardroom: Leading a Winning Team

As a pitcher I knew the importance of the other eight players on the field. If our defense did not make the plays or if our offense came up flat, no matter how good a job I did pitching that day, our chances of winning were slim. In the sport of baseball, teams win or lose, not individuals. It's the same in this career; I'm only as good as the people around me. My personal goal is secondary to the team goals. When everyone wins is when I feel truly successful.
—RICH HILLE, SENIOR VICE PRESIDENT, GLOBAL HEAD OF COMPENSATION AND BENEFITS, BANK OF AMERICA

Long before he entered the world of corporate finance, Rich Hille was a team player—literally. Beginning in high school in Queens, New York, and throughout college, Rich played both basketball and baseball, where he demonstrated a great aptitude for pitching. At St. John's University he played Division I baseball for four years. Though he still managed to graduate on time with a business degree, his high-profile baseball career and a wicked pitching arm got him drafted by the Cleveland Indians to play pro ball. His talent and hard work secured the attention of the scouts and got him drafted, but the ethos of athletics, the spirit and philosophy of teams, and the team-coach dynamic would later play heavily into his leadership and working style. He learned early on that the efforts and contribution of each team member were critical to the final result. In business and in baseball, "you rarely win without the help of your teammates."

After an injury took him from the world of pro sports, team-centered goals still made Rich a successful manager and leader, but so, too, did his approachability and positive energy. His impact on former employees and mentees is still palpable. At the very mention of his name their countenance shifts from guarded and tense to relaxed, familiar grins; voices soften and relax as former staff recount their tenure with him. He made people feel at ease, and brought comfort to even difficult work situations. This fluent leader was deeply loved and admired by his people, from the very start. "When I was being hired coming out of business school nineteen years ago, I had offers from JPMorgan and also from GE," remembers one former employee. "Rich took me to lunch and we got beer and fried chicken, and I remember thinking, this guy seemed way cool. Here I was; I had never worked in the corporate world and trying to decide what to do. And I picked JPMorgan without batting an eye because of Rich, because I wanted to work for him."

Rich credits his own former managers as modeling positive attitudes and approachability. They were all knowledgeable in their craft, with the addition of positive energy. "If you're negative and sarcastic it's hard to build trust and goodwill. You don't have to be Pollyannaish, but in the long run, if you're genuine, people respond to your positive energy and intent." That positive attitude and unconditional positive regard both trace back to baseball. "If I'm honest it goes back to high school. I remember in games I'd be pitching where I or the team did not perform up to expectations and the coach would just say, 'We'll get 'em next time,' instead of blaming me or one of our players for the mistakes." Howie Gershberg, Rich's pitching coach at St. John's, also modeled for Rich what leadership could look like, serving as a mentor, tutor, and psychologist to the young athlete, all wrapped up in one. Like many workers, "athletes are very frail with a lot of self-doubt at times. He provided the level of encouragement you needed when you didn't perform well. To see you through the dark times, if you needed an extra hour he gave you that extra time after practice, or a game to work with him. He would always lift you up and help you feel good about yourself."

This ethos clearly carried through to Rich's various leadership stints in Human Resources at JPMorgan, Bank of America, and Credit Suisse, among others. Unsurprisingly, the area where Rich really shone as a fluent leader was in his ability to manage at all levels and bridge the power gap. "We were an incredibly diverse team," a former employee said of her stint with Rich's "merry band" when he was at JPMorgan. "Here was Rich, an Irish Catholic man in his forties surrounded by younger women and men who, among others, were of Latino, Korean, and African American descent. Added to that, for many of us it was our first job out of college and we had a lot of learning to do." One by one, new recruits who went to work on Rich's team began their acculturation process into working in a highly demanding financial services organization. Many of them had newly minted BAs and MBAs in their hands but little experience. They spanned the ethnic and cultural continuum; some had children while others were single, and their ages ranged from twenty-one to thirty-six. Some of them were starting their careers, while others had come through the company's prestigious training program and were eager to make their mark. It was a situation rife with power gaps.

From the beginning, Rich was different from many other senior executives in the company. He approached his team without any pretense of title and sought to decrease any power gap with them from the start. Certainly they recognized that he was the leader of the team. No doubt he was the one who had the relationships with the senior business heads. Undoubtedly he was politically astute and capable of masterfully maneuvering inside the organization. Yet he never made them feel inferior, and he always went out of his way to let them know, "You're in charge. You're the ones who do all the hard work. You can be empowered to make the decisions with the line managers and should directly present your findings." He gave his team opportunity to interact with senior leadership in a way that they could demonstrate their skills and gain important sponsorship from the highest-level executives.

Through it all, Rich was able to connect on a personal and professional level with each of his reports, bringing out the best in each one. Rich was very intentional about connecting with each of his reports outside of just shop talk, which makes giving feedback and discussing difficult issues much easier. He also decreased the power gap by working in the trenches along with his team. One employee recalled, "He always stayed later during the day if we were going to be there all night. He wasn't out the door by four thirty; he was there working right alongside us. And after those 'house arrest' marathon sessions he would take the whole team out to breakfast on his own dime," giving the team an incredible sense of camaraderie and a safe place to share stories and rehash and work through any problems.

One former employee, who still names Rich as the best manager she's ever had, said when she first went to work for Rich, she felt very vulnerable, one of the newbies. "I had never even lived in New York City before, and here I was, working on Wall Street in a very difficult and demanding job." Yet she credits Rich with empowering her and giving her the skills and tools to succeed. She remembers well when a colleague tried to take credit for her work in a meeting. Rich knew that, as a young woman just starting out, she didn't yet have the skills or temerity to contradict the more senior person in the meeting and manage up effectively. So he did it for her, managing across by firmly interrupting the conversation and clarifying exactly who had done the work in question.

Another former team member, now in-house counsel at a large technology company, talked about how Rich was able to encourage him to get his ideas heard by managing down in such a way that he took Rich's feedback as both on point and encouraging. "He took me out to lunch," the former employee recalled, and said, "I know what you're going through. You're quiet. I was quiet, too. I know you know more than you are saying." In order to get ahead, his boss told him, he would need to let others know his ideas. Rich gave him a strategy. "This is what I do: You need a burst of insight in every meeting. Since it doesn't come naturally to you to speak up in the meeting, prepare ahead of time and decide on what that one burst of insight is going to be, and make sure that you voice it."

Rich seemed to hit his stride in helping his team members deal with messy issues and problems, often using humor or empathy to help smooth things over. One young former employee remembered when she was asked by Rich to do a task she didn't want to handle herself. "I didn't want to do it so I gave it to someone else and delegated it. The end results turned out okay, but I underestimated the total pricing of the program because I wasn't on top of it. At the end of the day, the numbers were inaccurate. It was clear that Rich wasn't happy about that because he had already shown it to his boss. At that moment, I learned a life lesson: never delegate something to someone that I didn't fully understand myself. At the time I thought it was a pretty serious issue, but throughout that experience Rich never put me in the doghouse. Instead the feedback that I remember getting from him was more lenient than I deserved. He said, 'I'm on to you . . . you procrastinate a little bit, don't you? You're a perfectionist.'" Giving her problem behavior a positive and humorous spin enabled her to reframe the issue and correct it without shame.

The respect and unconditional positive regard Rich held for each of his team members inspired them to exceed his expectations and allowed many of those just starting out in their careers to learn from their mistakes, show off what they knew, and continue to better their performance. In a corporate world that doesn't always favor long-term relationships, Rich has stayed present and available for a wide range of former employees. As a mentor he "always had great career advice and was the voice of reason and truth when we worked for him," one woman said, "but even after I didn't formally work for him anymore, he has always been accessible throughout my career. Even if you go six months without talking to him, it's like you're picking up from the last time . . . no time has passed." Like his relationships, the core of Rich Hille also remains constant, displaying now as then his strong personal values like the integrity, good humor, and humility that are his trademarks. "He's been working in financial services for over twenty-five-plus years and he's never let it change him. He always kept his values and stayed grounded and very down-to-earth. After all this time and after he's reached such a high level of seniority, he always treats us like he's known us forever. That level of friendship is always there." To give you an idea of how loyal his fellow team members are, I had no trouble getting any of the people I interviewed to get back to me in a relatively short time frame. As soon as they heard that we were going to examine Rich and his leadership style, their response was instantaneous. Once you were on Rich's team, you were a member for life.

CHAPTER 11

LEVERAGING DIVERSE THINKING FROM YOUR TEAMS TO DRIVE INNOVATION

Fast-growth companies must keep innovating. Companies are like sharks. If they stop moving, they die.
—MARC BENIOFF, FOUNDER AND CEO, SALESFORCE.COM

Considered one of the most innovative companies, Google always seems poised on the cutting edge on many fronts. Yet even innovators like this tech giant can provide cautionary tales on the dangers of allowing eureka moments to slip through fingers. Justin Rosenstein, now cofounder of a new software company, worked on the initial version of Google Drive, a software product that works across multiple platforms, allowing you to sync documents across multiple computers and share them out. Contributing to LinkedIn's *My Best Mistake* blog, Rosenstein writes compellingly about his own failing to help bring Google Drive to market at the time, in part because he lacked the clout and skills to make a persuasive pitch to leadership. Though Rosenstein's team wanted to launch, Larry Page, then copresident of Google, wanted the product to fully integrate with Google Docs before releasing the product. By the time Google Drive launched five years later, Dropbox, a company that makes a similar product, had filled the niche and was worth $4 billion with fifty million users. While Page perhaps didn't flex down to fully consider the alternate point of view, Rosenstein felt that his own mistake was in not fully articulating to his boss the positioning and strategy for Google Drive and finding a way to make his case compelling to management. As a manager now, he keeps his mind open when his employees seem very passionate or knowledgeable about an idea, and always gives them the opportunity to change his mind. The story demonstrates all too well the critical role flexing plays in creating an environment receptive to visionary thinking and creativity. It's not enough to listen to good ideas; individuals must reach up and down and close the gaps in order to fully explore ideas for innovation.

Visionary thinking requires intentional, diverse internal processes that value blue-sky thinking, as well as integrating different ideas and directions. The discomfort that accompanies this kind of thinking shouldn't be avoided, but instead must be explored if real breakthroughs are to happen. Throughout this book we have acknowledged that working though difference isn't always easy or comfortable. The good news is that if you can manage the conversations about difference fluently and use your skills to guide the process in a productive way, differences of opinion, thought, experience, and style can actually aid the innovative process.

It seems that innovation is the word of the moment. It is something that every global CEO has made a strategic priority for business survival and success. It is discussed in boardrooms around the country and tech conferences around the world, even in both sides' political speeches. Because it offers the thrill of discovery and the promise of the next big thing, innovation is a tremendously exciting and important objective for any organization looking beyond sustainability toward growth and increased prosperity. You might remember that innovation is also one of the hallmark traits of a fluent leader, which makes sense. By its very definition, innovation demands that you change things up and become open to new ways of thinking, accommodate different perspectives, and become attuned to fresh applications for existing products or strategies. Innovation asks for courage, integrity, and is the reward of taking risks instead of doing what is comfortable; in many ways innovation is integral to fluency. And so we think the question for modern businesses is: How do you innovate? How do you create a culture that rewards innovative thinking?

It certainly doesn't just happen. Conventional wisdom can in many ways be the enemy of innovative thinking. Do what you've always been doing, and you'll continue to do what you've always been doing. Even if we throw diversity at the problem of innovation, we need to be very intentional about what we mean to do by introducing people of diverse backgrounds into the picture.

FLUENT LEADERSHIP IS NEEDED TO FACILITATE INNOVATIVE THINKING

Hiring a diverse workforce is not enough. People must be trained to work with difference, and the importance of diverse ideas and process must be cultivated in order for a company to spur creative thinking. If done thoroughly, reaching across differences gives us the innovation tools we need in a global economy. In many ways, innovation is the utmost application of closing the power gap. It requires people to manage up, down, and across peers to work through differences, be receptive to good ideas no matter where they originate, and encourage risk taking.

LEADING WITH HUMILITY AND AUDACITY

Jacqueline Novogratz, CEO of Acumen, is continually working in uncharted territory, investing in fledgling companies and organizations that battle poverty on a global scale. As such, her reach is big and her message is one that encourages taking the leap. "I give our team outsize goals, and I have this mantra: just start and let the work teach you. We're building something no one has ever really built before, so don't be afraid of making mistakes. Let's just make the decision to do something." For Jacqueline, it goes back to the twinned principles of audacity and humility. "You've got to be audacious enough to set goals that make you stretch and give you clarity of vision and purpose. But you have to have the humility to know that this work is hard, and that you might not get there."

It also takes an organizational environment that encourages and incubates creativity and innovation. Companies should list it in their corporate vision and goals and make clear that it's a value foundational to how they do business.

HOW DIFFERENCE DRIVES INNOVATION

When you're forced to stay out of your comfort zone and are challenged by new information and points of view, the creative part of your mind is stimulated. Researchers found that multicultural experience—when people encounter or interact with foreign cultures or people—actually spurs creative thinking or the type of cognitive processes that result in the aha your company is always on the lookout for. In another experiment, the group that performed most creatively was the one that was made to hold differences or the juxtaposition of two things together in one cognitive space. Though it's painful and scary for some, staying in that space where different points of view, styles, means of communication, and cultural values are placed in tension without judgment causes an important shift in thinking that will bring innovative benefit to your organization.

Augmenting the above findings, another study found that the more intensive the immersion of someone into a foreign culture, the greater the boost in creative processes. People who were encouraged to follow the rules or received limits on exploring new ideas, however, did not receive the full creative boost the other participants enjoyed. Taken together, the research seems to hold that the ideas behind fluency (including investigating and leveraging difference) bolster the innovative creative process.

These findings support that many of the fluent leader traits profiled in this book are foundational to creativity: insatiable curiosity, adaptability, comfort with ambiguity, flexing across the power gap, confidence, and an openness to new experiences. One study found that people who are marginalized or different from the dominant culture were some of the most creative, a finding confirmed by our own experience and research. If you do not allow your employees to take risks and encourage them to develop their own ideas, you are helping to ensure that regimentation is the centerpiece of your company culture. Allowing for difference, encouraging positive risk-taking by putting mentors and sponsors in place and supporting employees in difficult moments, and encouraging the exchange of different points of view all help create a company culture fertile for creativity and inspiration.

We find that the environment is ripe for innovation when everyone is practicing fluent leadership and closing the power gap with others inside and outside the organization. How diverse perspectives are managed also plays a key role. If you need further proof that embracing and encouraging diverse perspectives spurs innovation in the workplace, these are just a few of the ways that having diverse teams can contribute to innovative thinking and processes:

- A diversity of opinions and experiences encourage creativity, adaptability, and original thinking.
- Diverse environments that value individual opinions are more likely to create a sustainable shift in one's mind-set.
- Diverse perspectives, broader expertise, and the critical evaluation of ideas within a team enhance decision-making and problem-solving processes.
- Diverse teams are able to leverage their more extensive networks and cultural capital to increase what is possible or thought to be possible to achieve.

ENCOURAGE MANAGEMENT STYLES THAT SPUR INNOVATIVE THINKING

Even if we know that difference enhances creativity, that still doesn't give us a concrete path toward innovative breakthroughs. Gary Hamel, in his contribution to the *Harvard Business Review*, offers the idea that companies must become "serial management innovators," systematically encouraging innovative thinking through the implementation of management systems designed to do just that. By taking what you already know about bridging the power gap and flexing to those different from you, you can go on to challenge your company culture and question whether you have the management systems in place that will allow you to leverage the difference to the company's benefit.

Hamel advises managers to "challenge" their "management orthodoxies" by asking themselves a series of questions very reminiscent of our three pre-engagement questions before dealing with someone different from you. Your managers and company leaders should get to the bottom of their innovation-dampening processes by challenging conventional wisdom and looking at internal beliefs for possible root causes of the problem, then asking:

- What *either/or*s can we turn into *and*s?
- What are we bad at, and how can we turn that around?
- What can we do to meet the challenges of the future?

How can you ensure that you are having this conversation with the relevant people within your company and even outside your company? How do you reach out to make sure that happens?

AWAKEN THE INNOVATIVE POSSIBILITIES

Amazing things can happen when diverse perspectives are brought together. Frans Johanssen talks about how innovative breakthroughs coincide with the convergence of diverse disciplines and fields, a phenomenon he calls the Medici effect. Just as the Medici family brought together individuals from a wide range of disciplines across the arts— sculptors, scientist, poets, philosophers, painters, and architects—to launch the creative synergy that produced the Renaissance, a similar innovative effect is achieved through cross-disciplinary collaboration.

So-Young Kang has done just that. A dynamic woman who recently moved to Singapore from the US, Kang created a company called Awaken Group, a transformation design (TD) company that helps companies rethink—in the broadest sense—their identity. Fundamental innovation is one of So-Young's primary goals. "I define innovation as bringing disparate things together for a different kind of outcome. If it's incremental change then it doesn't fit my personal definition—the innovation I care about must be fundamental. Fundamental innovation is where you're creating something or a function that did not exist before and you're challenging assumptions. You are challenging the status quo," she said. So-Young believes it is essential to stretch or flex in order to bring two disparate things together in a way that makes a difference. "I accept that some people refer to 'making tweaks and refinements to things' as innovation. Everyone wants to be innovative. But to truly be innovative you need to be open. Diversity and differences are an absolute requirement for innovation. You cannot innovate if you just stay within your comfort zone doing the same thing you did yesterday, in the same way, with the same people."

"Diversity and differences are an absolute requirement for innovation. You cannot innovate if you just stay within your comfort zone doing the same thing you did yesterday, in the same way, with the same people."

As such, So-Young brings together diverse teams of experts to solve client problems. She helps them ask the right questions, such as, How do customers experience our brand and products? How do our employees experience us as a company? The company is different from other consulting companies—innovative—in that consultants usually tackle one side or the other, but through Awaken Group she directs holistic change. She directs the execution with her strategists, marketing gurus, branding experts, designers, and executive coaches to help change leadership and the way organizations are managed. She partners with communications experts and architects, looking at all facets of the diamond.

To illustrate, So-Young uses McDonald's as an example of branding taken to the nth degree. There's a McDonald's experience in their commercials, in their philanthropy, in their décor, and in the attitude of their employees, and they want it to internally shape their employment as well as customer experience. This is applicable to airlines, too: if you walk into the first-class lounge, how do you experience an airline? Starbucks is predicated upon this whole concept—the interrelated experience of Starbucks from both the customer and employee viewpoints. In order to help her clients to the furthest extent, she needs to be able to reach and consider all those disparate points of view, then leverage them into an action plan.

"That openness to things or people different from you is key. You notice the most brilliant of creators and innovators in history were people whom you could not put in a box. They were not just scientists, just engineers, just teachers, or just philosophers. They were actually many different things. Because they had to draw from different courses of thinking and different disciplines in order to then start to bring these disparate or different pieces together."

OVERCOMING THE BARRIERS TO INNOVATION THROUGH FLEX

We've covered many of the positive results of leveraging a diverse workforce in an organization. However, without proper management, tensions rise when differences are brought to the fore and opinions are exchanged and critiqued. Some people dominate group conversations or strategy sessions, while others shrink back and lose their voice in the conversation. Realizing the innovation benefits of diversity without falling prey to increased conflict and tension is really dependent on the fluent leader who can acknowledge the different voices in the room and appropriately manage diverse teams, global projects, and cross-departmental collaborations. It is here that fluent leaders can get creative in how they manage up, down, and across.

Raudline Etienne is a senior director of Albright Stonebridge Group, a global strategy firm that believes in the power of putting diverse teams together to leverage the innovative thinking that can occur. However, as an African American executive, when she puts a team together, she thinks about the balance. She's had to be mindful about the fact that sometimes there's a power gap that already exists between her and others in the room because she's a black woman. There may be unconscious bias or resentment that can threaten the dynamics of the group—a not uncommon phenomenon when dealing with diverse teams. In a past role, Raudline had a "lieutenant"—someone on her team who helped bridge the gap between her and team members. Admitting that "softness isn't a core competency of mine," Raudline realized the benefits of leveraging the team member's strengths, especially in situations where confronting the unconscious bias might be disruptive. "A lieutenant needs to be a great navigator and very compassionate. Team members need someone to talk to who can build understanding and shift perspectives. We worked together to bridge gaps in our team dynamics." Raudline was very creative and intentional to find a way to still build a relationship with team members where this unconscious bias presented itself so that she could hear every voice in the room. Her technique can prove helpful for many managers who might use other employees or reports strategically to help bridge that gap in the team. You don't have to do it alone.

TAKING RISKS

In order to create a culture of innovation, new ideas and risktaking need to be encouraged and not penalized. As a fluent leader, approach each individual team member and assess how they might push into new territory and what that looks like for them. Help them try to anticipate any possible negative outcomes and come up with a plan B, and encourage their willingness to step outside their comfort zone. Consistently demonstrating unconditional positive regard toward your team builds a safe place to fall should they try something new. Forecasting possible negative outcomes allows for examining failures as learning opportunities. It's a strategy that works well across the spectrum. Remember that Rafe Esquith, the fifth-grade teacher at

Hobart Elementary School, practices this type of leadership every day with his students. " 'There is no fear here,' " he reminds them. " 'No one's scolding you, shaming you if you get some answer wrong.' We try to create an environment where they're not afraid to fail and not afraid to ask questions."

FLUENT MEETINGS: HOW TO BRING IDEAS TO THE TABLE

The age-old tactic of group brainstorming is nearly synonymous with the innovative process. Conventional wisdom says if you want to come up with creative new ideas you just put people around a table and let the wisdom fly. Come to the meeting with a blank slate. Say anything that comes to mind, write everything down, and there's sure to be a gem in there somewhere.

However, recent studies show that this might not be the go-to technique companies should reach for. One University of California, Berkeley, study gave different groups a problem and then asked them to come up with solutions. Some were given no parameters for talking it through, other groups were asked to brainstorm ideas, and others were asked to come up with ideas and hone them using a debate format. While the brainstorming groups did slightly better than the groups given no instructions, groups asked to use a debate format generated 20 percent more ideas than the brainstorming group. Individuals in the debate group came up with a greater number of additional ideas following the session—their brains were in innovative mode. As we noted above, there seems to be something about the critical process that allows people to adjust their initial offerings and come up with more creative collective ideas. Lacking the critical piece, groups tend toward affirmation of the most popular ideas. Even those who disagree with a proposal introduced in brainstorming tend to fall in line if the idea receives popular support. Dissenting views are silenced and truly innovative thinking goes out the window.

There are other issues with the brainstorming model. *Quiet* author Susan Cain wrote about a phenomenon she calls the "new groupthink," the popular philosophy that all creative work should be done in groups. As a self-professed introvert, Cain challenges the group creative process, and like her, others think best when allowed to do so privately and without interruption. These are the voices you are apt not to hear in a group brainstorming session where only the loudest (and those who thrive on interaction) will predominate.

To get all the ideas out on the table, it's important to know how each team member takes in information, processes it, and then spits it back out. Some people simply think aloud—it's how they process ideas. However, there will be a lot of people who want only finished ideas brought to the table. Consequently, you must have an awareness about different styles and be able to flex so individuals get heard and recognized. It is also important for managers to give their employees and mentees appropriate feedback for how people engage in a group setting. For the people who process internally, are they cutting down ideas too soon before bringing them to the group? For the verbalizing processors, are they putting so much out there that people can't see the stronger ideas?

As a fluent leader, you will need to be attuned to these differences in thought and process and create a variety of organizational opportunities for ideas to come to the table. Think through what creates a barrier for people against speaking up in a group; then, how do you listen and facilitate around those barriers as a manager? This holds true not just when soliciting ideas, but also in delivering feedback and pushing people to rethink how to handle and approach problems.

When Toni Riccardi was part of the management committee at Pricewaterhouse Coopers she was the only woman on the management committee. Five of the members, including Toni, were waiting at an airport for a delayed flight. "They began to reminisce about giving one of the male members a hard time when he first joined the management committee. Almost like hazing, they told him what he should and shouldn't do—the informal rules—because they wanted him to be successful. It was a natural thing for them to do. They didn't do that with me. I don't believe it was intentional, I am sure it never even crossed their minds. So, I had to find other ways to understand the ways of the group. Eventually, I began to develop a slightly more open relationship with the CFO. He came to me and admitted, 'When you talk about diversity, I have no idea what you are talking about.' I said, 'That's funny. When you give some of your financials reports, I have the same problem. We can do some mutual coaching!'"

In an atmosphere where only the dominant point of view got expressed and only certain individuals were pressed to rethink and retool their strategies, the organization loses out on a real chance to push the boundaries of what the management team was capable of, especially related to diversity and difference and the possibilities inherent in opening up that conversation.

DON'T BE AFRAID OF CONFLICT

Conflict is inherently something that people feel like they want to avoid. But the truth is, you need it. It's a good thing. And it will happen. The result of diverse work environments is that people hold different ideas, priorities, objectives, values, and beliefs. So if a manager can't manage past those conflicts, it's a deal-breaker not only in terms of innovative thinking, but even in a productive workplace environment. We would argue that perhaps your highest calling as a manager lies in not only resolving conflict, but using it as a driver of innovation. Innovative business cultures look for it and even initiate it, asking the questions, Why are you doing it that way? How could we do it better? What if it looked like this? The goal is not to pick a fight and not to make it personal, but instead to create healthy debate and a synergy of ideas. It is one way to make sure you're hearing all ideas. If done well, it's a way of getting the disparate factors out there—people could have an emotional or passionate tie to an idea, they could see it working in another environment, or it could be they've thought about it for a long time but never saw the opportunity to bring it up. The goal is to get all the ideas out on the table in an environment where they can be critically honed, not just blindly accepted.

Fluent leaders are therefore skilled in building an environment of constructive conflict resolution. If conflict is an opportunity and a driver to innovation, therefore managing conflict appropriately is the key to innovation within a diverse team. Flexing up, down, and across the hierarchy becomes an especially critical skill in this environment, though there is more a fluent leader can do to set up an overarching organizational structure and environment that teaches and values conflict resolution.

HARNESSING YOUR TEAM'S INGENUITY: REVITALIZING THE PLAYBOOK

We all have experienced the joys of a really well-run innovation session, where the group went beyond the goals you had hoped to accomplish and participants left feeling clear in their next steps, heard, even energized! And we have all probably experienced (and perhaps even run) meetings that fell short of expectations—no truly new ideas or action plans were elicited and participants left feeling at best flat or stymied and perhaps even angry or ignored. With some planning and attention to structure and goals and employment of flex principles, that tired old brainstorming session can become a true innovation session, producing creative, forward-thinking ideas and initiatives.

1. **Set up the team with ground rules for success.** Discuss ahead of time how you will deal with conflict and manage comments on other people's ideas.
2. **Know the styles of the people in the room.** For smaller teams, giving assessments will help you know how each person best contributes. If you are indirect and emotionally expressive, for

example, what does that look like for you, and what does it look like when you're in conflict? How do you focus on repairing that relationship? If it's a formal team or if they work together regularly, it can be helpful for each team member to know the others' styles and how to best communicate. Be careful not to box others in with assumptions like "You're the details guy" or "You're the processor." Assessments and inventories are tools meant to help you work together more effectively. Once people begin to use the assessment results as labels for each other, it's time to throw them out the window.

3. **When you facilitate the conversation, it is your opportunity to be the leader in the room.** It's your job to identify emotions and clarify objectives and ideas. In order to keep the flow of ideas going, encourage "yes, and . . ." interactions rather than "yes, but . . ." responses that can shut down dialogue. As facilitator it's your job to address criticisms and objections, and park ideas as necessary. Even heated dialogue or emotional reactions can be gifts for a skilled facilitator who is able to hear the opportunities in the room and direct the piece appropriately to create the right response in the group. Focus on the idea, not the person. Ask people to defend or evaluate the idea on its merits in a way that is both constructive and direct.

4. **Address criticisms and objections effectively.** As a fluent leader you need to be able to recognize that yes, criticism is affecting that person directly; or, in contrast, we need to stay on point. If issues arise meriting further examination or exploration, stay there and do it. Those can be critical breakthrough moments to get through difficult issues and make progress. If it's truly an aside, then table the issue for the time being. Make sure that you write the issue down so that the group can return to the open questions. Eliciting and managing criticisms includes thinking through all the elements of the idea, all possible outcomes, the stakeholders involved, budgets, resources, and timelines.

Leverage difference in the room as a strategy to critique ideas and invite participation. You might notice someone from finance in the room; what isn't being considered from a budget perspective? In general, feel out the comfort level of the people in the room and allow them to have the conversation they need to have.

DIVERSIFY YOUR FORUMS FOR DEBATE AND EXCHANGE

For all the same reasons the old open-door policy isn't enough, it's critical for an organization to allow for diverse channels to receive input and ideas. For some, the mere act of offering an idea or opinion that will be critiqued seems too daunting. For others, there might be one or more barriers keeping them from contributing to an exchange of ideas. Some might be perfectionists, held back from contributing because they want to present complete and/or perfect ideas before voicing them. Some people might have political concerns, worried they will offend someone with an idea if they step into others' territory, use their resources, or change their plans. There could be an issue of authority, wherein someone feels uncomfortable challenging a superior or feels it's not his place to bring up the ideas. There could be personal concerns of looking stupid or naïve if others don't receive an idea well. Based on experience with representing the minority voice, one might also carry the fear or expectation that an idea might not be heard, or be heard and taken by someone else. Someone could also simply be reticent to stand or speak out. Remember Susan Cain's position that the large-group dynamic is anything but ideal for the introvert.

Therefore, if you want to capture the widest possible variety of ideas and opinions, you need to offer a wide range of organizational opportunities where people can exchange ideas and debate their merits. These can range from something as small (and anonymous) as a suggestion box or feedback forms or designated blue-sky days. Take advantage of organic opportunities that naturally arise with conflict to set up a more formal place where you can tackle a real issue directly and provide a mechanism for ongoing feedback. For example, if your team is having a major disagreement with the finance department about budget costs, view it as an opportunity. Perhaps you might suggest, instead of just playing games, why not just get around the table and talk about it?

CREATE SPONSORS AT ALL LEVELS

Another way to help encourage risk is to create champions at all levels. As you're building this environment ensure there are sponsors for each team member and initiatives at all levels of the hierarchy. Could Justin Rosenstein at Google have gotten traction on Google Drive if there was a champion in a critical department who could have helped work the problem through? At PepsiCo, the president of Frito-Lay North America sponsored an employee affinity group to help create an innovative and unlikely collaboration. Create a culture where everyone at all levels is valued. If someone has a great idea, there is a forum or channel for that innovation to be tapped. Ensure people are open to a full team perspective.

Steve Miola of Merck encountered Dylan, a colleague who was quiet and reserved and rather isolated from the other team members. When Steve was assigned to a project with Dylan, he was immediately impressed by how good he was; Steve knew that not many others had any idea of what Dylan could contribute because of his low-key demeanor. "I thought to myself," Steve recalls, "'If I knew what he knows, I would be out there making presentations!' So I told his boss that he needed to be out there talking about his work, and we gave him that feedback. We ended up doing presentations together to the scientific groups. The material was so great! I loved making the presentations and he loved fueling the information. Together we teamed up to communicate. We had complementary skills and were able to leverage each other's strengths and get a new idea out there."

ACCESSING INTERNAL AND EXTERNAL VOICES TO DRIVE INNOVATION

Innovative thinking requires that you hear from all the participants at all angles. Internally, it's crucial that you are listening vertically down the command chain and that departments hear one another's perspectives. From an organizational viewpoint, you need to ensure every function, whether it's sales or an affinity network, is hearing from all the stakeholders. You also need to forge ways to connect to external points of view and close the customer gap. Speak to the people who are in direct contact with your customers—like a field sales group—or connect regularly with virtual and offsite teams to get their perspective. These are the voices that may not be in the room.

People are often very good at telling you what they need and want; sometimes the problem lies in making sure the right people are really listening. As an organization, have you developed channels for identifying needs/wants of different constituencies? Do you have processes in place for gathering ideas, then facilitating and testing them using the skills we discuss below? You need to be very intentional about hearing from minority interests and from the people who are not in the dominant group and develop this as a company value with processes in place to support it.

Some proven ways of accessing external voices and closing the gap include accessing user groups, industry groups, and verticals. With its growing business use, you may be able to leverage social media to get to those different perspectives. For example, Meetup is an organization that has helped create interest clubs in local communities around the world. You can simply go to the Meetup site, type in your interests, and get connected to a group of people invested in your focus area. Fluent leaders can leverage their input and interest to create a feedback loop into product development, sales and distribution, vendor relationship, and business partnerships.

In the last chapter, we explored how companies leveraged diverse talent in order to connect with consumers. The people mattered, but so, too, did the organizational channels built up to support and encourage that connection. When IBM launched its diversity initiative centered on the creation of employee networks, it meant to spur some much-needed innovative thinking on how to tap into new markets. Highlighting difference and provoking constructive critique is itself an innovative concept in the world of business where differences are often missed, or overlooked in the name of efficiency and cost containment. We think Ted Childs had it right when he termed their goal as "constructive disruption"—a seemingly unwelcome pause in daily operations in order to engineer a break in conventional processes and thinking.

Creating and leveraging affinity and resource groups is a smart and effective way to bridge the gap and bring together new ideas. The employees in your employee resource groups (ERGs) are your market—they can be subjects of vital market research or focus groups for new applications and products. They can be accessed to get out to their communities or used internally, giving real-time feedback at every point of development. We urge you to consider ERGs as an R&D and marketing resource already existing in your company. However, leaders should really reach across the power gap and ask ERGs for specific help, instead of simply setting them up expecting they will add value in some way. Remember, for an organization to have business results, diversity must be actively acknowledged and leveraged. If senior leaders are intentional and go to the group meetings, they should be direct in asking for the ERGs' input and ideas. You might say, "We have plans to grow this business aggressively over the next few years and we believe that you can guide us in our quest to drive this business strategy. I want to invite you to think about your own network and community. Are there organizations or groups in your network that we should be including? Your input is critical to our success!"

Each employee brings external networks and knowledge and insight to the direction of the business, and the more you can harness that cultural capital, the more engagement you will find in your employees. Putting the groups to work and employing the ideas and strategies they identify also helps overcome any initial distrust that can stem from the groups simply functioning as diversity window dressing. Sales leaders can take the initiative to reach out to affinity groups and ERGs to mine their ideas about how to connect to diverse markets. One idea would be to put a formal channel in place for ERGs to share ideas with leadership, as well as a senior-level executive sponsor for each group. Go directly to the group, soliciting its response, and bridge that power gap so that it is closer to you. In doing so, you will help ensure the free flow of ideas and a sense of empowerment on the part of the group.

However you decide to set up the formal processes, simply leveraging your diverse talent and staying open to all points of view will help fuel strategic innovation in your organization. Strategic innovation focuses on the integration of how things come together to become an idea, and looks for new applications of existing technologies. When a company employs strategic innovation, it can work with an existing product or idea but introduce it to a completely new consumer market, change how the product or idea is delivered, or change the end value for the consumer. Consider this example from PepsiCo. One day, an employee working the packaging line on the manufacturing floor had a flash of inspiration. He took some Cheetos being produced at the time and combined them with a spice mix used in another Frito-Lay product. He thought the spiciness would work against the flavor of the cheese. Yet Cheetos Crunchy Cheddar Jalapeño-to-be would never have made it on to store shelves if the line worker hadn't felt empowered to give the bag to Jacob Pak, who was then sales director at Frito-Lay. Jacob liked the combination so much he brought it to Tom Greco, who was then head of Frito-Lay Sales, to try. Tom tasted it and put it right into development. The Cheetos Brand Marketing team was very supportive of this project and was able to provide the financial resources to enable the commercialization of this new Cheetos

Cheddar Jalapeño flavor. Ideas can come from unlikely places, and innovative organizations create an environment where management listens to whoever is having the good ideas and stays receptive to that possibility, instead of being rigidly wed to the "correct" process and business as usual.

CONCLUSION

The best experts in any field constantly stretch their horizons so they can do something new. That is how they stay sharp. Nobel laureates do this; great composers do this—and so do the savviest judges of human potential. They refuse to become so habit-bound that familiar customs unthinkingly turn into ruts. Instead, they keep analyzing their own track records, looking for new opportunities and unexpected misfires. Doing so helps turn agility and continual improvement into a way of life.
—GEORGE ANDERS, *THE RARE FIND*

As we were writing this book, a women's leadership roundtable occurred at the *New York Times* headquarters, organized by IMPACT Leadership 21, a movement "committed to transforming women's global leadership at the highest level of influence in the twenty-first century." The event struck us because it gathered together CEOs, UN representatives, NGOs, nonprofits, and entrepreneurs to tackle the issue of women's leadership advancement at the top. And it captured our attention for reasons other than IMPACT's core values, all of which are in lockstep with the fluent leader principles we've outlined in this book:

I	Innovation
M	Multiculturalism
P	Passion
A	Attunement
C	Collaboration
T	Tenacity

What was most striking was who had been invited to participate, a core demographic listed by the organization as fundamental to achieving its goals: men.

Thought leader and IMPACT Leadership 21 CEO and founder Janet C. Salazar knows that to exclude men from the conversation would preclude the type of diverse thinking that spurs innovation and change. Without confronting head-on the issue of gender difference and disparity with each side would be to leave the issue unexamined to the fullest extent possible—it would be to stay in those ruts George Anders refers to in the quote above. In a *Forbes* article Salazar says, "Without a transformative approach to advancing women's leadership we will find ourselves thirty years from now still talking about the same old issues, still wondering why women's progress into top leadership positions has been a trickle. Men can be powerful ambassadors for change. Men are untapped, yet a critical resource in advancing women's global leadership and achieving parity. How do we harness this untapped resource? We engage them."

If there is one prerequisite to harnessing the full creative power of tomorrow's talent it is this: we must be able to address and navigate through difference. We mustn't be afraid to have the conversation and work through complicated, misunderstood, messy, or loaded issues. And we must become willing to go outside our own comfort zones and extend an invitation toward those different from us to meet in the middle.

The onus is on each one of us to notice and call out difference, to investigate the underlying values and assumptions that cause each of us to behave in the way that we do. But the responsibility is not necessarily equal. Those of us who operate outside of the majority culture—whether we are multicultural professionals, women, the newest or oldest worker in the company, or someone from a different country or culture—have always felt the pressure to change, to fit in to the existing leadership models. There is not so much an invitation to flex as a mandate to adapt and assimilate. But attempting to make us all the same isn't the answer—if it were even possible—and it minimizes the incredible opportunity and potential that lies in leveraging our differences and broadening our understanding and skills.

In his research findings, Anders focused on the importance of looking for talent in unusual places, and encouraging us not to focus on talent that "shouts" but rather seeking out talent that "whispers." When you're working with people not like you, you might miss talent that "whispers" on first pass because they demonstrate leadership differently, and maybe in quite the opposite way of how you would do things. Even as recruiting and talent processes have become more sophisticated and more data is available about people, the results have not always gotten better. To turn this around means leadership must readily investigate and explore difference and not be afraid of the conversation. If there is to be a change in how we recruit, reward, and advance our best talent it means committing to practice and persistence, continuing to apply the principles of flex while making it a part of your ingrained management process.

Throughout this book you have encountered in-depth profiles of fluent leaders who have demonstrated how it can be done. These are people and organizations that have astounded us, often through simple acts, by consistently demonstrating core fluency traits and flexing to close the gap. We trust that the profiles provide useful examples of leaders who are adept at managing across the power gap to build strong work relationships and, ultimately, achieve success in business. Their actions and integrity have compelled us to tell their stories here and, we hope, to encourage you to think about the flex leaders in your own experience.

This is hardly the last word on this topic: we want to hear from you! We invite you to share your ideas and inspiring stories of your experiences and the fluent leaders who have impacted you and your career at www.flextheplaybook.com.

We hope to see you there.

BIBLIOGRAPHY

Anders, George. *The Rare Find: Spotting Exceptional Talent Before Everyone Else*. Portfolio Hardcover; 1st edition (October 18, 2011).

Barsh, Joanna, and Lareina Yee. "Unlocking the Full Potential of Women in the US Economy." McKinsey & Company, April 2011, www.mckinsey.com/Client_Service/Organization/Latest_thinking/Unlocking_the_full_potential.aspx.

———. "Becoming Interculturally Competent." In *Toward Multiculturalism: A Reader in Multicultural Education*, 2nd ed., ed. J. Wurzel. Newton, MA: Intercultural Resource Corporation, 2004.

———. "A Developmental Approach to Training for Intercultural Sensitivity." *International Journal of Intercultural Relations* 10 no. 2 (1986).

Bennett, M. J. "Towards Ethnorelativism: A Developmental Model of Intercultural Sensitivity." In *Education for the Intercultural Experience*, ed. R. M. Paige. Yarmouth, ME: Intercultural Press, 1993, 21–71.

Birkman International. "How Do Generational Differences Impact Organizations and Teams?" Part 1, n.d., www.birkman.com/news/view/how-do-generational-differences-impact-organizations-and-teams-part-1.

Blanchard, Ken. *Leading at a Higher Level,* Revised and Expanded Edition: *Blanchard on Leadership and Creating High Performing Organizations.* Upper Saddle River, NJ: FT Press, 2010.

Boushey, Heather, and Sarah Jane Glynn. "There Are Significant Business Costs to Replacing Employees." Center for American Progress, November 16, 2012, www.americanprogress.org/issues/labor/report/2012/11/16/44464/there-are-significant-business-costs-to-replacing-employees.

Bryant, Adam. "Google's Quest to Build a Better Boss." *New York Times,* March 12, 2011, www.nytimes.com/2011/03/13/business/13hire.html.

———, ed. "The C.E.O. with the Portable Desk: The Corner Office." *New York Times,* May 1, 2010.

Buckingham, Marcus, and Curt Coffman. *First, Break All the Rules.* New York: Simon & Schuster, 1999.

Burkhart, Bryan. "Getting New Employees Off to a Good Start." *New York Times,* March 13, 2013, boss.blogs.nytimes.com/2013/03/13/getting-employees-off-to-a-good-start.

Burns, Crosby, Kimberly Barton, and Sophia Kerby. "The State of Diversity in Today's Workforce." Center for American Progress, July 12, 2012, http://www.americanprogress.org/issues/labor/report/2012/07/12/11938/the-state-of-diversity-in-todays-workforce.

Cain, Susan. *Quiet: The Power of Introverts in a World That Can't Stop Talking.* New York: Crown, 2012.

———. "The Rise of the New Groupthink." *New York Times,* January 15, 2012, www.nytimes.com/2012/01/15/opinion/sunday/the-rise-of-the-new-groupthink.html.

Carl, Dale, and Vipin Gupta with Mansour Javidan. "Power Distance." In *Culture, Leadership, and Organizations: The GLOBE Study of 62 Societies,* ed. Robert J. House, Paul J. (John) Hanges, Mansour Javidan, Peter W. Dorfman, and Vipin Gupta. Thousand Oaks, CA: SAGE Publications, 2004, 513–63.

CBS News. "Is Your 'Open Door' Policy Silencing Your Staff?" April 20, 2010, www.cbsnews.com/8301-505125_162-44440188/ is-your-open-door-policy-silencing-your-staff/.

Chao, Melody Manchi, Sumie Okazaki, and Ying-yi Hong. "The Quest for Multicultural Competence: Challenges and Lessons Learned from Clinical and Organizational Research." Hong Kong University of Science and Technology, New York University, and Nanyang Technological University. *Social and Personality Psychology Compass 5*, no. 5 (2011): 263–74.

Chen, Pauline. "Do Women Make Better Doctors?" *New York Times*, May 6, 2010, www.nytimes.com/2010/05/06/health/06chen.html.

Chhokar, Jagdeep S., Felix C. Brodbeck, and Robert J. House. *Culture and Leadership Across the World: The GLOBE Book of In-Depth Studies of 25 Societies*. Series in Organization and Management. *Psychology Press*, April 5, 2007.

Childs, Ted. "Diversity in the Workplace." *UVA Newsmakers*, November 12, 2002, www.youtube.com/watch?v=lgOTjSp6vwY.

Chong, Nilda. "A Model for the Nation's Health Care Industry: Kaiser Permanente's Institute for Culturally Competent Care." *Permanente Journal*, 2002, http://xnet.kp.org/permanentejournal/ sum02/model.html.

Chua, Roy Y. J., and Michael W. Morris. "Innovation Communication in Multicultural Networks: Deficits in Inter-cultural Capability and Affect-based Trust as Barriers to New Idea Sharing in Inter-Cultural Relationships." *HBS Working Knowledge*, June 17, 2009, http://hbswk.hbs.edu/item/6194.html.

Cognisco Group. "$37 Billion: US and UK Businesses Count the Cost of Employee Misunderstanding." *Marketwire*, June 18, 2008, www. marketwire.com/press-release/37-billion-us-and-uk-businesses- count-the-cost-of-employee-misunderstanding-870000.htm.

Cuckler, Gigi A., Andrea M. Sisko, Sean P. Keehan, Sheila D. Smith, Andrew J. Madison, John A. Poisal, Christian J. Wolfe, Joseph M. Lizonitz, Devin A. Stone. "National Health Expenditure

Projections, 2012–22: Slow Growth Until Coverage Expands and Economy Improves." Health Affairs, http://content.healthaffairs. org/content/early/2013/09/13/hlthaff.2013.0721.full.

Deloitte. "Only Skin Deep? Re-examining the Business Case for Diversity." Deloitte Australia, September 2011, www.deloitte.com/ assets/Dcom-Australia/Local%20Assets/Documents/Services/ Consulting/Human%20Capital/Diversity/Deloitte_Only_skin_ deep_12_September_2011.pdf.

Detert, James R., Ethan R. Burris, and David A. Harrison. "Debunking Four Myths About Employee Silence." *Harvard Business Review*, June 2010, httphbr.org/2010/06/debunking-four-myths-about-employee-silence.

Dychtwald, Ken, Tamara Erickson, Robert Morison. "The Needs and Attitudes of Young Workers." Excerpted from *Workforce Crisis: How to Beat the Coming Shortage of Skills and Talent*. Boston: Harvard Business Review Press, 2006.

Dyer, Jeff, Hal Gregersen, and Clayton M. Christensen. *The Innovator's DNA: Mastering the Five Skills of Disruptive Innovators*. Boston: Harvard Business Review Press, 2011.

Ernst & Young. "Women Make All the Difference in the World." In *Growing Beyond: High Achievers: Recognizing the Power of Women to Spur Business and Economic Growth*, Ernst & Young, 2012, www.ey.com/Publication/vwLUAssets/Growing_ Beyond_-_High_Achievers/$FILE/High%20achievers%20-%20 Growing%20Beyond.pdf.

Escamilla, Kathy, and Susan Hopewell. "The Role of Code-Switching in the Written Expression of Early Elementary Simultaneous Bilinguals." Paper presented at the annual conference of the American Educational Research Association, April 1, 2007, www.colorado. edu/education/faculty/kathyescamilla/Docs/AERACodeswitching.pdf.

Feldhahn, Shaunti. *The Male Factor: The Unwritten Rules,*

Misperceptions, and Secret Beliefs of Men in the Workplace. New York: Crown Business, 2009.

Fisher, Anne. "Fatal Mistakes When Starting a New Job." *Fortune*, June 2, 2006.

Friedman, Thomas L. *The World Is Flat: A Brief History of the Twenty-first Century.* New York: Farrar, Straus & Giroux, 2005.

Frontiera, Joe. "Living Your Values for Profit." Good –b, Good Business New York, May 20, 2013, http://good-b.com/building-a-values-based-culture.

Gallup. "Gallup Study: Engaged Employees Inspire Company Innovation." *Gallup Management Journal*, October 12, 2006, businessjournal.gallup.com/content/24880/gallup-study-engaged-employees-inspire-company.aspx.

———. "State of the American Workplace Report," Gallup, 2013.

Gamb, Maria. "Women and Men Need This Instead of Quotas." *Forbes*, June 30, 2013, www.forbes.com/sites/womensmedia/2013/06/30/women-and-men-need-this-instead-of-quotas.

"George Gaston Chief Executive Officer, Memorial Hermann Southwest Hospital." *Houston Medical Journal*, December 2011, www.mjhnews.com/george-gaston-chief-executive-officer-memorial-hermann-southwest-hospital.html.

Gladwell, Malcolm. *Outliers: The Story of Success.* New York: Little, Brown, 2008.

Glass Ceiling Commission. "The Environmental Scan." Executive Report, March 1995. Washington, DC: US Department of Labor, 1995. www.dol.gov/dol/aboutdol/history/reich/reports/ceiling1.pdf.

Gort, Mileidis. "Strategic Codeswitching, Interliteracy, and Other Phenomena of Emergent Bilingual Writing: Lessons from First Grade Dual Language Classrooms." *Journal of Early Childhood Literacy* 6 (2006): 323, http://www.sagepub.com/donoghuestudy/articles/Gort.pdf.

Graduate Management Admission Council. *GMAC 2011 Application Trends Survey—Survey Report.* http://www.gmac.com/~/media/Files/gmac/Research/admissions-and-application-trends/applicationtrends2011_sr.pdf.

Grossman, Leslie. "Why Women Need Men to Get Ahead . . . and Vice Versa." *Huffington Post,* July 3, 2013, www.huffingtonpost.com/leslie-grossman/why-women-need-men-to-get-ahead_b_3530821.html.

Hall, Edward. *Beyond Culture.* New York: Anchor Books, 1976.

———. *The Silent Language.* New York: Anchor Books, 1973.

Hamel, Gary. "The Why, What, and How of Management Innovation." *Harvard Business Review,* February 2006, hbr.org/2006/02/the-why-what-and-how-of-management-innovation/ar/1.

Hammer, M. R. "Additional Cross-Cultural Validity Testing of the Intercultural Development Inventory." *International Journal of Intercultural Relations* 35 (2011): 474–87.

———. *IDI Resource Guide.* IDI LLC, 2011.

———. "The Intercultural Development Inventory: A New Frontier in Assessment and Development of Intercultural Competence." In *Student Learning Abroad: What Our Students Are Learning, What They're Not, and What We Can Do About It,* eds. M. Vande Berg, M. Paige, and K. Lou. Sterling, VA: Stylus Publishing, 2012.

———. "The Intercultural Development Inventory: An Approach for Assessing and Building Intercultural Competence." In *Contemporary Leadership and Intercultural Competence: Exploring the Cross-Cultural Dynamics within Organizations,* ed. M. A. Moodian. Thousand Oaks, CA: Sage, 2009.

Hammonds, Keith H. "Difference Is Power." *Fast Company,* July 2000, www.fastcompany.com/39763/difference-power.

Hannon, Kerry. "People with Pals at Work More Satisfied, Productive." *USA Today,* August 13, 2006, usatoday30.usatoday.com/money/books/reviews/2006-08-13-vital-friends_x.htm.

Harris, Paul. "Boomer vs. Echo Boomer: The Work War?" *T+D*, May 2005, https://store.astd.org/Default.aspx?tabid=167&ProductId=17752.

"Health Care Industry Will Create 5.6 Million More Jobs by 2020: Study." *Huffington Post*, June 21, 2012, www.huffingtonpost. com/2012/06/21/health-care-job-creation_n_1613479.html.

Helgesen, Sally. *The Female Advantage: Women's Ways of Leadership*. New York: Doubleday Currency, 1995.

Hewlett, Sylvia Ann, Carolyn Buck Luce, and Cornel West. "Leadership in Your Midst: Tapping the Hidden Strengths of Minority Executives." *Harvard Business Review*, November 1, 2005, http:// hbr.org/2005/11/leadership-in-your-midst-tapping-the-hidden-strengths-of-minority-executives.

Hewlett, Sylvia Ann, Kerrie Peraino, Laura Sherbin, and Karen Sumberg. "The Sponsor Effect: Breaking Through the Last Glass Ceiling." *Harvard Business Review*, January 12, 2011, hbr.org/product/ the-sponsor-effect-breaking-through-the-last-glass-ceiling/ an/10428-PDF-ENG.

Hewlett, Sylvia Ann, and Ripa Rashid, with Diana Forster and Claire Ho. "Asians in America: Unleashing the Potential of the 'Model Minority.'" Center for Work-Life Policy, July 20, 2011.

Hofstede, Geert. *Culture's Consequences: Comparing Values, Behaviors, Institutions, and Organizations Across Nations*, 2nd ed. Thousand Oaks, CA: Sage, 2001.

Hofstede, Geert, and Michael Minkov. *Cultures and Organizations: Software of the Mind*, 3rd ed. New York: McGraw-Hill, 2010.

Howell, W. S. *The Empathic Communicator*. University of Minnesota: Waveland Press, Inc., 1986.

Hyun, Jane. *Breaking the Bamboo Ceiling: Career Strategies for Asians*. New York: HarperCollins, 2005.

———. "Leadership Principles for Capitalizing on Culturally Diverse Teams: The Bamboo Ceiling Revisited." *Leader to Leader* 64 (Spring 2012):14–19, http://onlinelibrary.wiley.com/doi/10.1002/ ltl.20017/abstract.

Ibarra, Herminia, Nancy M. Carter, and Christine Silva. "Why Men Still Get More Promotions than Women." *Harvard Business Review*, September 2010, hbr.org/2010/09/why-men-still-get-more-promotions-than-women.

Johansson, Frans. *The Medici Effect: What Elephants and Epidemics Can Teach Us about Innovation*. Boston: Harvard Business School Press, 2004.

Johnson, Donald O. "The Business Case for Diversity at the CPCU Society." Society of Chartered Property and Casualty Underwriters, 2007, www.cpcusociety.org/sites/dev.aicpcu.org/files/imported/BusinessDiversity.pdf.

Johnson, Lauren Keller. "Rapid Onboarding at Capital One." *Harvard Business Review*, February 27, 2008, blogs.hbr.org/hmu/2008/02/rapid-onboarding-at-capital-on.html.

Joyce, Cynthia. "The Impact of Direct and Indirect Communication." The University of Iowa. Published in *Independent Voice*, the newsletter of the International Ombudsman Association, November 2012.

Kanter, Rosabeth Moss. *Men and Women of the Corporation*. New York: Basic Books, 1977.

Katzenbach, Jon R., and Douglas K. Smith. *The Wisdom of Teams: Creating the High-Performance Organization*. New York: HarperBusiness, 2006.

Kaushik, Arpit. "Cultural Barriers to Offshore Outsourcing." *CIO*, March 31, 2009, www.cio.com/article/487425/Cultural_Barriers_to_Offshore_Outsourcing.

Kochan, Thomas, Katerina Bezrukova, Robin Ely, Susan Jackson, Aparna Joshi, Karen Jehn, Jonathan Leonard, David Levine, and David Thomas. "The Effects of Diversity on Business Performance: Report of the Diversity Research Network." *Human Resource Management* 42, no. 1 (Spring 2003): 3–21, onlinelibrary.wiley.com/doi/10.1002/hrm.10061/abstract.

Kovalik, Susan J. "Gender Differences and Student Engagement."

Rexford, NY: International Center for Leadership in Education, 2008.

Krishna, Srinivas, Sundeep Sahay, and Geoff Walsham. "Managing Cross-cultural Issues in Global Software Outsourcing." *Communications of the ACM* 4, no. 4 (April 2004): 62–66, dl.acm.org/citation.cfm?id=975818.

Lagace, Martha. "Racial Diversity Pays Off." *Working Knowledge*, Harvard Business School, June 21, 2004, hbswk.hbs.edu/item/4207.html.

Lauby, Sharlyn. "Employee Turnover Caused by Bad Onboarding Programs." *HR Bartender*, May 22, 2012, www.hrbartender.com/2012/recruiting/employee-turnover-caused-by-bad-onboarding-programs.

Lee, David. "Onboarding: What Is It? Is It Worth It? And How Do You Get It Right?" *Human Resources*, September 10, 2008.

Lehrer, Jonah. "Groupthink: The Brainstorming Myth." *The New Yorker*, January 30, 2012, http://www.newyorker.com/reporting/2012/01/30/120130fa_fact_lehrer?currentPage=1.

Leung, Angela Ka-yee, William W. Maddux, Adam D. Galinsky, and Chi-yue Chiu. "Multicultural Experience Enhances Creativity: The When and How." *American Psychologist* 63, no. 3 (April 2008): 169–81, psycnet.apa.org/index.cfm?fa=buy.optionToBuy&id=2008-03389-003.

Llopis, Glenn. "Diversity Management Is the Key to Growth: Make It Authentic." *Forbes*, June 13, 2011, www.forbes.com/sites/glennllopis/2011/06/13/diversity-management-is-the-key-to-growth-make-it-authentic.

"Losing Money by Spending Less: When Outsourcing Customer Service Doesn't Make Business Sense: A Case Study." *Customer Inter@ctive Solutions*, May 2004, www.tmcnet.com/call-center/0504/outsourcing.htm.

Medland, Dina. "Women Challenge Leadership Styles." *Financial Times*, July 5, 2012.

Meyer, Meghan L., Carrie L. Masten, Yina Ma, Chenbo Wang, Zhenhao Shi, Naomi I. Eisenberger, and Shihui Han, Social Cognitive and Affective Neuroscience Advance Access published March 20, 2012. "Empathy for the Social Suffering of Friends and Strangers Recruits Distinct Patterns of Brain Activation." UCLA Psychology Department, Department of Psychological Sciences, Vanderbilt University, Nashville, TN, and Department of Psychology, Peking University, Beijing, China, http://sanlab.psych.ucla.edu/papers_files/Meyer(2012)SCAN.pdf.

Mulder, Mauk. "Reduction of Power Differences in Practice: The Power Distance Reduction Theory and Its Applications." In *European Contributions to Organization Theory*, ed. G. Hofstede and M. S. Kassem. Assen, The Netherlands: Van Gorcum, 1976.

Nilep, Chad. " 'Code Switching' in Sociocultural Linguistics." *Colorado Research in Linguistics* 19 (June 2006), www.colorado.edu/ling/CRIL/Volume19_Issue1/paper_NILEP.pdf.

Nobel, Carmen. "Taking the Fear out of Diversity Policies." *Working Knowledge*, Harvard Business School, January 31, 2011, hbswk.hbs.edu/item/6545.html.

Pagano, Amy E. "Code-switching: A Korean Case Study." *Griffith Working Papers in Pragmatics and Intercultural Communications* 3, no. 1 (2010): 22–38, www.griffith.edu.au/__data/assets/pdf_file/0018/244422/3.-Pagano-Codeswitching-in-Korean.pdf.

Page, Scott E. *The Difference: How the Power of Diversity Creates Better Groups, Firms, Schools, and Societies.* Princeton, NJ: Princeton University Press, 2007.

Patrick, Josh. "Yes, You Treat Customers Well. But How Do You Treat Employees?" *New York Times*, April 25, 2013.

Pollak, Lindsey. *Getting from College to Career: Your Essential Guide to Succeeding in the Real World*, rev. ed. New York: HarperBusiness, 2012.

Racho, Maria Odiamar. "Attributes of Asian American Senior Leaders Who Have Retained Their Cultural Identity and Been Successful in American Corporations." A Research Project Presented to the Faculty of the George L. Graziadio School of Business and Management, Pepperdine University, August 2012.

Rock, David, and Dan Radecki. "Why Race Still Matters in the Workplace." *Harvard Business Review*, June 2012, blogs.hbr.org/cs/2012/06/why_race_still_matters_in_the.html.

Rosenstein, Justin. "My Best Mistake: I Could Have Launched Google Drive in 2006." My Best Mistake, LinkedIn, April 23, 2013, www.linkedin.com/today/post/article/20130423100225-25056271-my-best-mistake-i-could-have-launched-google-drive-in-2006.

Roter, Debra L., Judith A. Hall, and Yutaka Aoki. "Physician Gender Effects in Medical Communication: A Meta-analytic Review." *Journal of the American Medical Association* 288, no. 6 (August 14, 2002): 756–64.

Sandberg, Sheryl. *Lean In: Women, Work, and the Will to Lead*. New York: Knopf, 2013.

Sealy, Ruth, and Susan Vinnicombe. "The Female FTSE Report: Milestone or Millstone?" Cranfield, UK: Cranfield School of Management, 2012, http://www.som.cranfield.ac.uk/som/dinamic-content/research/documents/2012femalftse.pdf.

Sheehy, Kelsey. "MBA Programs with the Most International Students." *U.S. News & World Report*, March 26, 2013, http://www.usnews.com/education/best-graduate-schools/the-short-list-grad-school/articles/2013/03/26/mba-programs-with-the-most-international-students.

Sheffield, Dan. *The Multicultural Leader: Developing a Catholic Personality*. Toronto: Clements Publishing, 2005.

Shin, Sarah. "Conversational Codeswitching Among Korean-English Bilingual Children." *International Journal of Bilingualism*, September 2000, 351–83.

Sy, Thomas, Lynn M. Shore, Judy Strauss, Ted H. Shore, Susanna Tram, Paul Whiteley, and Kristine Ikeda-Muromachi. "Leadership Perceptions as a Function of Race-occupation Fit: The

Case of Asian Americans." *Journal of Applied Psychology* 95, no. 5 (September 2010): 902–19, psycnet.apa.org/journals/apl/95/5/902.

Tannen, Deborah. *Talking from 9 to 5*. New York: William Morrow, 1994.

———. "The Talk of the Sandbox: How Johnny and Suzy's Playground Chatter Prepares Them for Life at the Office." *Washington Post*, December 11, 1994, www.georgetown.edu/faculty/tannend/sandbox.htm.

Texas Medical Center. "George Gaston Named CEO of Memorial Hermann Southwest." Memorial Hermann, January 4, 2010, www.memorialhermann.org/news/george-gaston-named-ceo-of-memorial-hermann-southwest.

Thomas, David A. "Diversity as Strategy." *Harvard Business Review* 82, no. 9 (September 2004), hbr.org/product/diversity-as-strategy/an/R0409G-PDF-ENG.

Verdon, Joan. "Promotion Targets Diwali Holiday." *Record* (Bergen, NJ), October 15, 2009, www.northjersey.com/community/Promotion_targets_Diwali_holiday.html.

Vittrup Simpson, Birgitte. "Exploring the Influences of Educational Television and Parent-Child Discussions on Improving Children's Racial Attitudes." PhD diss., University of Texas at Austin, 2007, https://repositories.lib.utexas.edu/bitstream/handle/2152/2930/simpsonb80466.pdf.

Walker, Danielle, Joerg Schmitz, and Thomas Walker. *Doing Business Internationally*, 2nd ed. New York: McGraw-Hill, 2002.

Weingarten, Gene. "Pearls Before Breakfast." *Washington Post*, April 8, 2007, www.washingtonpost.com/wp-dyn/content/article/2007/04/04/AR2007040401721.html.

Wenner, Melinda. "Smile! It Could Make You Happier." *Scientific American*, October 14, 2009, www.scientificamerican.com/article.cfm?id=smile-it-could-make-you-happier.

Wittenberg-Cox, Avivah. *Why Women Mean Business: Understanding the Emergence of Our Next Economic Revolution.* Chichester, UK: John Wiley & Sons, 2009.

"Women in the Labor Force: A Databook." US Bureau of Labor Statistics, *BLS Reports,* February 2013, http://www.bls.gov/cps/wlf-databook-2012.pdf.

Xu, Xiaojing, Xiangyu Zuo, Xiaoying Wang, and Shihui Han. "Do You Feel My Pain? Racial Group Membership Modulates Empathic Neural Responses." *Journal of Neuroscience,* July 1, 2009, http://www.jneurosci.org/content/29/26/8525.full.pdf+html.

Zenger, John H., and Joseph Folkman. *The Extraordinary Leader: Turning Good Managers into Great Leaders.* New York: McGraw-Hill, 2002.

ABOUT THE AUTHORS

AUDREY S. LEE
Executive Coach, Global Leadership and Diversity Strategist

Audrey Lee is an executive coach and global leadership and diversity strategist who consults with Fortune 500 companies to develop integrated leadership strategies that impact business practices throughout the organization. She expertly combines program facilitation, coaching, and leadership consulting practices with more than thirteen years of experience in marketing communications, product/program strategy, and alliance and channel marketing. A seasoned stage performer for more than twenty years, she also integrates her onstage experiences with her business and coaching strategies to create global programs that focus on effective communications and presentation skills.

With her unique background, Audrey is a frequent speaker at international conferences, corporate initiatives, and community events. Her clients include professionals at Fortune 500 companies and entrepreneurial start-up enterprises in a variety of industries including financial services, high-tech, media/communications, automotive, and consumer products. She is the coauthor of Hyun & Associates' Through the Bamboo Ceiling® training series and other highly acclaimed leadership initiatives. As a Certified Boardroom

Bound® Boardology™ coach, she is also an advocate for building minority talent pipelines for corporate board roles. She is a graduate of
Georgetown University's executive certification program in Leadership Coaching (accredited by the International Coaching Federation),
and also holds degrees in Spanish and music from Indiana University
(Bloomington, Indiana).

Audrey currently maintains her own leadership practice and col-
laborates with Hyun & Associates as a senior consultant. Previously,
she was principal and vice president of Hyun & Associates. Prior to
her career in diversity and leadership development, she managed key
marketing initiatives in small and large high-technology companies
such as Adaptec, Fujitsu Computer Products of America, Network
Peripherals, Philips Semiconductors, Philips Components, and Ray-
chem. In 1999, she began her own marketing practice, working with
clients in multimedia, storage solutions, and application service provider (ASP) industries.

A second-generation Chinese American, she lives in New York
City where she serves on the advisory board for the New York Asian
Women's Center (NYAWC), an organization that helps battered
women overcome violence, and also works to raise public awareness
about domestic violence, advocate for the rights of battered women,
and create an agenda for social change.

JANE HYUN
Leadership Strategist and Executive Coach

Jane Hyun is an internationally renowned global leadership strategist, speaker, and coach to Fortune 500 companies, universities,
MBA programs, and nonprofit organizations. Prior to launching
Hyun & Associates, she held a variety of business and HR management roles, including vice president of HR/talent at JP Morgan and
director of recruiting at Deloitte and Resources Global. The firm's
signature programs (including Art of Cultural Fluency™ roundtables

and the Bamboo Ceiling® leadership series) have received acclaim from organizations that seek to leverage the cultural capital of their teams to win in today's global marketplace. She serves as an adviser to senior management teams and as research director for the Conference Board's Cultural Fluency/Identifying Successful Leadership Styles in Asia Research Working Group.

Hyun & Associates helps organizations grow their bottom line through the effective deployment of their talent. Their clients range from small companies to large multinationals in financial services, consumer products, pharmaceuticals, consulting/professional services, technology, retail, schools, and nonprofits seeking to adopt next-generation leadership practices.

Hyun appears regularly on CNN, CNBC, National Public Radio, and in the *Wall Street Journal, Time, Fortune, Chief Executive,* and other media. A graduate of Cornell University with a degree in economics/international studies, she serves on the Women's Alumnae Council and is an adviser to the Toigo Foundation and the Center for Talent Innovation.

Hyun's groundbreaking book *Breaking the Bamboo Ceiling* opened up a critical dialogue for the need for a culturally grounded approach to career development. She is passionate about helping individuals realize their fullest potential in the workplace and broader community.